THE
THEMATIC PROCESS
IN MUSIC

THE MACMILLAN COMPANY
NEW YORK · BOSTON · CHICAGO · DALLAS
ATLANTA · SAN FRANCISCO

MACMILLAN AND CO., Limited
LONDON · BOMBAY · CALCUTTA · MADRAS
MELBOURNE

THE MACMILLAN COMPANY
OF CANADA, Limited
TORONTO

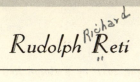

Rudolph Reti

THE
THEMATIC PROCESS
IN MUSIC

1951

The Macmillan Company · New York

Copyright, 1951, by Rudolph Reti

First Printing

Printed in the United States of America

Only when the form is quite clear to you will the spirit become clear to you.

—ROBERT SCHUMANN

In the organic theory a pattern need not endure in undifferentiated sameness. . . . A tune is such a pattern. Thus the endurance of a pattern means the reiteration of its succession of contrasts.

—ALFRED NORTH WHITEHEAD

ACKNOWLEDGMENTS

Since to the best of my knowledge this book represents the first attempt to analyze the particular type of compositional process described in the following pages, scarcely any of the customary bibliographical acknowledgments can be made. Certainly, in many books on musical subjects more or less interesting references to thematic connections occasionally appear; nevertheless, the reader familiar with theoretical literature will soon realize that even in cases where these references seem to approach the viewpoint advanced in this book, they invariably are concerned with isolated and specific instances and remain very remote in their whole purpose and direction from the ideas set forth in this study.

Some personal acknowledgments, however, must be listed.

For their help, through discussions, questions and suggestions, in furthering the growth of this book, I wish to express deep gratitude to Norman Dello Joio, Olin Downes, Wolf Franck, Roland Gelatt, William Kimmel, Kurt Oppens, Dragan Plamenac, the late E. Robert Schmitz, and Herbert Zipper.

For her untiring efforts during the preparation of the manuscript my particular thanks must go to Beverley Andrews Kalitinsky.

Of course, the greatest help came from my wife Jean. But her I do not thank, for I consider this book as much hers as it is mine.

New York, November 27, 1950.

RUDOLPH RETI

CONTENTS

ix

Part Three

THE
THEMATIC PROCESS
IN MUSIC

THE THEMATIC CONCEPT:
A FUNDAMENTAL ELEMENT IN THE
UNDERSTANDING OF MUSICAL ART

The prevailing technical approach to the understanding of musical art is based on theoretical disciplines such as harmony, counterpoint, and certain schematic ideas of musical form. One form-building element, however, and perhaps the most decisive of all, is almost completely neglected in our theoretical system. It is the sphere usually referred to as *thematic or "motivic"* [1] *structure*.

This lack of the thematic view has had a far-reaching effect on our whole approach to the technical and artistic problems of music. For on thematic conceptions, on thematic forming and construction, the actual creative process in musical composition is centered. Once we succeed in comprehending music in its innermost thematic mechanism, the structural and esthetic-dramatic content of music becomes incomparably more transparent.

In almost all accepted treatises on musical composition some indications are to be found on thematic structure, and in oral discussions between musicians remarks about a work's more or less elaborate "thematic" handling frequently recur. However, such references invariably remain mere indications, vague generalities, to which no detailed specification is added. Thus "thematic structure" has become an almost fundamental *term* in music, yet its full meaning and content have never been realized concretely. No real attempt

---

[1] The difference between these two related conceptions will become clear in the course of this study.

has ever been made to comprehend in a systematic analysis the working of this most essential process of musical composition.

It is such an endeavor that forms the content of the following
pages. They give no more, but also no less, than a first outline of
this discipline of thematic structure. But although the following
exposition points to a new theoretical discipline, it is not a new
"theory." It simply attempts to bring to the fore a sphere of compositional phenomena for which the accepted disciplines do not offer
an explanation. In this sense it neither contradicts nor confirms any
of the prevailing systems.

A great part of the phenomena to be demonstrated may appear
even to the most learned musician surprisingly new. For instance,
the forthcoming analysis proves through an abundance of examples
that in the great works of musical literature the different movements
of a composition are connected in thematic unity—a unity that is
brought about not merely by a vague affinity of mood but by forming the themes from one identical musical substance.

Of course, every musician will assert that a work of any quality
must naturally represent an artistic unit. But if asked in what exactly
this unity between the different movements—let us say of a Beethoven symphony—consists, he would probably point to some general affinities of style, mood, or key, but hardly to any concrete relationship within the material itself. True, in some cases he might
quote a specific feature, for instance, the rhythm of the opening
exclamation in the Fifth Symphony, the ♪♪♪ ♩ , which, as is so frequently demonstrated, permeates the whole work. But this is about
as far as the common view on thematic homogeneity goes. However,
the fact that the themes themselves are built according to one
identical pattern—this, if it can be proved, is certainly a realization
entirely new to the accepted conception of a symphony's structure.

In addition to this thematic homogeneity between the movements,
our analysis will demonstrate another phenomenon, perhaps on
the surface less "sensational," but which in a sense is no less striking;
namely, the different themes of *one* movement—in fact all its groups
and parts—are in the last analysis also but variations of one identical thought. The general view would hold almost the opposite.
For instance, the first and second subjects of a sonata are usually
considered as contrasting, certainly not as identical or even related,

manifestations. In reality, however, they are contrasting on the surface but identical in substance. In fact, it is this being "different on the surface but alike in kernel" in which is centered the inner process of musical structure of the last centuries.

The first part of our study demonstrates through numerous examples this homogeneity both between the movements and between the parts of one movement. Faced with the first of these examples, some readers may be skeptical, considering them as exceptional instances of casual coincidence, as a kind of analytic trick, rather than as serious evidence of a principle. Later, however, when the examples become so numerous and convincing that any doubt as to the reality of the phenomenon is no longer possible, the question may be raised: If these are facts, how can it be explained that this knowledge has no part in the musical consciousness of our time?

A complete answer to this would require detailed psychological and technical explanation, much of which will present itself gradually in the course of this study. One important point has already been stressed: this whole sphere of thematic connections and thematic technique has never been included in our theoretical system; it is entirely absent from our educational curriculum; a specific discipline of thematic structure analogous to, and complementing, the old disciplines of harmony, counterpoint, and the general schemes of form has never been developed. Such a fact can in its effect hardly be overestimated, as education and theory play an incomparably more important role in music than in any other art. Theoretical conceptions and formulations are the mediators through which, in great part, our understanding of the musical phenomena is formed and, indeed, through which our whole way of musical thinking is often directed. Thus, as this entire sphere of thematic structure was never really included in our theoretical knowledge, it is little wonder that neither did that part of it through which the homogeneity of the movements is understood enter the general musical consciousness.

In the following analysis this thematic unity between the movements is greatly emphasized, as it forms an integral part of the whole subject. Nevertheless, striking as it may appear, this phenomenon should not be regarded as the core of, nor even as the main issue in, this inquiry. Our endeavor is to lay bare a principle: to give a description, or at least a first outline, of *the thematic process in musical composition.*

In this light the whole first section of our study represents an extended introduction in which the problem of our investigation is developed and the reader is familiarized with the material and terminology of the subject. The second section leads us to the core of the thematic process, especially in its relation to the problem of musical form. But only in the third and last section will the unexpected scope and meaning of the thematic principle and its role in the musical evolution of our epoch be fully encompassed.

The author is well aware that in the presentation of his subject he will find himself faced with some difficulties. One main difficulty lies in the fact that thematic structure, being the manifestation of one compositional principle, should be conceived as a whole. But in its demonstration one detail must be patiently presented after the other; an example introduced in the beginning can be fully understood only after many later ones have been examined; and these later ones cannot be anticipated because they require comparison with still others.

There is another problem of which the reader should be particularly conscious from the beginning. Simply to examine and compare the ensuing quotations as theoretical examples, without recognizing them as parts and constituents of the works from which they are drawn, does not suffice, even if the theoretical connections are understood "on paper." In order to comprehend the full meaning of the following analytic deductions, with all their structural and esthetic implications, the examples quoted must be understood, indeed, *heard,* as musical utterances. For this reason almost all the following examples are chosen from the best known works of the great musical literature, which are more or less familiar to every musical mind.

Nevertheless, in reading and thinking through this book, doubts and objections may occasionally arise. Perhaps they will be more likely to arise the more firmly, the more "professionally," one's mind is entrenched in the theoretical conceptions through which we are accustomed to comprehend the compositional phenomena. The reader is by no means asked to suppress these objections. In fact, a book like this should be read (as it was written) as a ceaseless discussion, constantly enriched by new questions and suggestions. Objections should not be smothered, but final judgment should perhaps be postponed until the end. The reader may rest assured that most of the minor doubts that may bother him in the beginning will be cleared up two or ten or fifty pages later, and that the problems which will appear to him essential at the book's conclusion will be quite different from those which seemed significant at its start.

Without further preliminary explanations and abstractions, we may turn to the matter itself—to music. We shall begin with a sketched demonstration of the thematic plan in Beethoven's Ninth Symphony.

Part One

THEMATIC HOMOGENEITY
AND
THEMATIC METAMORPHOSIS

THE THEMATIC PLAN
OF THE NINTH SYMPHONY

After an introductory group of sixteen bars (harmonically a long extended dominant), the first theme enters (*a* in the following example). To obtain a basis for later reference, we divide this shape into its four motivic [1] elements (*b*):

Ex. 1

---

[1] We call *motif* any musical element, be it a melodic phrase or fragment or even only a rhythmical or dynamic feature which, by being constantly repeated and varied throughout a work or a section, assumes a role in the

We notice that motif II, after its first occurrence in bar 3 of the theme, reappears in bars 5 and 6, and a third time in bars 7 and 8, here transposed to a higher pitch.

Turning to the theme of the next movement, the Scherzo, we become aware that its shape surprisingly constitutes an almost perfect replica of the Allegro theme's [2] design. This becomes apparent once we extract, as in the following example, the four motivic parts from the Scherzo theme:

compositional design somewhat similar to that of a motif in the fine arts.

A *theme,* then, could be defined as a fuller group or "period" which acquires a "motivic" function in a composition's course. Since, however, as this study is about to demonstrate, in a work of higher structural form no group can be entirely outside the motivic unity, the whole conception of a "theme" becomes somewhat problematical. We shall elaborate on this more specifically.

In general, the author does not believe in the possibility or even desirability of enforcing strict musical definitions. Musical phenomena come to existence in the constant fluency and motion of compositional creation. Therefore any descriptions of them must finally prove but approximations. It is for this very reason that in the course of this analysis it was considered more useful to cling as far as possible to the familiar expressions, and to apply them even in instances when their accuracy could be debated, rather than to invent new terms.

[2] For abbreviation's sake the four movements may henceforth be referred to as Allegro, Scherzo, Adagio, and Finale. In this sense the themes also may be quoted as first Allegro theme, second Allegro theme, Scherzo theme, and so on.

Thus we see that all four motivic characters of the Allegro not only reappear but even succeed each other *in exactly the same order as in the Allegro theme*. In other words, not only the motivic fragments but the image of the Allegro's *full theme* are reiterated in the Scherzo.

Specifically speaking, the kernel of motif I reappears almost unchanged, and so does motif II. However, of this latter motif the particles are exchanged: while in the Allegro the first occurrence F, E, D, is later followed by its inversion D, E, F, in the Scherzo the inversion is first and the original shape comes after it.

Motif III has undergone the most visible change: it simply reads E, F, G instead of A, G, E, A, thus assuming simultaneously the shape of a transposed motif II. However, its appearance exactly between the two occurrences of motif II makes it certain that this E, F, G, is nevertheless meant as a corresponding substitute for motif III. For the kernel of these bars reads, as is easily seen,

Ex. 3

and the identity is obvious. But in the speed and concentration which the composer wished for the Scherzo, the leap to the A would have torn the design.

The analogy of motif IV (apart from its transposition to another pitch) is complete.

Let us dwell for a moment on the meaning of the features just described. They represent a first illustration of the fact, indicated in our introductory remarks, that the different movements of a classical symphony are built from one identical thought.

However, to comprehend this phenomenon in its true sense, the following should also be understood. It is by no means alleged that this identity implies that a theme from one movement is literally, or even almost literally, repeated in the next. Naturally, such a procedure would be nonsensical and would never lead to any compositional form of higher structure. The composer's endeavor is just the opposite. He strives toward *homogeneity in the inner essence* but at the same time toward *variety in the outer appearance*. Therefore he changes the surface but maintains the substance of his shapes.

Accordingly, we see the Allegro theme transformed in the Scherzo into quite a different theme. Tempo, rhythm, melodic detail, in fact the whole character and mood are altered and adjusted to the form in which the composer conceived them fitting to the new movement. Nevertheless, there can be no doubt, as the examples clearly prove, that it is one common musical idea, *one basic pattern,* from which both themes have been formed.

As for the individual motifs, I, II, and III are even audible at the same pitch in the Scherzo as in the Allegro. Only motif IV appears transposed. However, as the Scherzo develops into a fugato, it is interesting to note that when the theme is taken over by the violas (and later by the first violins), this motif too is heard in the Scherzo at the same pitch as in the Allegro. And this original pitch is maintained when the definitive statement of the theme in fortissimo climaxes the design of the Scherzo:

Ex. 4

Proceeding to the following movement, the Adagio, we realize, incredible as it may seem considering the entirely different picture which this movement presents at first glance, that here again the similarity of the basic substance is not to be questioned. After two introductory bars the main theme of the Adagio enters:

Ex. 5

There is no doubt that the kernel of motif I from the Allegro theme, the descending triad D, A, F, D, also speaks clearly from the Adagio theme. Of course, tempo, rhythm, and the whole character are again changed. Also, in order to adjust the motif to the desired mood of the Adagio, the melodic course had to be expanded and a B-flat and an E-flat included.

Through this a particularly interesting situation arises. The Adagio theme is in B-flat. Yet the old motif from which it is derived, the D-minor triad of the Allegro theme, is not transposed according to the new key but sounds through at original pitch. We hear a theme in B-flat with a D-minor triad, as it were, at its base. This method of *transforming a shape from one theme to another which is in a different key, but at the same time letting it sound at original pitch,* will in many of the later examples become apparent as one of the most effective means of structural transformation.

This same phenomenon is seen immediately in the continuation of the theme. For, of course, we have so far examined only the Adagio theme's beginning. Now considering also the theme's continuation, which in example 6*a* is given by omitting a few repetitions, and comparing it to the corresponding continuation of the Allegro theme (example 6*b*),

Ex. 6

it is not difficult to trace the identity in the outline, the contour, of these two groups, in spite of their contrasting surface and key.

Note how motif II plus its inversion (D to F, up and down) is again clearly spelled in the beginning of the Adagio group. Motif III may not seem as obviously identifiable in the Adagio, but the transposition of motif II (up to the B-flat) and the following motif IV are recognizable in full transparency, completing the familiar design.

Thus we have arrived at the symphony's Finale.

After a gigantic introduction, in which fragments of the former movements' openings reappear in striking flashes,[3] the Finale's first theme, the "Ode to Joy," enters:

---

[3] This feature alone, so well known to every musician—that in the Ninth Symphony bits of the preceding movements are quoted in the Finale—should have sufficed to evoke an inquiry among analysts as to whether the different movements of a Beethoven symphony are not, indeed, thematically united. Naturally, the feature is also intended to convey a programmatic idea. Nevertheless, seen from the technical point of view, how could a mind of a structural, a "symphonic," intensity such as Beethoven's ever have thought to include in his work an effect tending seemingly to the sphere of the potpourri rather than to serious music, unless he were convinced that these themes represented three different expressions of one identical idea.

The kernel of its opening is again motif I from the Allegro, the triad in D, though here transposed to major.

But while in the preceding movements the original triad was still more or less verbally preserved, in the Finale, where the work's architectural and emotional drama drives to its solution, it is filled with bridging notes, thus making it fluent, songlike. The theme has changed to a tune.

Through this, however, the transformation has gone so far that on the surface it is no longer discernible as such. But recognizing the unquestionable analogy in all themes, in the secondary themes no less than in the first ones (as shall presently be demonstrated), and, moreover, adding innumerable proofs of a similar ceaseless homogeneity in all the other works of Beethoven—indeed, of almost all great composers—we must conclude that in this instance, too, the identity of the *underlying* triad suffices to assure us of the basic homogeneity.

The following motifs are easily recognized in the theme of this movement also. The ascending and descending thirds of motif II appear as interwoven subphrases in the melodic course. In fact, they form, transposed and at original pitch, the very bridging notes by which the triad is filled to produce the tune of the "Ode." Motif III is indicated by lifting the theme from D, E, F-sharp (bars 8 and 9) to E, F-sharp, G (bars 10 and 11).[4] Motif IV, finally, the descending seventh, is expressed through bars 11 and 12:

---

[4] After this chapter was written, the author looked once more through Beethoven's sketches to the Ninth Symphony. He was rewarded by a striking confirmation of his analytic deductions. In our motivic specification above, bars 9 and following of the "Ode" are introduced as repre-

That motif IV is really meant becomes evident when, as the first counterpoint in the following repetition (variation) of the "Ode," the phrase just quoted is immediately imitated, but appears now in the following version, clearly mirroring the motif's appearance in the Allegro:

Ex. 10

Thus we come to realize that the Finale theme is derived from the pattern of the Allegro no less than are the other movements.

With this the cycle of identity in the four first themes of the Ninth Symphony is closed. A symphony, however, is built not only on its first themes but also on its secondary themes. And the true picture, the full intensity of the symphony's amazing architectural planning, will only reveal itself if we include these second themes as well in our examination.

Before the Allegro's second theme is introduced, we hear a few bars which we may term a bridge or intrada to it (*a* in the following example). Motivically this intrada group somewhat echoes motif II, the pair of thirds. Then the actual second theme of the first movement enters (*b* in the following example):

Ex. 11

senting motif III. However, we could merely state that the motif is here expressed "in indication." But in the sketches these bars appear in the following version:

Ex. 9

This is an exciting discovery. For it shows that in Beethoven's original conception the bars really and truly represent the motif. The whole shaping is here in exact analogy to the form in which the motif appears in the Scherzo. In the sketchbook version especially, there is no sign of the D which appears in the score and thus complicates the analytic proof. Without the D, as in the sketch, no one can doubt the motivic meaning.

At first glance one would think this shape quite different from the previous ones. And the difference would seem logical, for this is, after all, the movement's second subject, and as such, according to all accepted conceptions, it must not resemble but contrast with the first theme. Yet looking at it closely, we discover that its kernel, the ascending triad D, F, A, is identical with that of the first theme, or, to be precise, it is its inversion.

This fact becomes still more apparent once we notice that these opening bars of the second theme are immediately repeated in a slightly varied version. This version makes the similarity to the triad kernel of the first theme still more obvious, as it begins:

Ex. 12

However, to avoid any misconception, it must be emphasized: It is not averred that this beginning of the second Allegro theme is just a "variant" of the first theme. It should not even be termed a "transformation," such as we would consider the Scherzo theme. No, this opening of the second theme is a new musical idea, with every appearance of a "contrasting" shape. Yet a structural affinity cannot be denied.

That this affinity, although an affinity through inversion, is not merely analytic conjecture is definitely proved by the continuation of the two themes. For, as we recall, the continuation of the first theme is the little figure called motif II (*a* in the following example), to which the continuation of the second theme (*b*) must be compared:

Ex. 13

Startled, we realize that the group from the second theme is none other than an expanded version of the little motif from the first theme. The change from E-natural to E-flat is merely due to the change of key from D to B-flat.

And in the second theme, after the phrase quoted has been repeated in transposition, a further shape follows (*a* in the following example), which—another surprise—is clearly a replica of the subsequent group (motif IV) in the first theme (*b*):

Ex. 14

Thus in its outer appearance, in the gentle mood of its curved line, this second Allegro theme indeed "contrasts" with the energetic first, yet it is a complete reiteration of the latter's inner content and design.

Now the significant question arises: Can an image of this second Allegro theme be discovered *in the second themes of the following movements,* just as the first theme of the Allegro was mirrored in the first themes of the other movements?

This would seem unlikely as far as the next movement, the Scherzo, is concerned, since scherzos usually lack an actual second theme. Nevertheless, if it has no second theme, a scherzo has a trio. And the Trio of the Ninth mirrors the design of the second Allegro theme, as shown in the following examples.

As mentioned above, the second Allegro theme was preceded by a short intrada. Comparing this intrada group, which in the following example is quoted in a transposed key (example 15a), with the Trio's opening (example 15b),

Ex. 15

it is obvious that the Trio group (b), though it is said to have been taken from a Russian folk tune, nevertheless clearly echoes the group quoted above as a.

In the first movement the group that follows is the actual second theme (a in the following example), which thus should correspond to the group that now enters in the Trio (b). Etching out the corners, the contour, from the Trio group (given under c), we realize that here too the analogy continues:

Ex. 16

Proceeding to the Adagio, we must logically turn to its second section to discover whether this "affinity of the second themes" is integrated in this movement also. This second Adagio section enters with the following theme (*a*), from which we extract a contour (*b*):

Ex. 17

Again the analogy to the second Allegro theme cannot be mistaken. Note, by the way, motif IV at the end of the theme (see bracket in the example). Yet with regard to this last example, one might perhaps argue: In this contour, why was D notated as the first note, while in Beethoven's text the soprano clearly shows F-sharp, the D being confined to the bass?

Therefore, at the risk of being repetitious, it must be emphasized again and again that naturally the composer did not feel the slightest compulsion to produce a textbook example for the sake of "thematic identity." But considering that, according to his self-chosen structural plan, the Adagio's second theme had to be derived from the second Allegro theme (*a* in the following example), we must admit that a more transparent transformation than the shape quoted as *b* could hardly be imagined:

Ex. 18

In the Finale this principle of analogy is increased to a fascinatingly wide architectural pattern. We may follow this far-reaching analogy between the first and last movements step by step. It will be seen that in the Finale the single sections are expanded to much larger proportions, but that apart from this, the analogy and symmetry not only of the themes but of the whole architectural plan are indeed astounding.

The Allegro commences with an introductory group of sixteen bars, after which the first theme enters. In the Finale the introduction is extended to a huge section of improvisational passages, after which the "Ode to Joy," as the Finale's first theme, is sounded. The structural analogy of the first Allegro theme to the "Ode" has already been pointed out. In the Finale, however, the design is still further enlarged by expanding the "Ode" to a cycle of variations and by repeating this whole section (Introduction and "Ode") with solo voices and choir.

What comes next?

In the first movement, after the group of the first theme has been developed and before the second theme follows, a second statement of the first theme is introduced. While the original statement was in D-minor, this second statement is in B-flat major:

Ex. 19

etc.

Does the Finale also carry such a second statement?

In the Finale the group which follows is the section of the tenor solo (*b* in the following example), which at first glance would hardly appear to be a second statement of the "Ode" (*a*). But comparing the two thoroughly,

Ex. 20

we recognize the second example as literally identical to the first, merely with changed rhythm and transposed to B-flat. Thus the section of the tenor solo proves to be a repetition in B-flat (the

"seventh variation" of the "Ode"), or, viewed from a wider architectural angle, truly the "Ode's" second statement, to which the later
following tenor voice merely forms a contrapuntal enrichment
(though naturally from a programmatic view a most important one).

Therefore, only the section which follows after that of the tenor
solo would represent the Finale's second theme. This next section
is centered on the so-called "Hymn":

Ex. 21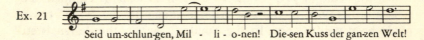

It becomes obvious that the second Finale theme of the Ninth

Here, then, a crucial question presents itself. If the averred
architectural analogy is a fact and not merely a casual similarity in
the movements' beginnings, this "Hymn" must definitely prove a derivative of the second Allegro theme. However, in this case it would
seem no affinity were to be traced.

Yet, probing more deeply into this melodic line, a striking realization emerges. This theme, though not a direct reiteration of the
second Allegro theme's idea, is an inversion of it. We must only, as
in previous instances, extract a kind of melodic contour from its
shape to make this clear:

 Ex. 22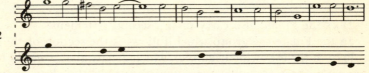

It becomes obvious that the second Finale theme of the Ninth
Symphony, Beethoven's venerated "Hymn to Mankind," is, technically speaking, none other than an inversion of the Allegro's
second subject. This certainly is a structural realization of the first
magnitude, and we should investigate the compositional core of the
phenomenon.

The author harbors some fear that readers may oppose his deductions, even if at a loss to contradict their validity concretely, for the
simple reason that they seem contrary to cherished illusions. "If the
shaping of a musical work," they might argue, "really evolves according to the preceding explanations, composing must be regarded as a
kind of musical engineering rather than as an emotional art—which
we refuse to believe."

Such objections, however, are not founded on reality. With regard to the *harmonic* sphere, for instance, we all know that there are certain basic ideas and cadential progressions that classical composers constantly apply in ever varying combinations when forming the harmonic structure of their works. Yet would anyone for that reason accuse Mozart, Beethoven, or Brahms of composing according to formulas?

In the same way *thematic* shaping evolves from some basic structural methods, even though these have not yet been comprehended in our theoretical system. But creative inspiration and emotional power are by no means hindered by these structural principles directing them—as the great compositional literature proves. For the creative mind structure is a means, not an obstacle, to the manifestation of its inspiration.

Let us try to envision the process of musical formation through which the last example from the Ninth may have evolved. The composer, having in the course of the work reached the point where the last movement's second subject had to be shaped, was aware that according to his own architectural plan this theme somehow had to be built as a kind of structural offspring of the second Allegro theme. However, he seems to have felt that any shape derived from the direct form of this theme would not agree with the concept of character and mood which he wished for the section in question. But the inversion seemed the right thing.

The second Allegro theme (*a*), to which the inversion is added as *b*, reads:

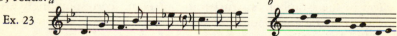

Ex. 23

In modeling the inversion, the E-flat of the theme was replaced by a D (added in parenthesis). This D was inserted as a variant by Beethoven himself in the theme's repetition. (See example 12.)

Adjusting the inversion to the rhythm and spirit of the text as the composer conceived it, it would have appeared in the version quoted below as example 24*a*, which in its melodic course is still the literal inversion.

But we can easily understand that this somewhat dry utterance did not yet please the composer. Hence he inserts some slight changes through which the final form of the theme, as we find it in the score of the symphony, comes to life (example 24*b*):

Ex. 24

a

Seid um-schlun-gen, Mil-li - o - nen, etc.

b

Seid um-schlun-gen, Mil - li - o-nen! Die-sen Kuss der gan-zen Welt!

In this inconspicuous, minute alteration [5] (apart from the ingenious rhythmical shaping) is centered the actual process of creation. Whether the composer came to it in the flash of a momentary vision or in a lengthy creative struggle, we do not know. We only know the result, which tells us that inspirational *and* structural forces—nobody can deny that it really is an inversion which lies here at the base—must have combined to bring this theme about.

Having thus outlined the architectural affinities of the symphony's main themes, this description would have to be complemented by much further detail if a full insight into this great work's structure were our immediate goal. This, however, would require a separate analytic study which is beyond our present purpose.

Only one specific feature shall be briefly elaborated upon, as it forms a decisive element, a central pillar, as it were, in the work's admirable architectural edifice. It is that *progression from D to B-flat* in which, as demonstrated above, the two statements of the opening theme present themselves both in the first and in the last movement. This step from D to B-flat develops to an ever recurring effect in the symphony's structural course and correspondingly also in its dramatic and emotional evolution.

Already in the opening theme, which climbs from D to its peak on the B-flat, this motivic progression forms its emphatic melodic contour:

Ex. 26

sf sf sf sf sf sff

---

[5] From a subtler structural view it will of course be realized that the "change" itself is also a motivic feature, as the phrase thus brought about (*a*) is, as such, a kind of inversion, or transformation, of the original (*b*):

Ex. 25

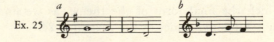

a   b

This motif is still more profoundly rooted in the second Allegro theme. For here it represents the innermost structural idea. It has already been pointed out how the essence of the first theme, the D-minor triad, also sounds through from the second theme. This second theme, however, is actually in the key of B-flat major. Thus, not only the D-minor triad, which is the Allegro theme's first statement, but at the same time the B-flat-major triad, meaning the second statement, is audible from its shape:

Ex. 27

In fact, the combining of the two statements of the first theme is the motivic idea from which the structure of the second theme came to life. Such a procedure, the building of a thematic shape from a blending of two previous ones, is one of the favorite means in the technique of classical composers, one which endows their creations with such astounding logic and consistency. In this instance the motivic progression from D to B-flat, as manifested through the Allegro theme's two statements, forms the core of this impressive structural feature.

This step is also heard in the opening of the Scherzo. Here D to B-flat is transposed to A to F. True, one could say that A to F is in itself a part of the D-minor triad and, therefore, naturally included in any occurrence of the first theme, and in this connection hardly to be understood as a separate feature. Yet in the Scherzo it grows to particular emphasis by means of the instrumentation. For, thus sculptured by a stroke of genius into singular transparency, the step A to F becomes a powerful expression of the described motivic progression:

Ex. 28

No more effective way could have been found to impress this A to F on the listener than thus lifting it from the regular course of the instrumentation by letting the F sound in a melodic thunder from the timpani. Indeed, it is this motivic relation which, once established, echoes in the listener's ear through the whole movement, rendering the later recurrences of these timpani F's (no matter where the soprano has wandered in the meantime) one of the most mysterious effects in all music.

This fundamental motivic third is, in the further course of the Scherzo, reiterated with such almost overemphatic vigor that the composer's conscious intention to impose this effect on the listener cannot be doubted. During the transition between the Scherzo's exposition and the development section, the following group is heard (of which only the bass line is quoted in full):

Ex. 29

In seemingly endless succession the motivic thirds march by. Though harmonic logic compelled the composer in some cases to change major thirds to minor, the continuity of the phenomenon is not to be mistaken. Bar by bar, the harmony progresses over the thirds into new and unknown regions: C, A, F, D, B-flat, G, E-flat, on and on. With each bar, each "modulation," there is a new and exciting surprise, until, in the last few bars, this dynamic as well as thematic crescendo reaches its peak.

It has already been demonstrated how this same relation from D to B-flat emerges in the opening theme of the Adagio, this

"D-minor theme in B-flat" (see example 5).

In the Adagio it is also audible as a concrete utterance, precisely at the summit of the movement's structural and dramatic development, when the horns and trumpets in utter fortissimo fall from the F to the D-flat of the full orchestra:

Ex. 30

However, not until the Finale is this phenomenon led to a climax. The Finale opens with a particular harmony:

Ex. 31

This multiple unprepared suspension, which, moreover, abruptly opens a movement, this combination—in fact, collision—of a D-minor and B-flat-major triad, so often in floundering attempts at explanation quoted as a proof of Beethoven's revolutionary style if not, stupidly, of his deafness, can be understood only from a *thematic* angle. For it is none other than an explosive expression of the D to B-flat motif compressed into a harmony, into one chord.

When later, before the entrance of the human voice, the opening section of the Finale is repeated, the chord is sounded once more, now increased to an utterance of apocalyptic power:

Ex. 32

Again we hear the collision of the D and B-flat harmonies, to which the dominant seventh of D (A, C-sharp, E, G) is added. Here the note B-flat need not even be interpreted as denoting a separate harmony, but it can be regarded as a part of the dominant harmony of D-minor; namely, the dominant ninth, A, C-sharp, E, G, B-flat. Thus any harmonic explanation of the chord must necessarily remain ambiguous and artificial. But from a thematic angle the feature assumes real meaning. For besides the basic motivic step D to B-flat, latent also in this increased harmony, the present chord discloses in its thematic sum total an expression, or rather a compression into one chord, of the full line of the work's main theme. The notes of this second chord read: D, E, F, G, A, B-flat, C-sharp. In other words, the chord consists of the notes of the D-minor scale, the very notes from which the Allegro's main theme (example 1) is formed, which is in turn the source for all the themes of the symphony.

Admittedly, it was a programmatic idea that led the composer to this feature. For the work's dramatic course had reached such a degree of overconcentrated intensity that the composer, wrestling for adequate expression, attempted to force, as it were, the entire thematic content into one chord. But through this the boundaries of the rational were almost burst asunder. Therefore the human voice is introduced, entering with the words, "O friends, no more of these sad tones, but let us intonate more pleasant and more joyous ones." The stimulus for this feature was indeed based on a programmatic vision. But this vision was materialized through musical, that is, structural and, in particular, thematic means.[6]

Through all this the dramatic function of the basic step D to B-flat gained greatly in power. For only when the listener has become accustomed to accepting this step as a fundamental motif, a symbol of one of the work's strongest impulses—no matter whether he

---

[6] The reaction of Hector Berlioz to this feature, which strongly attracted his attention, is extremely interesting. In one of his essays on Beethoven, after having convincingly elaborated on the programmatic idea and the harmonic problem of these discords, Berlioz confesses that though he had searched for Beethoven's reason for introducing them, it remained unknown to him. ("J'ai beaucoup cherché la raison de cette idée, et je suis forcé d'avouer qu'elle m'est inconnue.") Thus, since the programmatic and harmonic function was clear to Berlioz, it is obvious that what puzzled him was the *thematic* mystery.

knows the theoretical implications or grasps the phenomenon by instinct—only then will his ear and mind be responsive to the impact of the subsequent overwhelming appearance of this motivic progression at the peak of the work's architectural and dramatic climax, in the group, "Doch der Cherub steht vor Gott—vor Gott!":

Ex. 33

Seldom in the whole musical literature is a harmonic step to be found striking with a power comparable to that of these last two chords.

Through an example like this, a realization may dawn on us of how great an influence the thematic idea in music can exert. Such a step from D to B-flat (or A to F) is an almost neutral musical event that ordinarily would scarcely be noticed. Only through the motivic role that it gradually assumes in the course of the work as a regular element in the forming of the themes and in the establishing of relations between the themes; only through introducing it at the high points of expression, underlined by the effects of a striking instrumentation, as in the Scherzo or in the fortissimo of the choir masses; and, finally, through its connection with the stimulating text—only through all this, and through the whole web of conscious and instinctive conceptions which the structure spins, does this simple step from D to B-flat assume an almost magical importance and open the door to the highest spiritual and emotional spheres.

Thus, as a result of the symphony's thematic analysis, a picture of the most manifold, most effective, and most logical architectural interconnections has unfolded itself, far beyond that hitherto ascribed to a classical symphony.

Specifically, a far-reaching analogy, in fact a full identity in pattern, was seen between the first themes of the four movements (first Allegro theme, Scherzo theme, first Adagio theme, and "Ode") and also between the second themes (second Allegro theme, Trio theme, second Adagio theme, and "Hymn"). Since, in addition, the first and second Allegro themes themselves proved to be built from one common substance, it can be said in a wider sense that one thematic idea permeates the whole work.

This last must not be misunderstood. A close analogy is seen only between the four first themes on the one side, and between the four second themes on the other. In this twofold symmetry the actual architectural idea of the symphony is centered. Moreover, in the first and last movement this idea is intensified to an impressive, architecturally developed plan.

Finally, a specific architectural feature presented itself in this ever recurring thematic progression from D to B-flat. This motivic step, first expressed through the two statements of the symphony's opening theme, reappeared invariably at the high points of the work's evolution. Now attention may be directed to a most interesting fact. This same motivic progression also forms the keys of the work's movements, which are D, D, B-flat, D. This question of a thematic key relationship between the movements of a musical composition, on which we merely touch at this time, will become the subject of a more detailed investigation in a later section of this study.

2

SCHUMANN'S KINDERSZENEN:
A "THEME WITH VARIATIONS"

In reading the preceding analysis, the question may have arisen whether the astounding thematic permeation seen in the Ninth Symphony constitutes perhaps a specific case, or whether it can be accepted as an expression of a more general principle. Hence we choose as our next topic of discussion a work that represents an entirely different musical style and artistic endeavor; namely, Robert Schumann's opus 15. Yet, as shall be seen presently, the same idea of thematic unity and thematic metamorphosis discloses itself as the central architectural agent of this work too.

Schumann's opus 15, *Kinderszenen* (Scenes from Childhood), is generally regarded as a kind of suite or, perhaps more properly, as a selection of several small pieces held together by a common frame of mood and idea, a "program," as indicated by the title and subtitles. However, the following outline will show that this view is most incomplete. It does not correspond at all to the broader idea and impulse in which this set of charming miniatures was conceived by the composer. This work is not a selection of independent pieces but a *definite structural unit.* In fact, in its architectural design it comes very close to a "theme with variations."

Schumann at this period of his production especially cultivated a compositional type in which small pieces are accumulated to form a great whole. *Carnaval, Davidsbündler, Kreisleriana,* are other examples in this direction. In one instance, in his opus 13, the *Etudes symphoniques,* he even termed the pieces "variations." However, the *Etudes symphoniques* can hardly be regarded as much closer to the outspoken variation form than the *Kinderszenen.*

31

Actually, all these works lie somewhere between mere suites on the one hand and genuine variations on the other. It must be the task of the following analysis to test the truth of this statement.

1. *"Of Foreign Lands and People"* (Von fremden Ländern und Menschen)

We said that in the inner spirit of their architectural concept the *Kinderszenen* represent a kind of theme with variations. In this sense the opening piece would have to be considered as the theme of the "variations." Accordingly, we must examine its structural design in some detail, as this piece, if our view is valid, must represent the thematic source and sample for all the following ones.

The opening piece reads:

Ex. 34

Let us first look at the main melodic line, the soprano. In its course three elements, each of a different character, are discernible as melodic motifs:

Ex. 35

motif I, the *main* motif;
motif II, a little phrase, somewhat in the form of a *turn;*
motif III, a kind of *ascending scale.*

The piece starts with motif I, which is first repeated literally and then uttered again, this time in a slightly varied version to which is annexed a concluding phrase.

The difference between the new version and the original is that a falling third emerges as its melodic characteristic, which also appears in the concluding phrase:

Ex. 36

This falling third continues as a melodic feature throughout the next group, the "turn":

Ex. 37

Through this a motivic connection is established between the main section (characterized through motif I) and the intermediary group of the piece (motif II).

A connection between motifs I and III is then brought about through the fact that motif III, the "scale," is itself an ascending sixth and thus mirrors the beginning of motif I. Had Schumann notated the recapitulation which follows as a literal repetition of the beginning, it would have started with motif I. However, he altered the B to D (see asterisk in the following example):

In this way a variant of motif I, beginning with a fourth instead of a sixth, is brought about, which we may call I*a*

and, as will be seen, the composer, in the course of the work, uses both I and I*a*, interchangeably, as thematic shapes.

From this design emerges an interesting effect. Schumann imposed a fermata on the B before the recapitulation:

Thus endowed with melodic emphasis, the B connects itself to the ensuing phrase; through this, the original motif I sounds from this line together with I*a* (as shown in the above example).

Before closing our examination of the first piece, we may trace a few thematic features in the secondary voices, for so far we have dealt only with the soprano. In bar 5 (see example 34) the second chord in the left hand carries in some editions [1] two little marks;

---

[1] As everyone with some insight knows, the problem of authenticity in musical texts is often difficult. Since many composers corrected and recorrected their music endlessly, even original manuscripts, where still existent, furnish no answer as to the composer's final decision. Early editions, especially of Beethoven and Schumann, are invariably full of contradictions in phrasing, tempo, dynamics, accents, and even notes. Some of the accents quoted in our analysis of Kinderszenen may therefore be found only in

namely, an arpeggio and an accent, which performers usually ignore because they are not aware of their meaning. However, through these marks the main motif (B, G, E, D), which sounded in the soprano, reappears as a delicate contrapuntal imitation in the bass (example 41*a*).

Moreover, looking at the alto and tenor of the theme as a whole, we realize that these voices are by no means without thematic meaning. They spell variants of motif II, the turn (example 41*b*).

Also, when this turn becomes the leading thematic figure in the intermediary group, motif I is not forgotten. It sounds as a kind of inversion through a connection of the soprano and bass (example 41*c*).

Ex. 41

some editions and may be missing in others. The reader will realize that the content of our demonstration is in no way dependent upon which of these readings finally proves correct—even if they do not, as must often be assumed, actually represent the composer's opinion at different times.

2. *"Curious Story"* (Kuriose Geschichte)

Here our real investigation sets in. Is it thinkable, we must ask, that the theme, the gentle tune, which represents the opening piece is again manifested through the totally different shapes of the second piece? This second piece opens with this group:

Apart from its characteristic rhythmical feature ♩ ♪ 𝄿 ♪ ♩ we would at first glance hardly credit this piece with any similarity to the foregoing. However, shining out are some corner notes to which a deeper meaning should be attached. Connecting the accented notes, the following shape emerges (there are accents on B and D in some editions, while G is accented in all):

Thus there can no longer be any doubt: the main theme, motif I of the first piece (in fact, a combination of motifs I and Ia), discloses itself as the melodic basis, the inner contour, as it were, of this piece too.

Motif Ia appears also in the phrase of bars 2 and 3 of the theme (quoted as *a* in the following example), and even in the miniature of the grace-note ornament with which the piece begins (*b*):

Moreover, the astounding analogy continues. For here too, just as in the opening piece, motif II, the turn (plus the falling thirds), follows in the intermediary group:

motif II

Ex. 45

Motif III, finally, the ascending-sixth scale, appears in phrases such as that quoted as example 46*a*, or, on another occasion, as a canon to the fully worked out motif I (example 46*b*):

Ex. 46

a

I

b

III

III

3. *"Hide-and-Seek"* (Hasche-Mann)

The opening group of number 3 is given in the following example, to which a contour is added below:

Ex. 47

Again motif I, or, as we may now justly call it, the work's *prime thought,* is the melodic base. The motif, however, only frames the group. But looking at the phrase within the frame, we realize that it too represents none other than a transposed utterance of the same motif (example 48*a* being an expression of the [transposed] motif, example 48*b*):

Ex. 48

a   *b*

This transposed motif is thus interwoven, as it were, into the original one. Such a method of putting one motif on top of the other and thus creating a new shape is a frequent device in thematic technique. We will come across other instances in the course of our investigation.

In this piece too, not only the opening group but the whole outline is shaped as a mirroring analogy to the first piece. Perhaps more than through any explanation, this will become apparent by quoting the intermediary groups of the two pieces, one beneath the other, and letting the reader compare their melodic kernels. Though naturally considerably varied, the basically identical impulse can scarcely be questioned:

4. *"Pleading Child"* (Bittendes Kind)

The reader accustomed to thematic comparison will here recognize the analogy immediately:

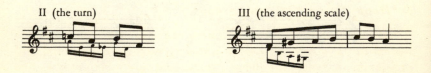

This analogy is the more impressive because these shapes are not figures chosen at random but the beginnings of the three groups of the piece—a design that mirrors the scheme of the opening piece completely.

To sum up what the analysis of Schumann's opus 15 has revealed so far, one fact stands out most strikingly: the thematic thought of the first piece is also the basic shape from which the following pieces were formed. It sounds from all of them through the same notes and *even at the same pitch,* different in appearance and key though the single pieces may be:

Ex. 51

In the analysis of the Ninth Symphony, similar phenomena became visible. But here, in the *Kinderszenen,* they appear transferred into a different language and orbit. The whole spirit of the romantic era speaks from this shaping, in which a charming initial thought emerges in a fourfold kaleidoscopic transformation of mood and key: first as G-major, then as D-major, then B-minor, finally, again D-major. Yet it always remains literally the same shape and pitch.

5. *"Happy Enough"* (Glückes genug)

Naturally, in a selection of thirteen pieces that the composer wished to build into an artistic whole of expanded emotional and programmatic range, the theme cannot continue indefinitely at one pitch. Sooner or later, not only the pieces but the themes themselves must modulate to different keys.

Therefore in number 5, which is in D-major, the theme itself is transposed to the key of the piece. At this new pitch it sounds from the soprano and answers, again transposed, from the bass:

Ex. 52

The theme reappears later in various forms and transpositions, according to the modulations of the piece.

Motif II, the turn, is also audible in such shapes as

Ex. 53

Nor is motif III, the ascending scale, missing. It emerges from the bass of the concluding group (example 54*a*). Again we should note one of Schumann's meaningful accents, appearing on the B-flat of the bass in the second to last bar. The accent lifts this impressively discordant note out of the general melodic course. Thus our ear will easily connect it with the following soprano, producing the phrase B-flat, G, F-sharp, E, D. Or, in other words, the work's prime thought at original pitch sounds again even from this piece.

In fact, this same phrase was already interwoven into the soprano in the preceding bars. The chart below (example 54*b*) demonstrates the group's amazing thematic design.

Ex. 54

6. *"Important Event"* (**Wichtige Begebenheit**)

In order to recognize this piece as a derivative of the first, we have only to visualize the theme of number 1 minus the opening note (*a* in the following example), instead of in its original version (*b*).

Ex. 55

But because in this way the group might have seemed too short, a few notes were added by the composer, expressing motif II. Thus the theme reads:

Ex. 56

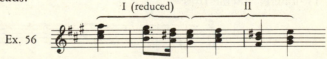

Moreover, motif II appears in this piece again, this time exactly in its appointed place; namely, at the beginning of the intermediary group. And the student may be interested to observe how elaborate is Schumann's thematic handling. For since motif II, as just indicated, was already interpolated in the opening theme, the composer, to avoid monotony, does not reintroduce it literally, but uses a slightly varied version, as is seen in example 57. In the second to last bar of this example he could easily have notated G instead of E in the soprano, by which the theoretical analogy to motif II would have been completed. But his compositional impulse called for the less obvious version, which adds a new melodic nuance, very fitting to the character of this piece.

Ex. 57

Finally, motif III, the ascending-sixth scale, also emerges from the bass:

Ex. 58

And at this point, when the bass rises to its melodic climax, the prime thought—the prime thought at original pitch, the shape conceived as G-major—rumbles also from this piece in A-major. By lifting the accented notes of the last example to a higher octave, this becomes clearly noticeable:

Ex. 59

7. "Träumerei"

In number 7 we find ourselves in an entirely different sphere, key, and mood. First it would seem that motif I*a* rather than I represents the leading thematic feature. However, it appears only as an indication in the theme's opening (C, F, E), from which the familiar "Träumerei" theme rises:

Ex. 60

And from this lyric ecstasy, motif I itself (transposed, yet in its full design) sounds as the theme's innermost melodic utterance. In fact, we hear it simultaneously from the soprano and the tenor:

Ex. 61

In this piece, owing to its individual character, the composer chooses to elaborate on the main motif only, omitting motifs II and III. No new analytical detail, therefore, has to be pointed out. One feature, however, cannot be overlooked, for it strikes us with an almost uncanny power; namely, that at one point a clear indication of the prime thought at original pitch sounds through again—even from these shapes in F-major:

Ex. 62

The thematic meaning, included in the above arpeggio, thus becomes understood.

8. *"By the Fireside"* (Am Kamin)

This piece, though in tempo and character quite different, may, with regard to its thematic substance, be regarded almost as an echoing variant of the preceding "Träumerei."

Here it is indeed motif I*a* (again transposed to F) from which the theme (example 63*a*) is formed. And, significantly, in this piece too, the motif at original pitch is indicated at one point (*b*)—in fact, through the same arpeggiated chord as in the "Träumerei."

Ex. 63

Here a few remarks may be inserted. It should be realized that, in addition to the main features to which we endeavor to direct the attention, an abundance of additional thematic connections can be traced in the design of this work, especially in the web of its secondary voices. Only by comprehending this fact in all its complexity can a conception of the composer's full intentions be gained. Yet, so far, we have ignored most of these secondary features, since

at this initial point our aim was above all to promote an understanding of the main principle of our subject, in the hope that as
the reader gradually becomes familiarized with the thematic view,
he will detect some of these ramifications for himself.

In this piece, however, one extraordinary example of elaborate
structural handling should be pointed out in detail; namely, the
thematic design of its intermediary section. For it may bring us to a
realization that the full understanding of a work's thematic design
is not merely of theoretical significance but may often have far-
reaching *practical consequences* concerning the work's interpretation.

The intermediary group of number 8 forms a section that is almost
always obscured in performance. If one looks at this part of the
score, a complete series of striking accents, all on weak beats, will
attract the attention. (In this instance, the accents are unquestionably from Schumann's own hand and appear in all editions.) Yet in
performance these accents are usually not observed, or if they are,
one has the feeling that the executant accepts them because they are
prescribed, unaware of their meaning and by no means convinced
of their artistic necessity and strength.

However, in reality these accents alone make of these bars a logical
and understandable design. They form not only the clue to this
group's actual content but at the same time represent a window, as
it were, which permits us to follow the true compositional process
from which the whole section evolved. This intermediary group
reads:

Ex. 64

Looking at this group, one can understand why from a purely rhythmical angle (apart from the thematic phenomenon involved) these accents appear as a rather whimsical, if not nonsensical, feature (note bars 4, 5, and 6 in the upper line of the above example). However, by etching out the accented notes together with the particles linked to them, a thematic design suddenly emerges, surprising in its clarity and transparent logic:

Ex. 65

As indicated by the braces, we see first motif I (in this instance opening with a falling instead of an ascending sixth, just as in the intermediary group of the first piece [see Ex. 41c]) after which three notes follow, forming a kind of echo of the foregoing; then the same motif I is again twice repeated (the second time transposed) in a charming canonic shaping. All these instances feature the falling sixth, and only just before the recapitulation which follows does the motif reappear in its original shape with a rising sixth. (The C in the bass of bar 8 of the example needed no accent, being at that moment the only note played.)

This is the picture that emerges through a linking of different voices according to the accents—representing, of course, only the secondary design. But does not the leading voice, the soprano itself, also express a thematic content? As is to be expected, the question must be answered in the affirmative. The soprano expresses the same ever recurring motif; it expresses it in a large contour, thus all the more emphatically. We have merely to notate the last two chords of this group an octave higher to make this transparent:

Ex. 66

Thus we see how strong is the thematic impulse permeating this group; but we also realize that no simpler and more effective way than these accents is thinkable, in order to make the full content of the group transparent to the performer and, if understood by the latter, to the listener.

9. *"Hobbyhorse"* (Ritter vom Steckenpferd)

The syncopated rhythm that, thematically so meaningful, sprang up in number 8 is carried over, intensified, and led to a climax in number 9. However, it is important to realize that in this piece the accents no longer emphasize hidden thematic figures but are here simply rhythmical features, expressing the programmatic idea of the hobbyhorse. Accordingly, the accents appear, indiscriminately throughout the whole piece, on the last crotchet of every bar, while the thematic lines emerge independently from this charming play of syncopated chords.

The opening group of number 9 is seen in example 67, from which a contour emerges, again clearly mirroring the work's basic shape.

However, here too we may search for the prime thought at original pitch. But it becomes apparent that here it is no longer audible. The most that can be said is that a remnant of it may perhaps still be detectable in the lower voices.

Ex. 68

Some readers, though now perhaps more accessible to the thematic principle, may still reject even this qualified interpretation as artificial. Since here again an essential point of the thematic technique is involved, we may supplement this example with a few general remarks.

Let us once more refer to the structural role of the accents in the foregoing piece (number 8). The thematic picture disclosed by these accents was composed as a musical reality. The motivic phrases brought to light by accentuation amid this web of voices were really intended as musical utterances to be heard in the performance.

In contrast, the feature now quoted is of a different nature. And to declare that the prime thought at original pitch is detectable even in this piece through the phrase given in example 68 means no more than that it is barely detectable. It does not imply by any means that this B, G, E, should be artificially accented by the performer, nor that it must be heard and understood as a motivic utterance by the listener. The unnoticeable influence that it may exert on the listener as a passing subconscious recollection—in fact, *its theoretical existence in the piece*—suffices. It constitutes a symbol of the ever recurring idea, nothing more.

We remember that phrases such as

Ex. 69

sounding from the work's beginning, emerged at the same pitch from the opening themes of numbers 2, 3, and 4. The themes of the following pieces, then, presented transposed versions of the same motif. But even in these pieces the utterance at original pitch was still heard, though, as the work proceeded, in ever less emphatic phrasing, in ever less noticeable indication.

Now, in number 9, a point is finally reached where it has almost entirely disappeared. Here only that remote remnant of it is traceable. And we must understand that this was the composer's clear intention. It would have been easy to bring the motif to the fore through a slight change in shaping or even through some accents, had he wished to do so. But his architectural vision called for a more elaborate plan. Just as in the harmonic sphere any effective modulation wanders away from the original key, without ever entirely losing the connection to it, so here, in the thematic domain, the original shape [2] has dwindled almost completely, only to reappear in full clarity in the following concluding pieces. In this emphatic reappearance of the motif at original pitch in the ensuing part of the work, the consciousness and intention of the architectural planning becomes visible.

10. *"Almost Too Serious"* (Fast zu ernst)

The opening, like all openings in the work, features variants of the prime thought, adapted, as usual, to the specific character [3] and key (example 70*a*, *b*):

Ex. 70

In the latter shape, as easily seen, motif III, the ascending-sixth scale, is also included. In the intermediary group motif II duly emerges:

---

[2] It should not be forgotten that all this refers only to the shape at original pitch, while, as demonstrated, the transposed shape forms the thematic kernel in this piece just as in all the others.

[3] From an architectural angle it is interesting to observe how the syncopated rhythm of the two preceding pieces still echoes in number 10, though this piece, as such, has returned to the peaceful lyricism that is the basic mood of the work.

Ex. 71

But now motif I at original pitch again becomes clearly audible. However, it is an original pitch that is, as it were, modified by the accidentals of this specific key—a "sharpened original pitch," if this expression is permissible:

Ex. 72

Here it should be understood that the reappearance of a thematic shape, *changed through the use of accidentals,* is not a casual feature merely introduced to strengthen our point. Such a change of accidentals is one of the frequent and basic devices used in thematic technique. Just as a shape first heard in major might later appear in minor, or vice versa, without its substance being touched, likewise a change in accidentals, while otherwise preserving the thematic essence, has become an established feature in thematic transformation. We will come across many more, often striking examples of this type.

11. *"Affrighting"* (Fürchtenmachen)

In Number 11, then, the circle is concluded. The main motif, the work's prime thought, sounds again as the theme of the piece. The opening bars themselves, in their course from B up to E and back over E-flat, D, C (see following example), would perhaps point to motif Ia. However, by listening to the larger contour (given below the theme in the following example), we recognize the full prime melody as the regained theme:

Ex. 73

Motif II, the turn, is, as always, expressed in the intermediary section. However, there are two intermediary sections in this piece; first, the group:

Ex. 74

In the soprano of this group the motif would call for an A on the third beat (see asterisk in the example above), but Schumann chose F-sharp instead, since the A sounds already from the bass.

But from the second intermediary group the motif sounds literally, echoing number I even in pitch:

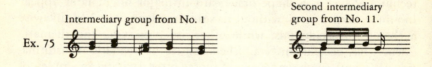

Ex. 75

Intermediary group from No. 1

Second intermediary group from No. 11.

12. *"Child Falling Asleep"* (Kind im Einschlummern)

This piece, which in a programmatic sense represents the last, gives prominence in its themes to the reestablished prime thought at original pitch, both in its true and "sharpened" version:

Ex. 76

Original

Sharpened

With this blending of the two prime versions, the transformation —indeed, the transfiguration—of the work is completed.

Also parallel to this, the poem, the programmatic "story," of *Kinderszenen* is concluded: the child's day is over; it has fallen asleep, perhaps, as the funereal rhythm of this piece might indicate, to eternal sleep. Now the poet himself steps before the curtain and adds his epilogue.

13. *"The Poet Speaks"* (Der Dichter spricht)

Though naturally this shaping could also in its essence have been derived only from the basic material of the whole, we feel that it has something of a tone language of its own. True, a reflection of the prime theme again forms its opening:

However, the interval with which this version starts is neither a sixth (as in motif I) nor a fourth (as in Ia), but a diminished fifth, an "intellectual" version of the prime thought, as a programmatic commentator might perhaps call it. And so we see that in this number 13, *for the first time in* Kinderszenen, *the main theme of a piece is not the prime thought of the work* but merely a variant, a truly new version of it. And this version persists:

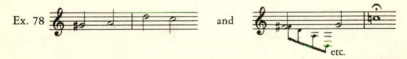

But in the midst of the piece, the poet seems to be overcome by the recollection of the happenings which he himself has created: he remembers, he quotes his own tune—indeed, the old Kinderszenen theme (here adapted to the present pitch and phrasing) reemerges in utter pianissimo, like a vision of things past:

Schumann, through small print and a notation free of bar lines, lifts this part out of the actual piece. This is a programmatic, a poetic feature, and it is not to be confused with those Lisztian small-print cadenzas of "brilliancy" that lack content, rhythm, and thematic meaning. The whole feature is truly on the border line of what, in the transcendental realm, can be expressed by rational shaping and notation. Accordingly, it is also revealing that within this notation in small print the composer still left a few notes in bold print (see last example). They are the very notes through which the specific thematic course of number 13 (with the characteristic diminished fifth) is continued.

After this episode the piece (and the work) concludes with a repetition of the opening of the piece and a few annexed bars, which read:

Ex. 80

and we recognize how the composer managed, almost miraculously, to let the work's first and prime thought sound again through this last utterance. *Kinderszenen* began with

Ex. 81   and

and though evolving from a different structure and assuming a different role, it ends with the same melodic shape. It is necessary to comprehend this phenomenon in its full meaning. We remember how the prime thought emerged, in the course of the work, in innumerable versions, in various rhythms, harmonies, and keys that expressed all kinds of different moods. But never in all this variety was the motif brought to a conclusion through its own shape. The last note, D, of the motif, though appearing in every imaginable harmonization, none the less never became a real end, a tonic. Once in the course of the work, at the end of number 5, the D in the motif seemed to take on a conclusive quality (see example 54). However, this conclusion was directed toward D-major, that is, toward a key that, within the work's architectural whole, could not form a definite solution. Thus even in this instance the motif remained but a wave in a ceaseless melodic stream, the goal of which remained out of sight. But now, through a new harmonic change, this same motivic thought becomes suddenly a harbor and end:

Ex. 82

With this transformation of the last D into a part of the tonic G—a change so simple, chaste, and convincing that only a genius could have invented it—all the structural and emotional tensions of the work come to their final resolution.

This last feature leads us to a specific consideration which, together with the insight gained in the working of the thematic principle as such, may have emerged as an additional discovery from the preceding analysis. It is the realization that there is, besides the familiar modulations and key progressions which the compositional course of a work represents, another progression formed by the keys or, perhaps more adequately expressed, *by the pitches and key qualities* of its thematic material. This second progression forms a modulatory cycle of its own in the work's architecture.

To indicate this, we may once more, in a kind of chart, recall the appearance of the prime thought in the thirteen themes of the work:

Group I (numbers 1, 2, 3, 4)

In this group *the motif at original pitch* forms the themes (either directly or integrated).

Ex. 83

No. 1   No. 2

No. 3   No. 4

Group II (numbers 5, 7, 8 and 6, 9)

In this group *the transposed motif* forms the themes. Note that the themes of numbers 5, 7, and 8 are even identical in pitch, save for the accidentals; also, the themes of 6 and 9 differ only with regard to the accidentals.

Group III (numbers 10, 11, 12)

The motif at original pitch reappears. It is heard at *"sharpened"* pitch in number 10; at *regular* pitch as the theme's contour in number 11; *regular and sharpened* side by side in number 12.

Group IV (number 13)

Here a *new and transposed version* forms the theme (13*a*). However, the original motif sounds from the last chords through a final harmonization concluding in the tonic (13*b*).

The amazing symmetry of this "modulation of themes" becomes all the more transparent in a final summarized chart, which may be drawn as follows (here number 8 appears almost only as an additional variant of number 7, *les agréments* of number 7, as it were):

Ex. 84

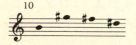

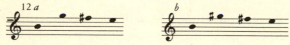

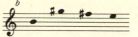

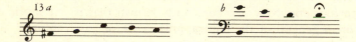

3

HISTORIC ORIGIN: IMITATION, VARIATION, TRANSFORMATION

One feature in our preceding thematic description may have puzzled some readers. As though to something natural and self-understood in a work of Beethoven or Schumann, reference was occasionally made to a theme or a phrase appearing as the inversion of a previous one. Now it is commonly known that in the music of Bach, or in general of the contrapuntal style of past centuries, inversions, retrogressions, augmentations, and various other such devices were constantly used in the composition's structural formation. But the accepted belief of today would hold that our time, and, for that matter, even the classics, rather abandoned such "academic" devices or, at least, applied them only in particular, exceptional instances, for example, when inserting a fugue. Yet even at this point it may be stated with emphasis that a closer examination of the classical technique proves such an opinion to be entirely erroneous. The classics by no means abandoned these contrapuntal devices. On the contrary, they intensified their meaning and enriched their use, though at the same time modifying the method of their application.

However, contrapuntal devices form only one element, a detail, within a problem of wider scope and more general significance, which must therefore be discussed first. It is the question whether the two styles in music, the one manifested through the structural type of the contrapuntal era, the second through the thematic technique of the so-called "classic" (or classic-romantic) period, *represent two essentially separate compositional principles or merely two different stages of one evolutional development.*

If the two styles represent contrasting principles, further questions arise: Through what alterations or innovations in the structural technique was the change from one principle to the other effectuated? When did it take place? At what period of history and in the works of which compositional schools or individual composers?

Any exhaustive answer to these questions would require an extensive sifting of historical detail, which is beyond the purpose of this study. Therefore, from the specifically historical aspect the following presentation may prove very incomplete. Yet the historic point cannot be omitted entirely. For as far as the principle of the problem is concerned, an answer must be attempted, since a clear understanding of the principle is an indispensable presupposition for the comprehension of the thematic process itself.

From the outset we must distinguish between two fundamentally different phenomena: *contrapuntal imitation* and *thematic transformation.*

In a *canon or a fugue* a shape is repeated or obviously imitated, either directly, or by inversion, augmentation, or similar devices. Any deviation from the repetition or obvious imitation would be considered an expedient. For an attempt to vary the original shape, instead of repeating and imitating it, would destroy the very idea and spirit that these compositional forms are meant to express. Logically the composer does not wish to conceal the fact that his next utterance is a reiteration of the preceding one; he wants to emphasize it. Indeed, the artistic strength and appeal of these forms is largely based on this very ability to reiterate literally the thematic shapes in as many voices and combinations as possible and still to build from these repetitions a unified whole convincing in its expressiveness and variety.

In a *sonata or symphony,* on the contrary, the spirit of the form is fulfilled only if the shapes are transformed in such a way that the new theme *seems* to be entirely different from the one from which it is derived. True, Haydn in his symphonies sometimes introduces a theme that according to all signs of the outer proportions represents a second theme but proves to be a mere repetition of the first theme. In the light of the ensuing evolution, however, this must be considered a problematic shaping—a shaping that may be explained simply by the fact that in this early stage the deeper idea of the symphonic form and the thematic technique through which it was expressed were not fully realized even by the same great musical mind who, in a sense, must be regarded as its father and discoverer. But in the advanced symphonic style, the era of genuine thematic transformation, a composer's ability to form a theme from a preceding one must be considered the more effective, the less the outer similarity of the two themes is recognizable, in spite of identity in kernel.

In this style, therefore, it must be the composer's endeavor not to emphasize the identity but to conceal it. To state this in a way perhaps still more appropriate: a thematic transformation must be regarded as most impressive from a structural angle if the identity is rooted strongly and firmly in the depths of the shapes in question and at the same time is as inconspicuous and little traceable as possible on the surface.

If this antagonism between imitation and transformation were the only distinction characterizing the two different styles, the contrapuntal on the one hand and the thematic on the other,[1] the problem would be a simple one. However, imitation was not the only structural means in the contrapuntal era. In that era too, themes were not merely imitated but were also varied. And in the thematic technique they were imitated, varied, and transformed.

A glance through history will make us understand how these various principles originated, how their interrelationships developed, and their forces were balanced.

Stepping far back in time, we observe that in the long period before our occidental evolution, contrapuntal conceptions were by their nature unthinkable, since music at that stage was, as every musician knows, confined to essentially monodic forms. However, we discover that even in these earliest examples of "composition" both repetition and variation present themselves as apparently a most natural means of structural formation. There is little ancient

---

[1] The author is well aware that in using the words "contrapuntal" and "thematic" to distinguish these styles he is employing an entirely inaccurate terminology. The music of the contrapuntal-polyphonic period makes ample use of themes and thematic shapes, while on the other hand the works of the classic, the "thematic" era are permeated by polyphony and counterpoint. Yet, because within the traditional, generally understandable terminology no more adequate expressions seemed available, the author contented himself with these familiar ones, trusting that no musician would be at a loss as to their meaning.

music of which we know, either through direct preservation or through reconstruction, be it Chinese, Indian, Jewish or Greek, in which, besides simple repetition, a varied reiteration of parts and particles does not constitute a foremost structural agent.

In the crowning phase of this monodic development, then, in the Gregorian chant, the compositional course very obviously, indeed, very emphatically, consists of such varied reiteration, or shall we say, reiterated variation of certain phrases.

The question whether such motivic variation should be termed a first attempt at our modern "thematic transformation" is rather unimportant. The composers, whoever they were, in this long remote period of music were certainly not too much concerned with what "thematic" principles materialized in their creations. They simply followed their musicality, their inborn structural trend, in which conscious and instinctive elements concurred and where, consequently, all shades and degrees of "imitating" and "varying" peacefully emerged side by side.

However, when polyphony is introduced into art music, in the centuries around the turn of the millennium, more specific problems present themselves for consideration. The question of prime interest, from the point of view of our subject, in this earliest stage of polyphony is: Did such thematic affinities, either through imitation or variation, appear in the second and third voices, which now were added to the basic melodic line?

For this initial period of polyphony, the question must decidedly be answered in the negative. These first contrapuntal lines, emerging from the originally theoretical form of the organum and the later practical attempts, do not reveal any thematic relationship to the main voice. At this primitive stage the musician's capacity was obviously fully absorbed by the endeavor to find any contrapuntal lines at all, which in sound (at least according to the then valid concepts) seemed fitting to the main voice. He could not concern himself as well with the possibility of establishing thematic affinities between the voices.

Gradually, however, in the course of the evolution, since it obviously corresponds to an inborn sense of musical formation, such affinities between the voices emerged in the compositional design, at first sporadically and perhaps instinctively, later more frequently and clearly intentionally. And though this development was not a uniformly continuous process but was often interrupted by periods in which the trend toward "thematification" seems to have paled, we still see that a few centuries later, at the bloom of the contrapuntal evolution, a definite and very close connection between the different voices of a musical composition was considered as a self-understood, indeed, as the basic structural phenomenon in music.

And from the beginning such affinities between the voices were achieved both through imitation and variation. Even in the very early, primitive polyphony of some twelfth and thirteenth century compositions, we occasionally see phrases of one voice reappear in another voice, either literally imitated or slightly varied. In the ensuing centuries this technique was greatly developed. In the fifteenth century, for instance, the technique of varying a given shape, for example, a Gregorian tune, by all kinds of figurate treatment, by freely expanding or reducing it, was already in full swing; in fact, it formed the center of the structural endeavor. Imitation was also practiced, but not as generally and extensively as was variation. It was mostly confined to specific canonic types of composition.

Here we come to a striking turning point. For within a century, in a quick, victorious evolution, imitation became the most emphatic structural device in the compositional technique. This technique of imitation rose to a peak of perfection, producing a treasury of great musical literature, though often also complicated compositional constructions—"artifices of the Netherlanders"—an evolution which reached its final clarification and culmination in Palestrina, Lassus, and others.

But while imitation strove to this height, the other principle, variation, was by no means discarded. Yet it did not at that time progress to as comprehensive and methodical an art of structural formation as did imitation. It rather remained at the comparatively simple stage that it had reached a few centuries before. No definite system, no concrete *technique of thematic varying* was yet developed. This decisive step from a simple stage of varying to an elaborate, subtle technique was not taken until the thematic, the classical style superseded the contrapuntal. This more elaborate, more complex method of varying a given shape we call *transformation*.

With regard to the structural principles just described, one difference is of specific interest. The "contrapuntal" composers, no matter whether they imitated or varied a theme, intended that the imitation or variation should be recognizable as such. They did not wish to create a new theme but wished to repeat the original, literally or with slight, well defined changes. In contrast, in the classical technique of transformation it is the composer's intent to produce a theme which is entirely new in appearance and character, though derived from the same essence and kernel.

Naturally, however, in practical music there is no clear border line between these different principles, and it is by no means always distinguishable when a change ceases to be mere "varying" and begins to be "transformation." At any rate, a definite terminology in this respect is rather unimportant. But it is important to distinguish between the different principles. *Varying* (plus imitation) represents the foremost structural agent in the period before the classics. *Transformation* (plus varying and imitation) is the main forming factor in the era from the classics on.

When this change from variation to transformation actually took place—in what period or compositional school or in the works of which individual composer—is not entirely clear. One is rather inclined to think that it must have been a very gradual process, untraceable in its detail. Or was it, after all, Haydn himself, in whose music we can for the first time *clearly* observe the working of this new technique of transformation, who as one man "invented" it? Even if this were so, it would merely mean that it was he who developed the thematic technique to the all-embracing, irresistible degree that we see in his and his successors' works. For, as mentioned above, the idea as such, the method of reiterating themes in changed versions, was valid and extensively practiced since ancient times. As the evolution progressed, this method was intensified, and it grew particularly strong in parts of the operatic production which set in at the beginning of the seventeenth century: here quite a few of the structural effects that characterize the symphonic period appear anticipated. And now we must even modify our previous formulation. For it must be stressed that at the very height of the contrapuntal era, when imitation and varying were the dominant principles in musical formation, still an ever increasing abundance of features emerge which do not prove mere variations but which may be called indicative forerunners or perhaps even the first manifestations of that process of "transformation" which became the structural basis of the ensuing epoch.

If in the following an illustration is given from a Mass by Palestrina, this by no means implies that these instances are thought to form the only or even the earliest examples of the type. They are examples to which, no doubt, many others from various composers and periods could be added.

The following theme sounds at the entrance of **Palestrina's** *Missa Papae Marcelli:*

and, as is natural in "contrapuntal imitation," the whole first section, the Kyrie Eleison, elaborates on shapes like this or their derivatives.

The next section, the Christe Eleison, opens with the following figures:

on which this section, in turn, elaborates. And it is easily seen that these bars are a reiteration of the second half (marked II in example 85) of the opening theme. This in itself is no surprise. For it is common knowledge that the thematic beginnings of different parts of Masses and other large compositions were shaped in structural affinity even long before Palestrina. (The whole principle of the cantus firmus tends to it.)

But the feature which we wish to demonstrate is more specific. For the first half (marked I) of the opening theme, with its characteristic leap of the fourth upward, is missing in the direct course of the second section's melodic shaping.

Nevertheless, in the performance this feature, too, miraculously becomes audible, thus complementing the thematic affinity of the two sections. This becomes apparent if we connect certain voices, as indicated by the arrows in the following examples:

Ex. 87

Effects like these emerge from the entire section; in fact, the whole of Palestrina's music abounds with features of this kind.

The "thematic" principle becomes still clearer in this "contrapuntal" environment through the following shaping. In the course of one of the next sections the following shape emerges:

Ex. 88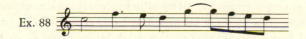

which is obviously a varied intensification of the first half (I) of the opening theme (example 85). Once, however, such variants have taken root in the composer's (and listener's) ear, it seems only natural that the second piece of the Mass, the Gloria, should open with a theme (example 89a) that compared to the theme of the first piece (example 89b) is very close to genuine "transformation."

Ex. 89

This almost resembles the manner in which in a classical symphony a "second subject" might have been developed from the first.

A century and a half later, in the music of Bach, true phenomena of thematic transformation become audible. Though they are used only as passing features, imbedded in a domain which in its structural spirit and substance still belongs to the contrapuntal world, the full intention of producing shapes *that on the surface seem different but are identical in kernel*—the decisive symptom that characterizes the technique of transformation—can here no longer be doubted.

An example from **Bach's D-minor organ fugue** may illustrate this. The theme of the fugue opens with the shape quoted in example 90*a,* which, be it noted, is merely a concentrated, rhythmically altered expression of the beginning of the preceding toccata (example 90*b*):

Ex. 90

After having completed its first utterance, the theme of the fugue reenters as usual in a second voice, with a counterpoint almost paralleling it. But then, before the theme reappears in the third voice, an interlude (still in two voices) is interpolated (example 91*a*), which certainly seems to unfold a picture quite different from that of the theme. Yet connecting the uppermost notes in the line, a contour emerges (example 91*b*) which clearly again expresses the main theme in a slightly modified version (the C-sharp instead of C-natural being merely due to the modulation from G to D).

Ex. 91

The author cannot conceal how deeply impressed he is by features like this (and Bach's music is full of similar ones). Is it not as though we were looking at a crossroad of history, witnessing how one idea of style and musical forming begins to supersede the other?

The whole problem of how this idea of transformation emerged from the contrapuntal realm will again confront us in the third section of this book. There, from a new vantage point, not only the answers but the questions themselves will appear in a different light.

4

VARIOUS CATEGORIES
OF TRANSFORMATION

When the classics replaced the principle of contrapuntal imitation and variation by thematic transformation, they did not have to invent something entirely new. As we have seen in the foregoing chapter, a part of the structural mechanism through which the thematic principle manifests itself was already in full usage in the contrapuntal era.

In particular, there was a specific group of features which the thematic technique could take over directly, ready-made, so to speak, from the contrapuntal sphere. These features were the well known devices of inversion, augmentation, and the like. The thematic technique, indeed, took them all over, but adapted them to its own purpose and spirit. While in the contrapuntal realm these devices were applied literally, the thematic technique used them in a free, flexible manner.

An inversion, for instance, in a mass of Okeghem or Palestrina or in a fugue by Bach, is a shape which note for note repeats in contrary motion, that is, "inverts," the original phrase. And an augmentation "augments" a preceding shape, that is, reiterates it "verbally" in notes of longer value.

But in a Beethoven symphony, as we observed in the analysis of the Ninth, an inversion is, upon a superficial glance, not even recognizable as such, as it may be garbed in a quite new appearance of different rhythm and accent and may even have undergone a considerable change in the melodic shaping itself.

Apart from these standard devices, of which every textbook carries a neat definition, the contrapuntal technique made ample use

66

of a host of others, as, for instance, the above-mentioned alteration of rhythm and accent or the change of the harmonic function of a melodic shape, and many others. They, too, were not simply taken over into the thematic style but were widened and intensified in their meaning and way of application.

Now it has to be understood that all these devices, and many others that were newly added, were seldom used singly in the thematic style, but more often in combination of two, three, or more. A shape, for instance, which was a theme in one movement would appear in the next in its inversion, simultaneously with shifted accents, in a new tempo, and so forth. In fact, this tendency to combine and intensify the devices became the main idea of shaping in the thematic era. It is the very phenomenon which we call transformation. Thus thematic transformation is in the last sense no longer carried out according to any specific device, old or new, that can be formulated, but is brought about freely, in whatever form the compositional inspiration envisions it. The possibilities are innumerable and every ingenious composer constantly invents new methods. In short, the thematic technique no longer inverts, augments, or simply varies the shapes, but transforms them in the full sense of the word.

Therefore, no real list of the different types of thematic transformation can be made, as is done with the contrapuntal devices; and the following enumeration certainly should not be taken as more than an attempt to add further characteristic examples toward the understanding of the thematic principle and of the thematic technique through which it is expressed. In fact, it is, above all, the examples rather than the definitions that count in the following demonstration.

Among these examples, as in our whole study, a greater part was chosen from works of Beethoven. This was done because it seems to the author that the thematic technique, though it unquestionably became the structural basis for our whole epoch's compositional endeavor, never was handled in a more intense, concentrated, and conscious manner than in Beethoven's music, so that most of its phenomena can best be described through quotations from his work. However, once the idea, as such, is understood, it may prove all the more revealing and enjoyable to observe how this principle is applied in different ways by other composers according to their style and individuality, tending toward different effects and a different spirit.

Inversions, Reversions, Interversions

We may start with the most common of all devices, the inversion.[1] Such inversions, as pointed out above, were, in the specifically contrapuntal style, outspokenly technical features, literally repeating a given shape in the opposite direction. (See example in the footnote.) In contrast to this, the idea of an inversion in a work by Beethoven may produce a new shape—a shape brought about

---

[1] To clarify the terminology, the following should be understood. In a strict technical sense *inversions, contrary motions, and retrogressions* (for which latter, for the sake of simplification, the term *reversions* may henceforth be used) are three different conceptions. The inversion of a fourth, for instance, is a fifth, of a third a sixth, and so on. But the contrary motion of the ascending fourth C to F is simply the descending fourth F to C. However, in musical practice these conceptions may often be almost mixed. And we would call it an inversion if, as in the following example from a suite by Bach, the phrase *a* later emerges as *b*:

Ex. 92

though strictly speaking only the first interval appears in inversion, while the remainder should be termed contrary motion. But since the term "inversion" is almost universally accepted for contrary motion, this usage will in general be retained in our analysis.

A reversion, then, is a transformation whereby the last note of a shape is used as the beginning of another, followed by the second to last, and so forth, until the first is reached. Interestingly, however, this does not differ from contrary motion, as long as it is applied only to shapes consisting of straight scales or chords. For instance, the particles given below under *a* would, both in contrary motion and reversion, appear in the forms shown in *b*:

Ex. 93

But as soon as less uniform shapes are concerned, this becomes entirely different. For instance, the shape given in the following under *a* would in contrary motion appear as seen in *b* but in reversion as in *c*:

through some variants of the literal inversion. And the composer carries these changes out freely in whatever way they seem fitting to the part of the composition in which he wishes to include the inverted shape.

In **Beethoven's Rondo in G-major** ("Rage over the Lost Penny") two of the leading themes read as follows:

Ex. 95

There can be no doubt that the second theme *b* was conceived as an inversion of the first *a*. Both themes consist of two symmetrical halves, which in their essence repeat each other. Each first half contains two motivic particles (marked I and II).

Particle I, in the first theme an ascending triad (*a*), appears in the second as a descending triad (*b*); whereas particle II, which in the

Ex. 94

Thus, however, when motifs are of a short, uncomplicated nature, reversions, contrary motions, and inversions are sometimes not to be differentiated.

first theme forms a descending fourth (*c*), becomes in the second theme an ascending fourth (*d*):

Ex. 96

As for the basic material, therefore, the fact of a clear inversion cannot be questioned. Nevertheless, in appearance, as musical expressions, the two themes are distinctly different, chiefly because the first theme has these characteristic figurations which the second theme lacks. Moreover, in the first theme particle II is literally repeated (*a* in the following example), while in the second theme the repetition is transposed (*b*):

Ex. 97

through which an entirely different shape finally emerges.

What we wish to demonstrate is that a shape can be *built as an inversion and still assume a completely new surface*. For the composer, of course, does not produce such a feature "theoretically," first deciding, as it were, upon an "inversion" and then trying to find out how it would read. No, whenever a theme rises in the ear of a structurally trained composer, all kinds of possible transformations will at once automatically flash across his mind. If among these, as in this individual instance, the inversion seems the most fitting, he would accept it as a basis but then shape the new theme as freely as his imagination requires, not caring, indeed, not wishing, that the detail of the second theme should strictly correspond to the first.

The working of the same phenomenon can be most transparently observed in a beautiful example from **Brahms, Two Rhapsodies, opus 79.** Now it can in general be assumed that whenever a composer of structural consciousness includes two or more pieces under one opus number, this should, and frequently does, mean that these items constitute an artistic unit, that they represent a higher architectural whole formed from a common thematic material. Indeed, examining the openings of these two rhapsodies, we will discover that in essence, independent as they look, *the one finally turns out to be the inversion of the other.*

We may put the main groups of the two themes one above the other to facilitate comparison (some questions which the reader may hold will be answered immediately):

Rhapsody I

Ex. 98

Rhapsody II

It hardly needs lengthy explanations to make one realize the affinity binding these two themes together. One must have been produced with the idea of forming a new shape that would mirror the other in the contrary direction. Comparing the corresponding parts (I and II in both examples), we might say that the parts marked I form perhaps a reversion (or contrary motion) rather than a strict inversion—though this question of terminology is of little importance to the matter itself—and that motif II in the second Rhapsody is not the literal inversion but is slightly changed. Yet the idea of an inversion cannot be mistaken. The reader may also have noticed that the opening bar of the second theme (Ia in the following example) was omitted in the above quotation. This was done because Brahms did not include this bar (which after all is a mere transposition of the next) when he built the inversion. However, to what degree of logic and symmetry even such "freedom" can be led by a composer with a highly developed sense of form may be seen by comparing the two themes in their entirety:

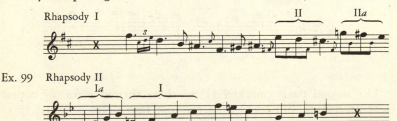

Rhapsody I

Ex. 99   Rhapsody II

We see that the bar at the beginning of Rhapsody II (marked I*a*) has no corresponding bar in Rhapsody I. But this "omission" is balanced at the end of the first Rhapsody's theme by an additional bar (marked II*a*) which, in turn, has no corresponding bar in the theme of Rhapsody II. Besides, just as motif I*a* is but a transposition of I, motif II*a* is merely a transposition of II.

Needless to say, here again the composer certainly has not constructed this symmetry "geometrically." A *musical* impulse must have told him that an inversion would satisfy his vision of the second Rhapsody's theme. Then, however, he worked musically *and* structurally on its final form.

We turn to a new and particular feature. It originates from the fact that, besides these inversions, contrary motions, and reversions, the classics introduced a further device in their technique never mentioned in any textbook—a device which, though somehow related to those inversions and reversions, nevertheless is distinctly different from them. It consists of interchanging the notes of a thematic shape in order to produce a new one. Since the current theory is so unaware of this type of transformation that not even a name has been designated for it, we are compelled to invent a new term and may call it an *interversion*.

Classical compositions in general, and the last works of Beethoven in particular, are full of such interversions. The opening movement (Adagio) of **Beethoven's quartet, opus 131, in C-sharp minor,** for instance, begins with a shape (example 100*a*) which in the last movement (Allegro) appears transformed as *b:*

The second parts (marked II) of these themes form, of course, clear inversions. But looking at the first four notes (marked I),

Ex. 101

we must admit that this is neither an inversion, contrary motion, or any of the accepted devices. Yet no musical mind discovering these two shapes as the main themes in one work would doubt that there is a definite affinity between the two. Therefore we must justly add these "interversions" to the list of structural devices of transformation.

Moreover, this conception of affinity between the two movements is, as in all works of Beethoven, confirmed by the other movements which furnish further examples of characteristic interversions. The pulsating rhythm of the fifth movement, the Presto, which in character seems a world away from the melancholy of the opening Adagio, nevertheless reveals itself on closer examination as springing from the same root. This is proved by the following example, in which the Presto theme is quoted in transposition (a). Comparing the contour (b) of this theme with the theme of the first movement (c), the analogy becomes evident:

Ex. 102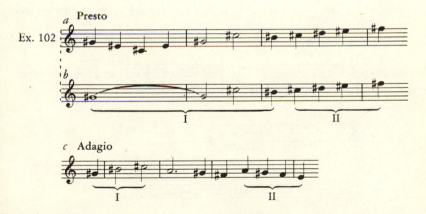

Here too, as in many previous examples, a "free" shaping is applied: three notes of the Adagio theme have no counterpart in the Presto. Yet the otherwise perfect analogy is obvious.

No less apparent is the basic identity in the second movement, the Allegro. molto vivace. Transposing its theme (example 103*a*) to the key of the first movement and comparing it with the latter's theme (example 103*b*), the analogy of the main elements again cannot be doubted:

Ex. 103

The same structural idea that appears in these interversions comes to life on an intensified scale when, as sometimes occurs, not only the single notes of a motif but full parts of themes are interchanged and melted together to create a new theme. Again particularly impressive examples may be chosen from the structural mysticism of one of Beethoven's last quartets, **opus 130.**

The three themes of its first movement, (*a*) the theme of the Adagio-Introduction, (*b*) the first Allegro theme, and (*c*) the second Allegro theme, read as follows:

Ex. 104

The second Allegro theme (*c* in the above example) is obviously none other than a rhythmically changed reiteration of the first Allegro theme (*b*). However, the above is only the second theme's beginning. Its full shape (divided between cello and violin) is quoted in example 105*a*. Examining it closely, we realize that not only the first Allegro theme but also the theme of the Adagio-Introduction (quoted in transposition as example 105*b*) becomes audible in the course of the second theme.

Ex. 105

We must grasp the full impact of this phenomenon: Beethoven forms a second subject by forging the first subject and the theme of the Introduction into one. The rhythm is varied, a few bridging notes are changed, but the whole melodic course of the new theme is clearly the result of a combination of the two preceding ones—clearly and consciously, as this shaping is too complex and too specific to have come about instinctively. As we termed the device of exchanging single notes within a motif interversion, we may call this parallel but increased phenomenon *interversion of the themes.*

Change of Tempo, Rhythm, Accent

Another way through which a thematic shape can be transformed into a new appearance is to change its tempo, rhythm, or accentuation.

Of course, a change of tempo was a device already very much in use in the contrapuntal period, forming the so-called "augmentations" (that is, a slackening of tempo) or diminutions (accelerating it). But what a difference there is between such an augmentation in the contrapuntal style and a transformation representing the same idea in the thematic technique may be shown in the following example from **Beethoven's Sonata in G-major, opus 14, No. 2.** In this work it must have occurred to the composer to form the theme of the second movement, the Andante, as a slowed variant of the first movement's opening figure, or to be precise, of this figure's inversion. This opening figure reads:

Allegro

Ex. 106

Since as a basis for a theme this figure seems somewhat too short, the composer prolongs it by repeating two of its notes:

Ex. 107

Omitting the first note as being identical with the second, the (transposed) inversion of this is the phrase given as *a* in the following example, which is, with a slight melodic license, the theme of the second movement (*b*), *if the tempo is greatly slowed.*

Ex. 108

Startled, some readers might perhaps remark: "Is this not mere coincidence? Is structural planning really involved here?" Yet by extending the comparison to the continuation of this shaping, all doubt must disappear. For in the first movement, after some repetitions of the quoted opening figure, a group (example 109*a*) follows, to which in the second movement example 109*b* clearly forms the corresponding shape:

Ex. 109

Notating the group *b* from the above example in a tempo four times accelerated,

Ex. 110

we realize that, apart from the first notes, this is identical with the above Allegro group (example 109*a*), literally identical in its minutest detail. Now two surprising affinities like these in succession, both based on the same change of tempo, are too realistic a coincidence to have come about by chance. The groups from the Andante are indeed "augmentations," first of the Allegro group's inversion, then of its direct shaping.

No less incisive than changes of tempo are rhythmical alterations. It is amazing how even a small phrase can, through a slight shift of accent and rhythm, often assume an entirely different appearance.

The Grave-Introduction of **Beethoven's Sonata, opus 13,** the so-called "Pathétique," opens with the shape given below as *a*, followed by its transposition (*b*), and later by a version in major (*c*):

Ex. 111

But then the following figures emerge:

Ex. 112

And here one might at first think that the picture has changed and that this is something new. Factually, however, these are still the same melodic phrases, merely with changed rhythm and accent.

Notated without rhythm and rhythmical repetitions, the sonata's opening shape, example 111*a*, and the shape quoted as example 112*a* are identical. That one's ear, however, unless attention is drawn to this fact, is inclined to ignore the identity is merely due to the changed rhythm, especially since the last note in the opening phrase is on a weak beat, while in the second version it is on a strong one.

Thus the next phrase (example 112*b*) needs no further comment.

In spite of its lengthened rhythm and its entirely different accentuation, it again turns out to be in its *melodic* course the sonata's opening figure (with a chromatic note included).

This feature of change of accent was deliberately demonstrated on a short motivic phrase rather than on a full-length theme, since its nature could thus be described more transparently. Moreover, as will soon be realized, such rhythmical changes of small thematic particles rise to a paramount role in the music of the later classics, particularly Brahms.

The mechanism of Brahms's orchestral technique is largely based on this art of cutting out particles from one theme, changing their tempo and rhythm and integrating them in, and linking them to, other themes. Brahms almost regularly delineates the secondary parts with which he accompanies the second subjects in his symphonies with figurations that are differently accented particles from the same work's first theme.

We may follow the beginning of the thematic course in **Brahms's Second Symphony** a little more thoroughly than required for this specific point, as through this not only our list of rhythmical transformations will be enlarged, but our whole understanding of a symphony's compositional design enriched.

The symphony opens with this shape:

Ex. 113

As seen by the braces, this group is built from two motivic figures (I and II). This first group is followed by another, reading:

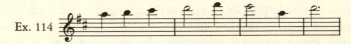

Ex. 114

which represents a slightly varied reiteration of the last three bars from the preceding group. The two groups together (example 113 plus example 114) form the first half of the opening period.

In the construction of this theme a delightful, genuinely Brahmsian feature becomes apparent; namely, that during the last bar of the above-quoted opening group, a bass corresponding to the opening bar is sounded, representing the beginning of the next group. Through this the connection between the two groups becomes all the more intimate, producing two overlapping symmetric groups, each of five bars (A and B):

Ex. 115

This part, forming the first half of the whole theme, is followed by a corresponding (prolonged) half, which again commences in the bass during the last bar of the first half (indicated as A*a* in the above example). Moreover, during the last bars of the opening period a new group (again built from the initial motifs) is started, this time by the violins; this bridging group leads to the tonic D, intonated in pianissimo by the timpani. From here on the conclusion of the whole first part reads:

Ex. 116

The last two bars of this are taken over to start a new theme— and here the main point of our demonstration begins. One might surmise that this new theme is the second subject. However, as the whole further course of the movement proves, this theme, according to all that the term implies, cannot yet be classified as the second theme, but forms a new group within the first thematic section. Now it is noteworthy and most impressive from an architectural angle that an examination of this "intermediary theme" reveals that, as far as its shaping is concerned, it lies precisely between the first and the later following second theme. It has just as much startling resemblance to the first theme on the one side as to the second on the other.

Let us test the validity of this statement. This new (intermediary) theme reads:

Ex. 117

Taking the second half (marked II) of this theme, a comparison shows that its shape is formed as a kind of replica of the first theme.

First theme

Ex. 118

Second half of new theme

The analogy between these two groups cannot be mistaken. Motif *a* is transposed, while motifs *b* and *c* appear at original pitch; motif *b* in the new theme merely expanded through a figuration.

Surprisingly, however, the second theme is equally mirrored in the first half (marked I in example 117) of the new theme:

Second theme

Ex. 119

First half of new theme

This must strike us most forcibly. We are looking into the innermost ramifications of compositional formation. The composer states his first theme, which is followed by an intermediary theme that reiterates the substance of the first. But this intermediary theme is in turn, and at the same time, a foreteller of the second theme.

We should be conscious of the intricate shaping through which this phenomenon is brought about. In some bars of the intermediary group, contours of both the first and second theme sound through. *If we single out certain notes, the first theme comes to the fore; if we single out others, the second theme appears.*

With this we come back to our first point of discussion. For the difference in appearance and character of these three themes (in spite of their identity in kernel) is caused, in great part, through shifts of accents and rhythm in the basic motifs.

In this respect an additional, impressive feature should also be noticed; namely, that the second theme, while introduced by the violas and cellos, is accompanied in the violins by figurations which are clearly expressions of motif II from the first theme. To summarize this we could say: the second theme is accompanied by parts of the first. And looking closer at this "accompaniment," it also reveals itself as an astounding play of transformation through rhythmical variety:

By connecting different voices (as indicated by the braces) a whole collection of rhythmically differentiated versions of motif II, succeeding or even overlapping each other, becomes audible.

This technique was eagerly taken over and even increased by modern composers. As an illustration we may quote some examples from **Béla Bartók's fourth string quartet.**[2] Before referring, however, to the specific devices here in question (once more these changes of rhythm and accent), we must first draw, in brief outline, a part of the quartet's thematic picture. It may give us a more lucid conception to start with the Finale, its fifth movement.

The Finale begins with an introductory group which is virtually a repetition of one harmony stretching over eleven bars, whereupon

---

[2] In this chapter all musical quotations from Béla Bartók's fourth string quartet are published by permission of the copyright owner, Boosey and Hawkes Inc. Copyright, 1939, by Boosey and Hawkes Inc.

it changes into a typical accompanying figure (bars 12 and following):

It is significant to observe that, with the exception of the grace note (A-flat), the notes which form the accompanying figure are identical with those forming the chords of the preceding introductory group. Then, after a few bars, a theme rises above the accompanying figure, the latter continuing throughout the whole theme (example 122). And the melodic line of this theme itself is again built from the same notes as the chords of the introductory group (merely with the change of one accidental). The whole design is an instructive illustration of how in the thematic technique even the harmonic sphere is often permeated by the thematic principle. These harmonies are clearly expressions of the movement's thematic idea compressed into chords.

The theme reads:

As we see, this theme consists of four groups (always interrupted by a few accompanying bars), of which the second group (marked I*a*) is an inversion of the first (marked I), while the fourth group (II*a*) is a (transposed) inversion of the third (II). All the groups are built from the same motivic essence. However, the groups I and I*a* (example 123*a*) are characterized by a diminished fifth, while the groups II and II*a* (example 123*b*), by a diminished octave (sometimes notated as a major seventh):

Ex. 123

From this we may turn to the first movement. This movement opens with an introduction of fifteen bars, after which the group of the theme enters. In the following example we give only the decisive thematic voices, to render the idea more transparent:

Ex. 124

We recognize here, too, the outline of the Finale theme: first a series of motifs with diminished fifths (I), which later are increased to diminished octaves (II).

However, in spite of the inner identity between these thematic groups of the two movements, we would hardly call this whole feature an actual "transformation" but rather a kind of thematic varying. For the similarities are too obvious, the beginnings even identical. And similar conditions are to be seen in the second movement, where the thematic shape (II) emerges, also in "verbal" repetition, in the following canonic passages:

Ex. 125

Yet, whether transformation or varying, of particular interest to us at this point is that constant change of rhythm and accent of otherwise identical shapes. In the first movement, for instance (example 124), the first four occurrences of the thematic thought appear each time in different accentuation, entering first on an eighth quaver, then on a seventh quaver, then on a first, then on a third. In the last movement, owing to the jubilant Finale character, the theme itself (example 122) sounds in a clear, straight rhythm. Nevertheless, in the later course of this movement, too, the play of shifted accentuation and rhythm is taken up again and led to a climax:

Ex. 126

However, a picture like this, though it represented at the time it was written a peak of refined, audacious shaping, is today almost a matter of routine. The gifted among our young composers frequently display remarkable adroitness in this technique of motivic detail, through which parts of their scores acquire the attractive appearance of an elaborate thematic embroidery. However, such traits are less frequently matched by an equal understanding for the larger thematic forming and the technique and function through which these structural connections, relations, and transformations build the architectural whole of a musical work.

Thinning, Filling of Thematic Shapes

Assuming that one of the basic motivic particles from which the themes of a work are built were to read,

Ex. 127

it would be only logical that the composer wishing to achieve variety would in the later course of the same composition sometimes use the following versions of the motif:

Ex. 128

the first representing a "thinning" of the original, while the second may be called a "filled" version.

These examples, by the way, are not fictive abstractions but indicate literally the motivic picture in **Beethoven's First Symphony.** The openings of its first three movements read:

Ex. 129

All the other themes of the work likewise give prominence to variants of the same motivic figure:

Ex. 130

The second theme of the Finale, for instance (*a* in the above example), is an inversion or, perhaps better, an interversion of the original, while the second theme of the first movement (*b*) combines both a "thinned" version and a "filled" inversion. Even the beginning of the whole work, the famous chords with which the Adagio-Introduction opens (*c* in the above example), are also a manifestation of the same motif compressed into chords.[3] And the same idea is expressed in a more gentle way in the theme of the minuet's Trio (*d*).

---

[3] This opening with a "dissonance" was in Beethoven's time much stared at and questioned as a revolutionary feature. Much more revolutionary, however, than this mild dominant seventh, was the then new idea to express motifs, that is, thematic thoughts, through harmonies.

Thus there remains only the first Finale theme, of which, however, merely its opening, Ex. 131 is formed by the familiar motif, while the main course of the Finale theme is not centered on this motif but is derived from another motivic shape of the first Allegro group—from a shape of which the Finale theme is, in fact, a *reversion:*

But back to our discussion on "devices." The theme of the second movement not only opens, as shown above (example 129*b*), with the thinned motif but also continues thus:

which is melodically the literal motif, rhythmically changed, of course. In fact, this is a classical illustration, as it were, of how completely a simple shift of accent can alter the whole meaning and appearance of a musical shape. For the shapes

are in their concrete course literally identical. Yet each expresses in character and mood something entirely different, chiefly because the second note, which in the first version is the least accented, becomes in the second version a strong beat. Naturally, the change of tempo from Allegro to Andante also plays an important role.

Thus having pointed out the prevalence of this basic little motif in all themes of the symphony, it seems only a natural consequence that the keys of its movements also spell the same idea. And indeed, the keys of Beethoven's First Symphony read, C, F, C, C.

Of course, it was motivic particles rather than actual thematic shapes to which our last examples referred. But that there is in all these relations a full architectural intention involved may be seen from the following quotation. For comparing the Andante theme with the second Allegro theme, and thus no longer dealing with particles but with actual themes, the analogy of the full pattern becomes evident:

Second **Allegro** theme (transposed)

Ex. 135

Andante theme

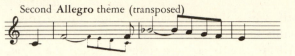

The example speaks for itself.

Cutting of Thematic Parts

That parts of a theme are used to create a new one was demonstrated in numerous preceding examples. Sometimes, however, this is done in a peculiar way, on which we may elaborate somewhat in detail, as it will increase our insight into the methods of thematic forming.

In **Beethoven's Sonata, opus 81a, "Les Adieux,"** the opening of the Adagio-Introduction, the famous "Lebewohl," and the beginning of the first Allegro theme read as follows:

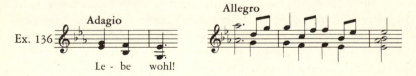

Ex. 136

Is there any relation between the two? True, the notes G, F, E-flat, of the first shape conform with the melodic course of the last part of the second group. Yet were the two shapes played to us independently (that is, without our being told that they open two sections in one movement), we would certainly not consider them related at all. Apart from all differences in character and phrasing we would, even as a matter of principle, refuse to accept the melodic idea expressed by:

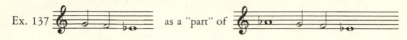

Ex. 137 ⟨music⟩ as a "part" of ⟨music⟩

The latter appears to us, according to all musicianly concepts to which we are accustomed, as a musical entity of its own, from which no note can be "cut off."

Yet Beethoven proves that this is not a cogent conclusion. As he chooses the two shapes as the alternating thematic utterances of this movement, we must, according to all structural principles as manifested in all his works, take it for granted that the one is a "derivative" of the other. This is a fact that becomes all the more certain by comparing the whole outline of the Adagio figure with the Allegro theme:

a **Adagio** opening

Ex. 138

b **Allegro** theme

The analogy of the two is unquestionable.[4]

Another, perhaps still more striking feature of the same type, presents itself in the **Piano Sonata, opus 110,** which opens with this theme:

---

[4] The author may here recount a little experience which he had during the days when these pages were written and which once again may prove how unawareness of thematic connections often produces awkward results in the performance.

In a rendering of this opus 81*a* in Carnegie Hall, a well known pianist completely misconceived the poetic idea of the work by unleashing the Allegro theme as a sudden explosion of overaccented fortissimo beats. Had it dawned on this otherwise gifted musician that owing to its shape this Allegro theme must be understood as a more passionate utterance, an intensification, as it were, of the inherent woe of the sonata's initial

Ex. 140

According to the usual way of hearing and comprehending such a melodic shape, many of us would deem it impossible, in fact, musically entirely unnatural, simply to cut off the first, most important opening note of this theme, the C, in order to develop a thematic variation or transformation from the remaining "fragment."

Nevertheless, this is exactly what Beethoven does. For the theme of the fugue which forms the last movement of this sonata reads:

Ex. 141

and it is obvious that this is formed as a perfect image of the first movement's theme, after having discarded the opening note.

There is a striking revelation that must be drawn from these examples. The customary view that musical shapes which form a composition are firm, "static" beings which cannot be tampered with

---

thought, he would have heard the cry of the "Farewell" sounding no less from the Allegro than from the Adagio of the Introduction. He would have played forte (significantly Beethoven notates *f*, not *ff*), but still with greatest "espressivo,"

Ex. 139

Le - be - wohl!

instead of converting it into a drum effect:

does not hold true for the inner process of musical creation. *In the actual process of creation shapes and themes are not rigid but in a state of constant change and fluctuation.*

A rather meticulous example from **Beethoven's opus 27, No. 2,** the so-called "Moonlight" Sonata, may add further testimony to this fact. The first theme reads:

Ex. 142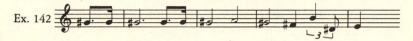

This theme, still alive in the composer's mind after the conclusion of the movement, gradually increasing in fluency and speed, shifts from a four to a three rhythm. Thus the original melody, transposed to a higher pitch, becomes:

Ex. 143

which still, in spite of the change in tempo and rhythm, remains literally the original melodic design. In fact, even something of the original rhythm echoes through:

Ex. 144

At a later stage the line, still revolving in the composer's ear, may appear in this reduced form:

Ex. 145

which is almost too small a shape for a theme. Therefore, the composer finally interpolates, as it were, the lost C from the beginning into the midst of the phrase. The result is:

Ex. 146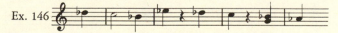

the theme of the "Moonlight" Sonata's Allegretto.

Now it may have been noticed that the end of the Adagio theme, according to the original text appearing as given below under *a*, was quoted in the form of *b*

Ex. 147

that is, by inserting in the upper line the D-sharp from the accompaniment. And this is the point where, according to our preceding explanations, objections might be raised. "It is by no means permissible," one might argue, "to insert the D-sharp from the accompaniment into the thematic line of the soprano." Such objections would be justified as long as this first movement only is in question. As for the theme of the Adagio, its ending must indubitably read, F-sharp, B, E, and to insert a D-sharp from the accompaniment would not only be a falsification but utterly unmusical.

Yet at the moment when the movement is finished and the composer searches for his second and third movement (or, for that matter, even once the theme is uttered and the composer is about to form the next one), all these "laws" become invalid. For at this stage the composer hears merely *that which sounds,* and cares little whether what revolves in his mind was written in the soprano or alto. He uses the emerging shapes to build a new theme, entirely according to his forming will and free imagination.

That Beethoven wished to form the theme of the next movement from that of the preceding—in the "Moonlight" just as in all other works—is proved by the continuation; namely, the third movement. For by extracting from one of the Finale themes (*a* in the following example) the melodic contour (*b*), and comparing it to the (transposed) Adagio theme (*c*),

Ex. 148

the amazing identity becomes so obvious that it disperses all doubts as to instances when the formation is freer.

The Conception of a Thematic Contour

The last example from Beethoven's opus 27, No. 2, brought to light an astounding inner similarity between the opening theme of its first movement and one of the main themes of the Finale. These two themes proved on closer examination almost identical, though they are in character and appearance entirely different utterances, and do not seem, at first glance, to have anything in common at all. As we may remember, the same idea presented itself as the underlying structural feature in numerous previous examples. Hence it might be worth while to try to proceed to the core of this phenomenon. "What exactly," we may ask, "constitutes the common denominator linking these two themes together?"

The answer is that the melodic line of one is expressed in the line of the other, though not in the latter's concrete melodic course, but indirectly, through a connection of some of its corner notes. In other words: *The Adagio theme sounds from the contour of the Finale theme.*

Such a "thematic contour," repeatedly indicated in our preceding demonstration, is one of the central conceptions in the structural realm of the classics. Since, as sufficiently described, shapes are not literally repeated in the thematic technique but always somehow varied, this phenomenon of contour, or at least a touch of it, will to a greater or lesser degree become audible in almost any transformation. *Thus it proves in the last analysis the archetype of thematic metamorphosis.* For be there an inversion, augmentation, change of tempo or rhythm, or whatever specific device, in one way or another the original shape will invariably sound from the contour of that shape into which it was transformed—or vice versa.

To illustrate the general principle of this phenomenon we could, therefore, refer to almost any instance of thematic transformation. For our immediate purpose, however, we may single out a more specific example, one in which the idea of contour comes to life in a more outspoken, concrete form. It is once more an example by Beethoven; namely, his last **Piano Sonata, opus 111.**

This composition bears in its grandeur and mysticism all the characteristics of Beethoven's last, much discussed period. In its general plan, with its two so different movements, it represents a particular if not unique way of shaping a sonata. The work's dramatic plot, as it were, seems entirely concentrated in the passion and tensity of its first movement, at the conclusion of which one has the feeling that emotion has reached such a peak that nothing more can be added. Accordingly, the second movement, the theme with variations, appears at first more like an annex, an unpretentious tune like a folk song, intonated to calm the storm when the actual drama is ended, though later the variations themselves in renewed transfiguration lead to summits of a transcendent world. At any rate, the two movements seem so contrasting that one would hardly be prepared to discover any structural tie between them. And it is almost like a miracle that the Adagio theme (example 149*a*) when reduced to its melodic contour (example 149*b*) reveals a striking similarity to the theme of the first movement, the Allegro, quoted as *c*:

Ex. 149

The affinity is unmistakable: the Allegro, changed to major, sounds from the contour of the Adagio. The only note missing in the Adagio theme, the A-flat, is merely a dissonant passing note which did not fit into the character of the Adagio's shaping.

It should be added that the Maestoso-Introduction of the first movement,

Ex. 150

complements this scheme of unity. The Allegro theme's opening, the C, E-flat, B, appears in the first three bars in interversion as E-flat, C, B (marked I), while the remainder is expressed through the following group (II). (In this instance the A-flat is actually included.)

Thematic Compression

Sometimes a theme of one movement is transformed to that of another by compressing the initial shape to a kind of abbreviated version, or if we look at the procedure from the opposite angle, by expanding the body of a theme to a wider shape.

Let us compare the themes of the first and last movement in **Schubert's Fantasy-Sonata, opus 15,** the "Wanderer" Fantasy. The theme of the Finale, (*b* in the following example) is obviously none other than a much compressed version of the opening section of the first movement (*a*):

The two groups of the Allegro theme (marked I and II) clearly reappear in the Finale, though now in abbreviated statements.

Another beautiful example of such thematic compression is seen in **Schumann's Piano Concerto, opus 54.** The first themes of its first movement (Allegro affettuoso) and its last movement (Allegro vivace) read:

Ex. 152

and it is evident that the latter is but an abbreviated expression of the former, transferred to major. A comparative chart makes this clear:

Ex. 153

Still more intensely is this idea of thematic reduction pursued in

the theme of the second movement, the Andante. The Andante
theme, reading,

is factually built from only two little phrases of the Allegro theme,
though its most essential ones; namely,

The Andante's opening bar is clearly sounded as a recollection of
the first of these phrases, which, after having been several times repeated in an improvisational manner, leads to a second phrase, an
octave leap. Such a crescendo leap to the octave formed the climax
of the Allegro theme. Now, as a double leap, it represents the core
of the Andante theme.

Moreover, that the themes of the first movement and last movement were in the composer's full architectural consciousness conceived as two different versions of one and the same thematic idea
is proved by an interesting feature, which may now be described.

The concerto, in announcing the main theme, opens with a short,
toccatalike group:

Ex. 156

ff

etc.

This group surprisingly reenters (in slight variation) at the end of the second movement. To understand the meaning of this feature, we must trace the section in which the reentrance is embedded. Toward the end of the second movement, a few phrases from this movement's opening are reiterated by the orchestra, reading:

Ex. 157

pp

Then suddenly a bar follows which is a clear replica of the first bar of the Allegro theme, merely changed to major:

Ex. 158

mf espr.

Obviously the conjuring influence of the preceding particles, being the opening phrases of the Andante theme and at the same time a part of the Allegro theme, was so strong that the composer could not help returning to the latter itself. However, he quotes it, as seen, in major, directed, as it were, by a subconscious vision of things to come. This magic recollection of a shape from the first movement is followed immediately by an even greater surprise. For now the soloist comes in with these toccatalike bars, recalling the concerto's opening:

Ex. 159

The orchestra, in turn, replies with a repetition of the first bar, but now in minor, the original form:

Ex. 160

Again the soloist follows with the toccata group. All this takes place in an improvising, searching mood. But then the improvisation is at an end; a third time the decisive bar is sounded from the orchestra, this time again in major; and now, through an attacca the last movement, the Finale theme enters.

How could all this have happened, had the composer not been conscious of his intention to form the Finale theme, so to speak, as a second statement of the first movement's theme? To insert a few bars of the concerto's opening, particularly with this toccatalike introduction, in the midst of the lyrical Andante would appear a nonsensical, indeed, childish idea, unless it was the purpose through this to announce the reappearance of the first theme, now in its transformed, concentrated form as the Finale theme.

Change of Harmony

Since in the process of transformation a theme often undergoes a complete change, becoming a quite new shape, it is by the very nature of this procedure that the original thematic line may in its new appearance often emerge with an entirely different harmonic basis. Such change of the harmonic idea is of course a very incisive alteration.

Taking, for example, the first Finale theme in **Beethoven's "Waldstein" Piano Sonata, opus 53** (quoted in the following in transposition as *a*), and comparing it with the second theme of the first movement (*b*):

Ex. 161

one has to admit that the similarity of the two melodic lines seems striking. If nevertheless this similarity has gone unnoticed, this is undoubtedly due to the entirely different harmonic formulation in which these almost identical melodic lines appear in the work.

It may be interesting to delve into this difference more specifically. Ignoring the harmonic meaning, were we to compare only the two melodic lines (transposed Finale theme and second Allegro theme), we would simply say that the line has been changed from major to minor by replacing the E-sharp by E-natural. However, the new line, allegedly having been changed to minor, appears now harmonized as E-major. Thus, in addition to the change in tempo, phrasing, and so forth, the two themes have now become entirely different musical enunciations. Yet the common kernel cannot be denied.

The common essence is no less apparent in the sonata's opening theme, reading as follows (to which a contour is added below):

Ex. 162

Comparing this theme to the Finale theme (example 161*a*), it becomes obvious that the former is in essence an inversion of the Finale theme's idea, though its figuration makes it a different utterance.

Identical Pitch and Change of Accidentals

The last two features to be described as important devices in the technique of transformation are the idea of identical pitch and the change of accidentals.

Logically, it is of tremendous effect if, in the course of a composition, the kernel of a theme is heard in a later transformation at the same pitch as before, though not only tempo, rhythm, and the whole appearance, but even key and harmonization may have been changed. Such simultaneity of identical pitch and different key is in many of the great works of musical literature, a central phenomenon to which the current theoretical approach has failed to direct attention.

In our previous analysis many instances of identical pitch were quoted. Now we will try to demonstrate that a work's architectural plan itself may often be focused on such identity of pitch uniting different transformations of one thematic shape.

Schubert's "Wanderer" Fantasy, to which reference has already been made in this chapter, opens with a theme quoted in example 151. The second theme of the same movement commences with a shape that is almost entirely identical to the opening theme; it is merely transposed to the key of E-major. Because of this, the melodic line that in the first theme was centered on E appears in the second on G-sharp:

Ex. 163

But now we may turn to the following movement, the Adagio, where the same theme (here as the work's prime message, the "Wanderer Song") sounds again at the pitch of G-sharp, though it is now harmonized in the key of C-sharp:

Ex. 164

Thus the over-all keys of the two first movements of the "Wanderer" Fantasy are C and C-sharp, which certainly represents an unusual relation between movements in classical times. However, this relation becomes quite a natural organic feature because of the very phenomenon of identical thematic pitch that links the two movements so effectively together.

Let us repeat the compositional procedure here involved. The Allegro's opening theme in C reappears as the Allegro's second subject at a new pitch, which is centered melodically on G-sharp.

This G-sharp is taken over as the melodic pitch in the theme of the second movement, but now in the key of C-sharp (example 164). The identical pitch of G-sharp uniting the two themes of the different movements is thus in fact the architectural bond linking the two movements together.

The following movement, the Scherzo, is in A-flat. Its theme, again a variation of the basic shape, reads:

Ex. 165

We see that in this movement, too, G-sharp (though now in enharmonic notation as A-flat) is maintained as the uniting pitch, thus again assuring the connection to the preceding movements. At the same time the key of A-flat (moreover, here with G as the opening note) brings the work gradually back to the original C, from which it seemed far removed in the Adagio. But there is one more feature which places this Scherzo theme in close connection to the work's opening theme. The work's basic thematic figures appear in the Scherzo theme in bars 3 to 4 and 9 to 10. And they appear at a pitch which, compared to their occurrence in the first Allegro theme, is "identical" *save for changed accidentals.* (Naturally the 4/4 rhythm of the Allegro theme is altered to the 3/4 rhythm of the Scherzo):

Ex. 166

We would call this feature a "flattened identical pitch," just as on a previous occasion we spoke of a sharpened identical pitch. These conceptions are by no means artificial analytic constructions. Within the thematic technique they express a principal device which is in general use throughout the whole literature. In one specific application, as a change of a theme from major to minor, or vice versa, the existence of this principle is of course common knowledge. However, just as a major third or sixth can be shifted to minor without changing the structural essence of the shape involved, so accidentals may in general be altered; yet the theme to which such alterations are applied will remain intact. Innumerable examples prove the validity of this fact, which, as will be demonstrated later, can be traced far back in history as an inherent principle of structural formation.

As has been shown in our last examples, such changes of accidentals combined with the retention of identical pitch produce specific effects and at times even constitute a decisive form-building element. The concluding bars of the opening theme in the Scherzo of the "Wanderer" Fantasy form a further striking illustration. These bars are essentially identical—even in pitch, save for some accidentals—with the concluding bars of the opening theme in the first movement:

Ex. 167

In both movements these bars announce the reentrance of the main theme. In the Scherzo, moreover, the same passage reappears several times and is finally heard toward the movement's close, shortly before the entrance of the Finale theme. In fact, the bars here form the very modulation through which the Scherzo is brought back to the C-major of the Finale, which is the work's original key. But such reintroduction of a passage from one movement in the midst of another would in itself have to be considered as a somewhat strange procedure—a procedure to which great composers would not resort, unless for specific reasons. Indeed, we encounter here an architectural device in some respects similar to that in Schumann's Piano Concerto quoted above. For only if the composer conceived the themes of the Allegro, the Scherzo, and the Finale (the entrances of which were announced by this passage) *as identical in their inner-most essence,* does this whole feature make sense and appear as a logical procedure. Thus, through the effect of identical pitch plus changed accidentals, the work's architecture becomes an uninterrupted cycle.

This leads us, for a final consideration, back to Beethoven's opus 53, the "Waldstein." For now we may more easily explain the thematic transformation of the two decisive themes quoted earlier. The "Waldstein's" first Finale theme and second Allegro theme,

are in fact two similar thematic utterances at identical pitch with changed accidentals.

The phenomena just described, in connection with various other features emerging from our preceding analysis, must have evoked a whole sphere of speculation. One may well wonder whether our current theoretical schematisms, dividing compositions into all kinds of sections, subjects, bridges, and so forth, can really account for the whole of what constitutes musical form. Even if these schematisms should prove to be right—that is, to bear some resemblance to the reality of the great compositional practice—they can only describe the more outward, ephemeral attributes of the complex and mysterious process through which "form" manifests itself in music. There must be stronger forces at work, shaping a composition's content, determining why one section follows the other, influencing its proportions and interrelations, and establishing *that the whole has not only quantitatively but also qualitatively a different effect from its single parts.* Perhaps the following pages will bring us closer to the solution of this problem.

Part Two

THE THEMATIC PROCESS
AND THE PROBLEM
OF FORM IN MUSIC

5

TWO FORM-BUILDING
FORCES IN MUSIC

There are two form-building forces in music.

The one, the *inner* force, comprises those thematic phenomena, the demonstration of which is the purpose of this study.

However, there is also a second form-building force in music, which models its *outward* shape. It is the *method of grouping*.

To group, to divide and demarcate the continuous course of a work or a movement into sections and parts is a natural means by which a musical composition assumes a comprehensible form.

To be sure, many people are aware only of this second form-building method. They conceive a work's architecture only through its outer picture, as brought about by the proportioning and sectioning of its parts. However, the great composers invariably develop the true form of their creations—that "form" which at the same time is content and essence—also through inner structure, through the evolution and relationship of the thematic material.

In practical composition these two forces exert a concerted influence. Thus it will be necessary to give some thought to the phenomena and effects brought about through this second form-building force, the outer grouping of a composition, although the subject is in itself somewhat aside from the purpose of this study, or at least is not its primary concern.

What makes a musical utterance appear as a unit, an entity, is first its melodic-rhythmical shaping as such.[1] As a composer would

---

[1] The author is well aware that this is an inaccurate, vague, even evasive statement. But to explain and define what constitutes elementary musical entities would require a special analysis, largely based on psychological

hardly wish to express musical thoughts which the listener is unable to follow (analogous to endless sentences in literature), he will invariably choose utterances which sooner or later come to repose not merely through their content but through their shape. This molding of a musical series into a group is usually supported by the harmonic shaping.[2]

Through a succession of several of such groups or "periods," a small piece or a part of a larger piece, a "section," can be developed.

To render such a section, such a series of groups, comprehensible as a unit within the larger frame of the work, another device is used; namely, the composer shapes one group in such a way that this one group shines out amid the others, melodically, rhythmically, and in all respects, as a clearly defined and particularly characteristic musical utterance. A perception, or at least some recollection, of this group dwells more firmly, more transparently in the listener's mind throughout the work. Such a group would thus assume a leading role and would be termed a *theme*.[3]

A succession of such theme-carrying sections, then, brings about a larger piece, perhaps even of symphonic proportions.

Here compositional technique as a rule makes use of another device, which we may call thematic resumption. For simply to link together parts and thematic sections, as it were, indefinitely, even if clearly grouped, would hardly create a convincing architecture. The listener would scarcely feel, even if the parts in themselves appeared understandable, that together they form a unit. But if

---

and philosophical, if not speculative, rather than musical grounds. Thus the above should serve only as a directive enabling us to proceed to actual musical problems.

[2] In classical music this harmonic grouping is brought about through the familiar "cadences," leading to the tonic or dominant or their substitutes. But the same principle was to some degree no less alive in the preclassical epoch, even if in some periods the harmonies were not directly audible but rather immanent in the contrapuntal design. Again, in a different way, it is today at work in "modern" music, through a harmonic shaping in quasi-tonics or in any harmonies which the composer is able to endow with concluding or at least grouping effects.

[3] This definition of a "theme" is, of course, quite different from that given in the beginning of our study. But the difference corresponds precisely to the two angles from which, according to the above deductions, a compositional course can be understood: either in its motivic function as a specifically "thematic" element or, as here, as a means of grouping.

groups which were heard, for instance, near the beginning of a work were to reappear, literally or even somewhat varied, toward the end, the listener would connect the two identical (or nearly identical) groups and the parts between to one entity. Such thematic resumption, or recapitulation, forms one of the most commonly used and most effective means of shaping a musical course into a comprehensible whole.

The devices just described:

1. grouping as such;
2. making some groups appear as themes;
3. thematic resumption, that is, resumption of previous groups, constitute the fundamental principles from which were developed the theoretical patterns of musical form, the terminology of which is familiar to every musician. They comprise a few over-all, central conceptions such as the binary form, the ternary form, and others, which represent the basic schemes of such "musical form through grouping."

By applying these schemes to different rhythms, tempos, and architectural proportions, also to various national idioms, to certain combinations of instrumental and vocal settings, the abundance of specific "forms" described in our familiar theoretical classifications came to life. They culminate in the sonata form, the well-known pattern for symphonies, sonatas, quartets, concertos, and so forth.

Yet, as indicated, we must always remain aware that all these schematisms, in fact, the sum total of the current theoretical definitions and explanations on "form" still interpret only the outward picture of a musical work's shaping. For, if these simple methods of grouping really comprised the whole phenomenon of musical form, one could take at random five groups from five different pieces, fit them into a close key relationship, and thus forge them into one "work." It is obvious that this could yield only an absurd result.

Therefore, there must still be some other essential qualities necessary to mold musical groups into an architectural whole. And we know from our previous deductions that these necessary qualities are none other than the thematic and motivic affinities. But before including these latter in our present investigation on form, we must still devote some consideration to certain specific aspects of the method of grouping.

The above-mentioned patterns of musical form set up by theoretical classification, the sonata form or any other pattern, do not of course represent any inherent law of musical formation. They are mere abstractions deduced from musical practice. The composer may follow or ignore them, change or mold them to his idiom or invent new ones, entirely according to his structural vision in each individual instance. Especially in our time the patterns have become problematic if not obsolete. The patterns themselves, therefore, are not, and strictly speaking never were, important. But the *timeless phenomenon of grouping as such* is as decisive a feature today as ever. For largely on the extent and degree to which the grouping of a musical work is carried out depends how transparent its form becomes to the listener. If the composer groups his work distinctly, making the demarcation of its parts lucid, the composition's "form" will quickly become perceivable. If he obscures the grouping, letting the parts flow into each other without noticeable demarcation, much effort on the part of the listener will be necessary to follow the compositional course and perceive its idea.

Yet one cannot say which of these two ways of shaping is preferable or, for that matter, whether a clear, obvious grouping points to a higher artistic level than a less emphasized, subdued one. Works of the highest standard have been written in both ways. It is a question of style and of individual taste, whether composers or whole schools, either in general or for certain types of works, apply a more or less distinct grouping. Naturally, the gayety and dance atmosphere emanating from a minuet by Haydn or Mozart call for a straightforward, symmetric grouping, while the religious mysticism of some of Bach's chorale preludes is more adequately materialized through a style in which the demarcation is not emphasized but almost concealed.

Beethoven's last quartets form a significant example in this respect. Since many people conceive "form" only according to outward appearance and proportions, it is understandable that the label of a certain formlessness, of composing according to the dicta of an unbounded imagination rather than according to the approved structural conceptions, has so frequently been attached to these works. However, as will be shown specifically in a later part of this study, all that could justly be said is that some movements (by no means all) in the last quartets adhere to the method of less transparent grouping, described above. But as far as inner, thematic consistency is concerned, stricter, more logical, and more completely structural music than these admirable works is hardly thinkable.

How far a composer dare go toward endangering the easy perceptibility of his architecture by "obscuring" the grouping depends, as has been indicated, on his own artistic intentions in each individual case. But he must realize that a less transparent state of the outer proportions inevitably calls for compensation through an all the more intense and compelling handling of the work's thematic evolution—a fact which is so convincingly demonstrated by the last quartets.

This brings us back to our initial subject. For the compositional process is a dual phenomenon working from two architectual directions in constant interrelationship—the result of which we call musical form.

With regard to this interrelationship we may advance a few more thoughts.

Until now in this analysis we have, as far as the thematic sphere is concerned, given prime attention only to those thematic connections which are, as it were, hidden in the depths of musical structure. However, we must understand that besides these hidden ones there are also truly thematic affinities that are quite obvious features, as easily detectable as any transparent grouping. And now we must include in our examination these obvious thematic relations no less than those which are hidden.

To explain this issue, we may for an instant return to our previous fictive question: Why do several groups from different works, linked together, not bring about a composition? Because, as we have said, they lack thematic unity, while a glance at a Schubert impromptu or a Chopin étude reveals such unity in that all the groups of one piece are permeated by the same or similar passages, even perhaps only by the figuration of the so-called "accompaniment." And in a larger piece, for instance in a symphony, at least within the single sections, some unity is usually brought about by such figuration. Such a homogeneous motivic figuration is doubtlessly a truly thematic feature; moreover, it is an obvious one.

Nevertheless, we must understand that through such motivic figuration alone no entirely convincing architectural whole can be brought about. Once again taking our "groups from different pieces": were they merely linked together by the superficial motivic homogeneity of some accompanying figures, this might perhaps appear to an indiscriminate listener as a fairly acceptable structural bond. This is precisely the technique often utilized in the so-called "potpourris." Still it does not suffice to create true musical form. Unless the thematic shapes themselves are also connected through deep inward affinities, as amply described in our preceding analysis, no amount of homogeneous figurations and motivic surface connections would suffice to forge different groups into a musical whole. On this question we shall elaborate in detail later in this study.

At this point, to avoid misunderstanding, the following should be stressed. This differentiation between obvious and hidden thematic affinities, important though it is as a question of principle, cannot always be maintained in practice. In a last analysis "obvious" and "hidden" are subjective distinctions, often depending on the observer's analytic training. But factually there is also no clear border line between the two; rather, one type passes into the other.

Therefore, a work's architecture must be understood as the result of a manifold yet entirely elastic process, mirroring the composer's always mobile inspiration. And the true structural dynamism of a composition, its "form" in the fullest meaning of this term, can be conceived only *by comprehending as a concerted stream both the groups and proportions of its outer shaping and the thematic evolution beneath.*

In our forthcoming analyses we will see what a decisive influence a work's thematic course exerts on its outward grouping, but also how these outer proportions in turn often direct the thematic shaping. In an attempt to obtain a concrete conception of this fascinating interplay, we may, as a first example, turn to **Mozart's Symphony in G-minor.**

The symphony opens with the following theme:

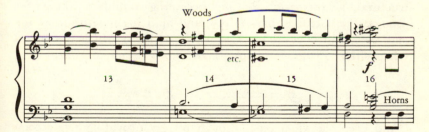

The actual thematic melody, as expressed by the violins (bars 1 to 9), hardly needs any structural explanation. Thoughts like these enter a composer's mind as entities that occur to him, without much "forming" activity on his part. This does not imply that this theme is not, even from a structural point of view, extremely well shaped. Twice within the opening group (bars 1 to 9), in two analogous halves, the line rises to a high sixth and falls back. This whole group is built from two motivic bricks:

Ex. 170

A summation of these two brings about the first rise (*a* in the following example). The descending scale which follows (*b*):

Ex. 171

is a kind of contrary motion of the same shape, prolonged to the C in order to reach a basis for a transposed reiteration of the opening bars.

All this, of course, concerns only the thematic "melody" itself, which the composer might have released in an instinctive musical impulse. But turning to the other voices we find the first signs of a structural, a "thematic" shaping becoming audible. Taking, for instance, the bass line (bars 1 to 8) and omitting repetitions of the same note, a little figure emerges (example 172*a*), which is a literal transposition of the symphony's main motif (example 172*b*):

Ex. 172

And even the viola part, though merely providing the accompanying flow, likewise indicates the thematic idea; namely, motif II. The viola part opens thus:

Ex. 173

and this rising B-flat to G is all the more significant, as it constitutes in the opening bar the only audible feature, since the violins do not enter until the fourth beat.

We may proceed to the continuation of the theme. From the opening group the figure around the high B-flat (bar 3), the theme's melodic peak, still sounds in the composer's ear. He takes it over and produces bar 10. For drawing a contour from the phrase around bar 10, the following shape emerges:

Ex. 174

and we realize that it represents a sort of expanded version of the second half of bar 3 plus the G of bar 4. Yet this does not imply that bar 10 is merely a reiteration or even a "variant" of bar 3.

Let us try to retrace the compositional process which might have led to bars 10 and following. The composer having formed the first part of his theme (bars 1 to 9), searches for a continuation, for something new, as of course he does not wish to repeat himself again. Yet the high point of the first group, bar 3, naturally still echoes in his ear. All kinds of variants revolve in his mind, such as the aforementioned contour (example 174). Now his forming capacity grasps the idea that satisfies him and he notates:

Ex. 175

and that is the shape we see in the score.

In the light of Mozart's much lauded creative facility, we can assume that all this may have been accomplished in less than a few seconds. Of course we do not know whether the whole theme or only a part of it arose first in his mind, nor even whether quite another of the symphony's shapes may not have been his initial thought.[4] Therefore, however, it must be understood that the preceding description of Mozart's personal, subjective procedure of forming was introduced merely as a working hypothesis, to render the objective structural process more comprehensible.

What is the result of this objective structural process?

_____

[4] That the compositional process is not always as straightforward as the finished work might lead us to believe is charmingly illustrated by a passage from a letter which the twenty-five-year-old Mozart wrote to his sister. Sending her a prelude and fugue which he had just finished, Mozart apologizes for the poor legibility of the fugue, "which I had written down while I was thinking out the prelude."

Bar 10 is a *new* figure, a *new* melodic idea, characterized by a diminished fifth:

Ex. 176

We may call this figure *motif III*.[5] Yet this new motif is imbedded in a line in which, as explained, a recollection of bar 3 is still alive.

That this is more than mere analytic conjecture is confirmed by the continuation. Bar 3 is followed by the aforementioned descending scale (bar 4). Correspondingly, bar 10 (after having been repeated as bar 12) is followed by a somewhat contracted but similar descending scale (bar 13).

Bar 3 and its continuation

Ex. 177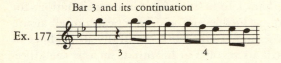

Bar 12 and its continuation

Thus the structural idea of bar 10 cannot be doubted. The composer formed the second part of his theme by taking over a phrase from the first part and interweaving into it a new thought (motif III).

We now distinguish two parts in the theme: the first part (bars 1 to 9), characterized by motifs I and II, and a second part (9 to 14), characterized by motif III. To this the composer now adds a third part, which brings the theme to a conclusion. The basic line of this third part reads:

Ex. 178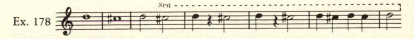

---

[5] Note that the diminished fifth appears punctually in this group in the viola (already presaged in bar 5), and also a few bars later (13–14) in the bass.

This is obviously a resumption of motif I, first in whole notes, then in halves, finally in quarters. And even the original eighth rhythm is resumed in the D's of the accompanying voices (see example 169 and note there the discords between the C-sharps and D's, which in themselves express the motif).

While the violins thus resume motif I, the winds enter, enriching the design with a contrapuntal figure, which represents an echoing indication of motif III (here shaped as the "scale" up and down, recalling the beginning):

Ex. 179

To be sure, this whole "grammatical" excursion into the theme's detail was only an unavoidable introduction to the work's actual architectural analysis. First, however, as a résumé, let us draw an outline of the theme's full course. It turns out to be a scheme strongly reminiscent of the well-known ternary form A, B, A. For the first part of the theme is centered on motif I plus II, the second part on motif III, while the third part returns to motif I. And since motif II is also indicated in the resumption, through the following figure in the violas:

Ex. 180

the scheme A, B, A, seems indeed complete.

However, we must realize that this whole conception is valid only if we view the theme from a thematic angle. *Omitting the thematic view, not the slightest trace of the ternary or any specific architectural idea can be discerned.* In the current theory, that is, with regard to its outward proportions, the theoretical description would simply read: This is a regular theme of sixteen bars, to which a few bars are annexed, repeating the last notes, and thus extending the theme to twenty bars. If any specific explanation were to be added, it would merely read that a part of the theme is permeated by the characteristic motivic figure of the beginning.

If the discrepancy between the thematic and traditional concepts has been here so strongly stressed, it was not for the purpose of questioning or criticizing the latter. For both conceptions are valid, each in its own realm. They reflect precisely the working of the two forces through which "form" is brought about in music. Certainly

Mozart was conscious of both. He really wanted this dancelike symmetry of sixteen bars, to which a repetition of the last notes is merely annexed. Such a symmetry was very important to him—it was part of his idiom, of his personal expression. Yet beneath this surface regularity, his thematic thoughts grow freely in complex variety, crossing, overlapping, competing with each other, and producing an inner design, entirely different from that which the simple grouping would lead us to believe.

In this higher thematic sense, as indicated earlier, even bar 1 assumes a deeper meaning. For the violas now form not merely an introductory accompaniment but the work's first melodic call, with their rising sixth, B-flat to G, of which the following actual theme, sounding from the violins, appears almost as a "canonic" intensification.

One should also note that this first bar is factually outside the symmetry. For the "eight-bar symmetry" begins only with the seventh quaver of bar 1 (as an auftakt), stretching through the sixth quaver in bar 9. Had Mozart been concerned with academic rhythmical symmetry—academic even at his time—he might have extended the "asymmetric" introductory accompaniment of the first bar to produce a more symmetric group of two bars, as indicated in the following fictitious example:

Ex. 181

In this way the opening group would have consisted of two introductory bars followed by an eight-bar period, a combination preferable from the angle of puristic regularity to the one-plus-eight scheme in the score. However, one need only listen to both versions to realize how much more exciting and musicianly is Mozart's "asymmetric" version.

After this group of nine bars, it is still not a "symmetric" group of eight bars but a group of seven bars that follows (10 to 16), reading:

Ex. 182

wherein two motivic ideas—the end of motif III and the beginning of the "descending scale"—collide in the high B-flat of bar 13. And this collision is the very means by which the contraction to seven bars is brought about. Again, had the composer insisted on eight-bar regularity, the group would have had to be extended in the following or some similar manner:

Ex. 183

No wonder that here, too, Mozart preferred his own shape of seven bars. Looked at in this way, the opening period of sixteen bars presents itself, interestingly enough, as a summation of 1 plus 8 plus 7 bars. And the last three notes, D, C-sharp, D (in bars 14 to 16), are not only the end of the preceding group but also the beginning of the "annex" with which the theme concludes. Also the eighth notes in the annex are a most convincing bridge to the following resumption of the theme:

Ex. 184

Thus the whole outer symmetry is but a charming attire, almost a camouflage—though for that matter not any less important in its artistic effect—beneath which everything is motion and fluency, abounding in thematic utterances and implications. It is in this very combination of outer symmetry and inner complexity that Mozart's twofold musical heritage may be detected; namely, the Mannheim School and his Italian and French predecessors on the one side, and Haydn and even Bach on the other. Of course, this was but the ground out of which grew his own individual genius.

Having dealt rather exhaustively with the first twenty bars, the tempo of our examination must now be accelerated. The next group constitutes a repetition of the opening group, the only difference being that the second part (bars 25 to 27) now rises a tone higher than the first part, while in the opening group it was heard a tone lower than the first. Through this, the present group concludes in B-flat, the relative major of the symphony's basic key. The whole first thematic section is then brought to a conclusion in the dominant (F) of this B-flat. The skeleton of this design (bars 28 to 43) reads:

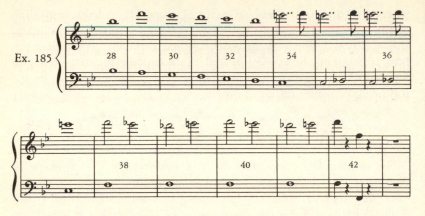

Ex. 185

Here there are first a few bridging bars (28 to 33) which recall the work's basic phrasing, that is, the "rise" followed by the descending scale, though here the rise is a fifth instead of a sixth. Then, in bars 34 to 36, motif I is again featured both in the soprano (E, F, E) and in the bass (C, D-flat, C). The above example is of course only a chart, a skeleton, and the reader should study in the actual score the manifold figurations which, in themselves thematic, fill this skeleton with life.

Only one of these figurations may be mentioned here specifically. In the flute part (bars 38 to 42) the F, E, is varied to F, E-flat, D-flat, E (example 185), a small, inconspicuous, yet fascinating nuance. For the little phrase presages the symphony's second subject, which is about to enter (see following example). In this way the first and second thematic sections are delicately knit together. However, turning to this second theme:

Ex. 186

we realize that the nuance mentioned is not the only bond between the two sections. True, taken by themselves, the above bars constitute a totally new, independent musical utterance. The gamboling eighths of the opening theme are replaced by a phrasing of almost lyric sensitiveness. In its whole appearance this second theme expresses a melodic impulse and flavor entirely different from that of the movement's first theme. Indeed, at this point the thematic evolution and outer demarcation of the movement meet as though at a crossing.

Having not only admitted but emphasized the contrasting qualities, the affinity between the themes must also be stressed. What strikes us first is a resemblance to the group around bar 10 or rather its repetition as bar 12. We remember having drawn in example 174 a contour of these bars, proving them to be a kind of varied reiteration of bars 3 and 4. Comparing this contour with the second subject (quoted in transposition):

Contour of group around bar 12   Second subject (transposed)

Ex. 187

it is obvious that a recollection of the former must have made itself felt in forming the latter. Yet these bars are only the beginning of the second theme. The full theme reads:

Ex. 188

Taking bars 46 to 50, is it not as if through them an echo of the symphony's very beginning (transposed) were to become audible?

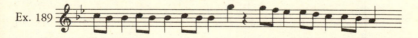

Ex. 189

In numerous examples from Beethoven, Schumann, Brahms, and others, we observed how this same idea of inner identity and outer variety presented itself in many forms. And it was interesting to recognize each composer's artistic individuality not only in the flavor of his melodies and rhythms but also in his personal *structural* conception; in the different technical mechanisms through which each of them realized that great law of thematic coherence. It is a fascinating experience now to see this mechanism applied in Mozart's inimitable manner, so unpretentious, ethereal, and yet so profound.

The lovely theme is repeated (bars 52 to 57), whereupon over a few bridging groups, which reiterate familiar motivic shapes, the concluding section of the movement's exposition is reached. Glancing first at the general picture of this part, figures obviously mirroring the symphony's prime motif catch the eye. According to all our previous experience this would not seem to indicate anything new. These are simply, one would surmise, different transformations of preceding shapes, produced in the course of the composition. Yet we shall soon see that we are here faced with a new and most important phenomenon—one which may lead our inquiry in new directions.

True, these features, too, are transformations, as are almost all thematic changes in the realm of classical music, but they are transformations of a particular, decisive type. There is first a shape of four bars (example 190*a*), followed by a group of which we give the full orchestral sketch (example 190*b*):

Looking at the first of these examples, we quickly notice that the thought of the work's opening phrase is integrated in it. Yet the endeavor to grasp the full difference in idea and expression between the opening and the present shape will bring us to realize that this is more than an ordinary transformation. The present bars are not merely one of many possible variants of the opening shape, but are rather an amplification, *an intensification of the opening shape's structural and emotional idea.* The opening thought appears here, as it were, on a higher spiral of expression. Comparing the first part of this line to the symphony's beginning,

we see that the rise to the sixth is accomplished in the beginning of the symphony on a weak beat, the B-flat (E-flat in the above transposed example) having merely the quality of a charming melodic lift, without much structural or emotional emphasis. But now, apart from the change of the phrasing as such, the corresponding sixth, E-flat, occurs on a strong beat. Thus emotional forces which in the initial version were latent have now become active. And the idea is still further intensified by the fact that, while the opening theme merely rose to a peak on the sixth, this peak has now become a new starting point from which the line climbs to a still higher summit (example 190*a*). And though this second rise is formed not by a sixth but by a fourth, the idea of intensifying the original thought is very effectively materialized. Such alternating rises of sixths and fourths themselves become from now on an important motivic feature throughout the work.

A similar idea, even increased in effect, is seen in example 190*b* (bars 72 to 80). From its artful polyphony, in which almost any part can be considered the main and none a secondary voice, we may single out the following thematic line:[6]

Here the phenomenon presents itself in utter transparency. The work's opening thought emerges first in piano (rise from B-flat to G–F), though with exchanged motivic particles: II plus I, instead of I plus II; whereupon the line soars in sudden forte to the sixth on E-flat and a third time (through a fourth) to the high G, before it falls back to the tonic. This last rise, beginning with the sudden forte on the E-flat, and occurring at a moment when we almost expect the group to end, stretches to the G as its highest point. Again, as in the previous example, the rise culminates on a strong beat, with a long sustained note, on which a natural forte is thus inserted. The dramatic meaning of this change of the initial thought from the gentle opening version to this highly emphasized shape is evident, and we become vividly aware that the function of these transformations is not only to transform but to intensify the musical and emotional content.

---

[6] Any other combination expresses a similiar idea, however, as:

showing a sixth from D to B-flat, then a fourth to E-flat plus a following descending cadence (analogous to example 190*a*).

But the full weight of this phenomenon only becomes apparent if we consider the whole role that these bars assume in the course of the movement's exposition. Here is an architectural device, a means by which "form" can be created in a musical composition *through the thematic shaping itself,* quite apart from the grouping of its outer course into sections and parts. When, as in this symphony, a lovely opening shape is led through various changes and adventures, until it finally emerges as a triumphant exuberation of its own inherent idea, then we have the feeling that this whole exposition has become one musical utterance, almost, if we may say so, one huge bar. A content, a "story" is thus developed through thematic forming. Just as it is the purport and essence of a good play to develop the fate of its hero as a consequence of his own being and character, so the narrative of this symphony, or of any musical work of higher structure, is centered on the structural and, through these, the emotional possibilities which can be evolved from a musical thought. In the symphony's opening theme a musical thought of charming grace was presented to us. It was the exposition's fundamental purpose to bring to full expression whatever structural and emotional possibilities were latent in this initial thought.

This idea is pursued throughout the remaining part of the movement, in fact, of the whole work. When the theme in the so-called "development" is carried through a further series of colorful changes and variations and then, in the recapitulation, the movement's whole course is recounted, the bars corresponding to those in the last example appear in a slightly changed version. And this last version forms the most intense expression of the thematic idea imaginable. The original gentle rise to the sixth is here effectuated no less than five times, as the following chart signifies (only the octaves are here exchanged):

Ex. 194

Follow this fivefold rise from B-flat to G, to E-flat, to C, to A-flat–G and to E-flat again.

One must comprehend the terrific emotional tension embodied in this constant reentrance of the thematic idea. Each entrance draws the listener's attention, until finally, at a point where he almost thinks that the theme has lived itself out, it embarks on its most emphatic utterance. And in this last resumption, centered on the rise to a natural sforzando on the E-flat, the line through a jubilant cadence finishes on the tonic. Thus the most intense expression of the musical idea, slumbering in the symphony's opening shape, has now become reality and fulfillment.

In this evolution from the modest opening shape, culminating in B-flat, to the manifold rise, culminating in the towering E-flat, is symbolized in briefest indication the whole story of the symphony's first movement. In fact, and in a wider sense, the symphonic idea as such, even the phenomenon of musical form in general, becomes apparent in such symbols.

Once the principle is understood, the architectural meaning of the remaining part of the symphony will quickly become clear. The theme of the Finale opens as follows:

Ex. 195

What is the structural meaning of this?

This theme is a kind of reversion of the symphony's opening theme. While the Allegro theme was built through:

Ex. 196

in the Finale theme (example 195) motif II precedes motif I. Of course bridging notes are now added to the motivic design to produce a mood of fluency and intensity. Thus bar 3 (motif II) from the first movement (*a* in the following example) appears in the Finale transformed to *b,* while motif I (*c*), enriched with eighth notes, becomes *d.* (Note the identical pitch, save for one accidental: E-natural instead of E-flat.)

Ex. 197

If we read the last shape omitting the F-sharps, the similarity of the underlying thematic root becomes obvious.

From an architectural angle one of the most significant features in this Finale theme is the fact that it rises to an *accented* sixth, while in the first movement this accentuation was only reached as a last intensification. Now, in the Finale, this accented sixth is, as it were, an established fact, as the movement already opens with it. Thus we recognize even in the first bars the architectural (and through it the emotional) function of the Finale. This function is to let the work's opening and basic theme sound in transformations which express in tempo, accent, dynamics, and mood a feeling of urgent pulsation, of an approaching goal. Or in other words, if a tautology in definition is permissible: the architectural function of the Finale is to change the opening thought into a Finale theme.

But the meaning of this Finale theme becomes only fully apparent with its continuation. The architectural idea of the whole first movement was symbolized, in utter concentration, as a progression between two shapes, culminating respectively in B-flat and E-flat—a progression from the opening theme to the "intensified version" which appears at the end of the movement's exposition or (once more) in its recapitulation. This progression from B-flat to E-flat, which stretches in a huge arc over the whole first movement, *now itself becomes the theme*. For the full Finale theme reads:

Ex. 198

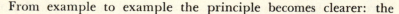

From example to example the principle becomes clearer: the

meaning and role of architectural sections is determined, more than through their outward position and demarcation, by what their thematic connections and transformations express. Obviously Mozart felt the impact of this jubilant rise from the B-flat to the E-flat so strongly that he let the second half of the theme, in which the rise is accomplished (bars 5 to 8), sound no less than four times in brief succession within the beginning of the movement. First, it is sounded twice by repeating the opening group (bars 1 to 8). Four bars are then inserted, in which, between heavily accented D's, the original motif (I) charmingly reappears: E-flat, D,. D, as seen in the following example (the glittering trills of the violins on the E-flat add emphasis to the feature):

Ex. 199

whereupon that important second half of the first group again enters. And since bars 9 to 16 also carry a repetition mark, the shape is heard four times within the first sixteen bars.

The Finale theme is followed by an expanded group of passages, recalling similar sections in the first movement:

From first movement

Ex. 200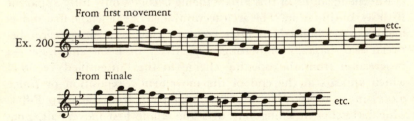

From Finale

Here, too, it is significant that in the first movement these sections form the end of the exposition, while in the Finale they follow immediately upon the opening theme. This exemplifies anew the different, though usually complementary, function fulfilled by the outer and inner design of a composition of superior quality. According to its outer form the Finale is shaped in a clear sonata pattern, almost identical in its main proportions to the first movement. As for the inner substance of the Finale, however, the first movement's final utterances here appear merely as points of departure. Note also how in the last example the three-bar pattern of the first movement is accelerated to a two-bar pattern in the Finale, through which the mood of urgency and intensification becomes all the clearer.

Upon the close of this section, the Finale's second subject is introduced and we realize that it mirrors—as could almost have been expected—the second subject of the Allegro. This becomes even more transparent in the versions in which the themes appear in the recapitulations of their respective movements, quoted in the following example (*a*, second Allegro theme; *b*, second Finale theme):

Ex. 201

The notes lifted into relief show the line of the Allegro theme shining out from the Finale. Again we see that the version in the Finale is not only a changed but an intensified expression of the Allegro theme's idea. Everything has gained weight: phrases which in the Allegro theme form mere particles (*a*) are now heard in full melodic emphasis as *b*:

Ex. 202

Now, as each theme occurs four times during its respective movement (twice in the expositions and twice in the recapitulations), it is worth while to observe that each occurrence forms a new variant and that the similarity between the Allegro and the Finale is demonstrable in each version. But the astounding fact is that the resemblance to the theme of the other movement is *in each variant materialized in a different way and through different nuances.* Comparing, for instance, the second appearance of the Finale theme from the movement's exposition (*a* in the following example) with the Allegro theme (*b*), an affinity emerges as striking as that seen in the former examples, yet brought about through a different shaping:

Ex. 203

Mozart's unbounded imagination, which ceaselessly invents new variants for his musical thoughts—he hardly ever repeats a shape literally—has with justification been greatly admired. But the true value and scope of this is not fully understood unless one also realizes how deeply and strictly this abundance of ever differing shapes is entrenched in thematic unity.

To return to the technical aspect: the second subject is again followed by a section of passages with which the Finale's exposition concludes. And since the Finale is, in its outer design, built on the same scheme of sonata form as the first movement, this exposition is further followed by a development and recapitulation. Here, then, at the work's conclusion, the work's prime thought again sounds in heavy strokes from the winds.

However, before quoting this group, some explanatory remarks should be added. For this whole concluding section of the work so clearly confirms the composer's consciousness of the architectural idea to which our present analysis points that we must elaborate on its thematic course in some detail.

Already in the Finale's opening theme the main melodic line in the violins was accompanied by some strokes of the winds mirroring the symphony's opening thought (motif I) or, more accurately, the variant heard in bars 16 to 20 of the first movement (see example 169). In the Finale theme these strokes appear as:

Ex. 204

This motivic figuration is continued in many parts of the Finale and now reappears in the Finale's concluding section. The way in which here, toward the symphony's conclusion, this figure becomes a decisive factor in the work's architectural resolution is noteworthy.

The concluding section is preceded by the second Finale theme. This second Finale theme is here three times repeated, appearing the third time in the following version:

Ex. 205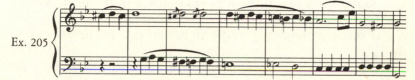

We see that the aforementioned figure, expressing a variant of motif I, is here twice interwoven, both in the soprano and in the accompanying line. This figure was not included in any previous occurrence of the theme. But having been thus introduced, the architectural importance of the following reentrance of these same motivic strokes is greatly stressed. Sounded again by the winds, over the glittering web of the violin passages (which, naturally, are themselves thematic), they actually form the opening of the concluding section:

Ex. 206

Indeed, the full idea of the symphony's opening theme, with the rise to the sixth, appears in contour in these strokes of the winds. Moreover, here again the sixth enters on heavily accented strong beats, with an annexed cadence concluding in the tonic. Besides, the regular crotchet rhythm in which the theme now sounds, in contrast to the original ♫ ♩ ♫ ♩ , intensifies the idea of resolution.

In the next bars, then (if we but adjust the octaves which Mozart had to keep within normal limits), an expression even of the "increased" version, the version with the ever rising sixths, soaring to a climax on the high C, becomes audible:

Ex. 207

Follow this line: from B-flat–A (motif I) to the G (a sixth), from here to the E-flat (sixth), from here in an arc to the final peak on the C (another sixth). And even the very last bars of the symphony repeat this progression in sixths, until the line finally resolves in the tonic.

Thus the work's thematic "story" is brought to a close. In it the relation between inner and outer shaping plays a significant part. In its outer shaping the concluding section is merely a symmetric repetition of the end of the exposition, without any "coda." But by interweaving into this concluding section a variant of the oft-mentioned "intensified version" of the symphony's opening theme, Mozart endows the concluding part with a new meaning. The work's prime thought is thus heard at the symphony's end—no longer with the dramatic effect and emphasis of the first movement, but in a transformation conveying ease and liberation.

Once the Finale's thematic meaning is understood, the other movements need little comment.

In the third movement, the Menuetto, the Finale pattern (motif II followed by motif I) is presaged in the theme's first bars (see braces in the following example). From these opening bars the charming dance tune is developed through a similar "intensification," as in the first and last movement—though the idea is here less outspoken. The full thematic line reads:

Ex. 208

Note in bars 7 to 9 the second rise of the motif (B-flat, A to F) (flutes) before the final descent in the concluding cadence; in the cadence a nice indication of motif III (diminished fifth) is included (bars 11 and 13).

The second movement, then, the Andante, unfolds in its thematic essence an analogous picture, though in an entirely different mood and musical character. The Andante's opening theme reads:

Ex. 209

Here the first melodic utterance emerges from the violoncellos and bass. This line expresses the motifs in the same order (II plus I) as in the third and last movement. (This succession is, in a sense, already heard in the opening of the symphony, with the violas sounding motif II, whereupon motif I follows in the violins.) This pattern is taken over in the next bars by the first violins.[7] Moreover, in the bars immediately following (as one might almost expect) the diminished fifth (motif III) punctually appears.

Thus the same thematic order and idea appear in the Andante as in the other movements, notwithstanding the contrasting picture that its shapes convey.

---

[7] At the same time this violin phrase continues in its repeated eighth notes the figuration of the violas and second violins. In these throbbing eighths the beginning of the symphony is mirrored. For the repetition of the E-flat in the opening of the Andante (*a*) is the form in which the Andante reiterates the opening of the symphony (*b*):

Ex. 210

Above we compared a symphony's theme to the hero of a dramatic play who is led through the vicissitudes of his fate to the solution of his life problem. Seen thus allegorically, the first and last movements could be thought to constitute the actual drama, wherein the central idea is developed, while the other movements represent episodes which take the hero through different events and environments. Yet, as throughout all these different events we encounter the same hero, *the theme,* these sections, too, become organic parts of the work's artistic whole. The new environments influence the "hero," who in turn influences them, and the final outcome is the result of this interplay, both in a symbolic and in a technical, that is, thematic sense.

In this analysis of Mozart's work it may have been noticed that more than before, ideas and expressions from the esthetic and even emotional sphere were touched upon. Now, although this study is an endeavor to explain the compositional phenomena on technical grounds, this does not mean that this author considers the creation of a musical work a purely technical process. The technical ground is maintained in our inquiry as long as possible only because it is in their technical appearance, that is, as structural features, that compositional phenomena can be most readily perceived, their validity tested, and a fruitful discussion engendered. Nevertheless, any analysis of artistic creations will finally reach a point where an abstention from all esthetic evaluation must necessarily lead to complete academicism and even to a misconception of the technical phenomena themselves. This is especially true with regard to the thematic process.

Here an intriguing question may be broached. *Why in music do technical and esthetic analyses live almost entirely separate lives?* Esthetic descriptions of a musical work's content and meaning indulge either in philosophical transcendency or in poetic or even programmatic aberration. Occasional attempts, however, to explain in technical terms the dramatic evolution of a composition prove even more sterile than the poetic ones.

Why?

Because the current theory hardly provides any firm technical ground on which such esthetic or dramatic interpretation can be based. For certainly it cannot, with any satisfactory result, grow from the harmonic or contrapuntal mechanism. And even the models of form, according to which the course of a sonata or any other piece is usually described, are, if taken alone, ephemeral concepts, much too schematic to serve as adequate guides through the spiritual forces which permeate a creative musical work.

But a composition's *thematic* evolution does provide a sensible technical basis for the comprehension of its dramatic course. The-matic phenomena and thematic structure are more directly, more obviously than harmonic, contrapuntal, or form-schematic features the immediate expression of the emotional and even intellectual energies which moved the composer. This was most transparently seen in the particular feature described in the preceding analysis of Mozart's symphony. As the examination disclosed, the symphony's architectural idea was centered on the progression of the work's almost chaste opening thought to its thematic intensification in the concluding sections. All the other shapes, variants, and ramifications which were passed through on the road from the initial to the final version constitute in some sense intermediaries intended to strengthen, to dramatize the pulsating drive to the goal, to prepare the denouement. Here structural and emotional expression indeed become one, each fully comprehensible only through the other. We may choose a name for this method of so transforming a thematic thought that it expresses and symbolizes the work's whole archi-tectural and even dramatic solution. We may call it *thematic resolu-tion*. Sometimes we may also specifically speak of a symphonic reso-lution, for, as will be seen, this device assumes particular significance in the symphonic domain. In the following chapter we shall ex-amine more works in an attempt to clarify their architectural totality and the architecture's possible interconnection with the dramatic course. In this investigation the work's "thematic resolu-tion" is apt to play a decisive part.

However, the foregoing conclusions should not lead to a miscon-ception. It is not averred that this method of deducing a musical composition's dramatic content from its thematic mechanism pro-duces an infallible clue to the work's spiritual and emotional mean-ing. The last magical content of any work of art, and of musical works in particular, will never yield entirely to intellectual compre-hension. The specific dramatic emotions and possible relations to other spheres of life active in a composition, and their esthetic im-plications, must always be decided individually. For in the last sense everyone sees in a work of art only what by his own predisposition he is able or inclined to see. Yet, on the basis of one's individual capacity and inclination, the understanding of a musical work's thematic architecture undoubtedly constitutes the solidest technical ground from which its spiritual values may be perceived, or at least divined, and perhaps to a certain degree interpreted.

Therefore when in the following chapter our presentation approaches still more closely to esthetic evaluation, it is not for the purpose of adorning our analysis with poetic or programmatic suggestions. What is to be demonstrated is only that an interrelationship between the thematic and spiritual spheres does exist—and that it must have existed while the composer formed his work. In our presentation any dramatic or allegoric comment will be introduced only to render the structural content more lucid by hinting at the underlying spiritual impulses. Once the structural idea of a composition is thoroughly established, it is left to the individual to reproject the structural idea into the spiritual sphere and interpret the work according to whatever symbolism may seem to him fitting.

6

THEMATIC EVOLUTION
AND THEMATIC RESOLUTION

The preceding chapter led us into the heart of our inquiry. No longer were we content merely to investigate such questions as: Of what does the thematic principle consist, from whence did it grow, and in what manner and by what devices is it materialized in musical composition? The principle was taken for granted, and we were free to follow its working in the real action and life of a composition. Our prime interest was no longer thematic transformation as such, but the problem of how a theme *moves by transformation toward a goal* and how in this process the dramatic development of the work and its thematic course are intertwined.

Brahms: Two Rhapsodies

To unravel the detail of this process Mozart's G-minor Symphony was chosen as a first example. Expanding our investigation to different works and styles, we may turn to Brahms's opus 79, the Two Rhapsodies for piano in B and G minor. The structural interrelationship between the opening themes of these two pieces was already demonstrated on a previous occasion (see examples 98 and 99). As explained there, the opening themes of the Two Rhapsodies are in essence inversions of each other. However, the work contains shapes other than its opening themes, and we must now delve into these wider connections and follow the course of this elaborate work in some detail.

In the following, almost the whole of the First Rhapsody's opening section is given:

139

Agitato

Ex. 211

The opening theme (bars 1 to 4), immediately after having been introduced, is reiterated in transposition in bars 5 to 8. However, this reiteration (though the left-hand part at first repeats the opening theme literally) is not a pure repetition but a true transformation. By transposing the right-hand part of bars 5 to 8 to the pitch of the opening group and comparing it to the latter,

the essential identity becomes quickly apparent. Such immediate transformation of a work's opening is a rare feature, highly characteristic of Brahms's restlessly active structural mind.

In the ensuing group (bars 9 and following) it seems as if the composer wished to reintroduce the theme two further times; however, he confines the reintroduction to the theme's first bar, which we now hear, twice transposed (left hand in bars 9 and 10), in a powerful crescendo leading to the climax and conclusion of the opening period on the F-sharp in bar 16. Bar 11, in which the climax is focused, is in its melodic essence a reutterance at original pitch of the opening bar of the piece. At the same time this part (bars 11 and 12) is presaged in the accompanying figures of bars 1 and 2— a fact which becomes especially clear by quoting the line of bars 11 and 12 in the form in which they appear later in the recapitulation, since here even the pitches conform:

Bars 11 and 12 (transposed)   Figure from bars 1 and 2

Ex. 213

The identity, save for accidentals, is evident.

Upon the conclusion of this group, a bridging group is inserted (bars 16 to 21), evolving from an augmentation of the characteristic figure in the opening bar,

Figure from opening bar

a   *b*   Bar 16

Ex. 214

of which the following bar (17) is but a sequence. The line of bars 18 and 19, then, is derived from the alto of the opening bars. Compare:

Bars 18 and 19   Alto from opening bars

Ex. 215

The ensuing bars (20 and 21) anticipate an important shape which follows later in the Rhapsody; namely, the second half of the so-called Interlude theme (the full course of which is quoted in example 219):

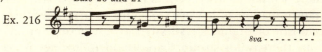

Bars 20 and 21

Ex. 216

Second half of Interlude theme (transposed)

With a kind of codetta, formed by a (varied) recapitulation of the opening group in the following bars (bar 22 and following), the section of the first theme is brought to a conclusion, whereupon the second theme enters, reading:

Ex. 217

Here, from a thematic point of view, we are approaching more vital questions. This beautiful theme is built from two motivic shapes. The first, motif I, appears twice; the second, motif II, follows. However, a third occurrence of motif I is built into motif II, forming this motif's beginning. Comparing this second theme with the opening theme (example 211), we realize that the second theme's first part (motif I) is a new thought, of which a corresponding part is not traceable in the opening theme. Perhaps one might say that an inversion of motif I is intimated in the opening theme's first bar (through F-sharp, C-sharp, B), but this is at best a theoretical, analytical similarity. As an actual musical utterance, motif I in the second theme does truly form a new thought. Motif II, however, the rise to the seventh followed by a stepwise descent, appears clearly as the melodic idea also in the second half of the first theme:

Ex. 218

That this identity was a structural intention of the composer is shown through another feature which is a most impressive proof of how thoroughly the thematic plan of the piece was thought out. This Rhapsody I is built in ternary form (A, B, A), its principal part being developed from the two themes just quoted. Between the two appearances of the principal part a middle part, a sort of *lyric interlude,* is inserted. The theme of the Interlude rising to a seventh is in its first half a literal and obvious reiteration of the Rhapsody's second subject (merely transferred to major). But the Interlude theme is expanded to a second half which rises to a ninth.

This Interlude theme, formed by the two halves, reads:

Ex. 219

dolce espr.

Now since the Interlude theme is identical with the second subject, it would also have to show some similarity to the first subject, from which, as explained above, a part of the former is derived. And indeed, the Interlude theme not only shows this similarity but, though it is an almost literal reiteration of the *second* subject, reveals this affinity to the *first* subject much more strikingly than does the second subject itself. For the twofold rise, first to the seventh and then to the ninth, which forms the core of the Interlude theme (and which was missing in the second subject) is clearly apparent in the first subject:

From first subject

Ex. 220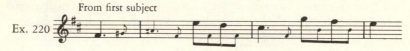

The identity is complete even to pitch, again save for accidentals, as the opening theme is in B-minor while the Interlude theme is in B-major.

But now note in the Interlude theme (example 219) the charming counterpoint of whole notes in the soprano, which in itself—follow its line from F-sharp to B, A-sharp—reflects the work's opening. The four successive F-sharps quite specifically reflect the version of bars 22 and 23 (see example 211).

However, this counterpoint indicates more. For through a combination of these two voices the opening bar of the Rhapsody resounds *in its complete shape* from this otherwise so contrasting Interlude theme:

Opening bar   Interlude theme

Ex. 221

This is a most startling example. New vistas of the work's architectural connections are opened. We first considered the first and second themes of the Rhapsody as two in essence unrelated utterances merely held together by a slight similarity of their second parts. But now we hear the first theme unmistakably resounding from the Interlude theme, which itself is a clear copy of the second theme. Only through this do we gain a true insight into the compositional process through which the Rhapsody was formed. Here the core of the composer's structural conception becomes apparent. For that he conceived an agitated first theme contrasted with a lyrical second theme and at the same time developed these themes so that one resounded from the other: this is the fundamental idea behind the Rhapsody's architecture.

After the Interlude section the whole first part is repeated literally, whereupon an annexed coda group concludes the piece. This coda—most logically from an architectural angle—expresses the idea of the two themes in contrapuntal combination. The second theme rises in the bass, while in the soprano a figurate counterpoint is heard, through which there sounds an intimation of the first theme. Compare:

Ex. 222

Shape from opening theme   Figuration from coda

Here a problem becomes apparent toward which at present our main interest is directed. This contrapuntal combination of the two themes in the coda, though it represents the most concentrated expression of the Rhapsody's inherent idea, still constitutes merely a reaffirmation of its tensions and challenges rather than an answer and solution. It does not bring about a structural solution, for the initial themes have been maintained literally without any decisive transformation; nor does it bring an emotional solution, for the initial stress and melancholy appear in the coda by no means eased but rather confirmed and intensified.

This lack of a "solution" does not signify a weakness in the architectural plan of the Rhapsody. To carry on the utterances and mood of the piece to the end, to "confirm" rather than to "resolve," is, within the frame and idea of the first Rhapsody alone, of powerful effect. But since the first Rhapsody is followed by a second, the two together forming one greater whole, the real plan of this whole becomes apparent when the first Rhapsody is not only complemented but almost contradicted, and so "resolved," by the structure and idea of the second.

This second Rhapsody opens with a theme which, as described

previously (example 98 and 99), is an inversion of the opening theme of the first Rhapsody. And it might also be called an inversion in the emotional sense, as its straightforward rhythm conveys a cheerful, almost jubilant atmosphere. Yet if the design of the second Rhapsody were in turn to evolve from its opening theme merely according to the organic musical law, we would still be confronted with two pieces, the effect of which would not amount to more than the sum of the detail of their shapes. However, as will be seen, Brahms's plan lifts the architectural and dramatic content of the Two Rhapsodies as a unit to a much more meaningful enunciation.

The opening theme of Rhapsody II is followed by a group reading:

Ex. 223

Now just as the opening theme of Rhapsody II proved an inversion of the first theme of Rhapsody I, this new group is in its basic concept an inversion of the second theme of Rhapsody I. The A, D, E, of the first Rhapsody's second theme (example 217) appears now in contrary motion as E, D, A, thus conforming even in pitch. And by including secondary voices, the inversion of the full theme can also be heard. Compare the contour of the group in question (*a* in the following example) with the second theme of the first Rhapsody (*b*). But to understand the full depth of Brahms's thematic concept, we should also note the bass of the group (*c*), which mirrors the phrase from the opening of Rhapsody II.

Ex. 224

Also of specific importance, both structurally and emotionally, is the group that follows:

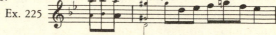

Ex. 225

The opening particle of this is taken from the characteristic figure in the work's opening bar, which in the first Rhapsody appears also in a more lyric version (see example 214). But the main content of the group quoted is a reflection of the first Rhapsody's second subject (see the notes in bold print in example 225 and compare with example 217). The two shapes are even identical in pitch. It is particularly significant that the group of example 225 is also emotionally a reminiscence, a resumption, of the lyric melancholy of the first Rhapsody. Of course, the composer does not dwell too long on this relapse into the melancholic. For this shape does not become the essential, the definite shape of the piece but merely a bridge leading to the next group. This next group, however, is no longer a mere "bridging" shape, but the decisive utterance of the second Rhapsody —in fact, of the whole work—its "resolution." We quote this group in the form in which it appears in the recapitulation, concluding the work:

Ex. 226

Viewed first from a structural angle, this group discloses itself as a combined expression of the opening theme in Rhapsody II and the second theme in Rhapsody I—thus in a wider sense, since these two themes contain the essentials of all important shapes of the work, as a final extract and résumé of the entire work's thematic content. The opening of Rhapsody II, D, E-flat, G, B-flat, clearly reemerges in the beginning of the present group. Compare:

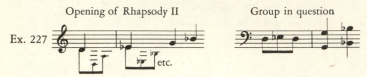

Ex. 227

And the second theme of Rhapsody I reappears in full contour in the melodic bass of the present group—however, with one decisive alteration: *its melodic line is lowered by a whole tone.* Thus the original fourth and fifth is now changed to a third and fourth, while correspondingly the original seventh must now become a sixth. Compare the (transposed) second theme of Rhapsody I (*a* in the following example) with the bass of example 226 (quoted below as *b*):

Ex. 228

Of course, in combination with the melodic alterations the harmonic meaning of the whole shape is also decisively changed. The theme is now firmly entrenched in the tonic, and the lyricism of the original shape rising to the yearning seventh of the F (see *a* in the last example) becomes in the new marchlike tempo, with the figural accompaniment and the cadencing conclusion added, an expression of cheer, almost of victory.

Indeed, an architectural spectacle similar in principle to that encountered in Mozart's G-minor Symphony here becomes apparent. There the original theme was transformed mainly by an alteration of accent into an utterance which brought the structural and dramatic course of the work to its solution. Here the alteration is chiefly melodic, brought about by a change in the theme's intervallic structure—yet the result is somewhat similar. The melancholy of the first piece is transfigured into a mood of tender jubilation. What was, structurally and emotionally, search and problem now becomes finality and solution—or to use the term introduced in our previous chapter: the work's "thematic resolution" is completed. True, the "jubilation" is in the beginning still subdued by a touch of tragic mysticism which is never entirely missing in Brahms's music, but finally it rises to a triumphant climax.

Again we see how—almost unnoticeably, inevitably, and inseparably—structural and emotional forces coincide. Again, as in the Mozart Symphony, it is not merely *any* transformation which forms the plan of the work, but only transformations which lead to a solution. Similar phenomena, though they may be effectuated in various technical forms and express various dramatic ideas, lie at the bottom of the architectural plan of every work of higher thematic conception.

Returning to the Rhapsodies, the decisive, jubilant shape rising to the sixth appears both in the bass and soprano. In the bass it is formed by a rise from G to E-flat, in the soprano by a rise from D to B-flat (see bars 109 to 112). From the F-sharp in bar 113, however, the line does not yet proceed to the tonic G but rises once more to a sixth, D.

This sixth in the soprano, D, and the sixth in the bass, E-flat, here clash in a wonderful climaxing discord (asterisk in the example above), thus expressing in one chord the characteristic motif D, E-flat, D, with a variant of which (see example 214*a*) the work also began.

In this whole feature also another point of interest is included. The groups quoted in examples 223 and 225 correspond thematically, as has been demonstrated, to the group which in the first Rhapsody we termed the second subject. This term would hardly be debated, as the main part of the first Rhapsody somewhat approaches the sonata form.[1] But in the second Rhapsody it is not clear whether the term "second subject" should be attached to any group and if so to which one. When Brahms shaped the group of example 225, he obviously had a second subject in mind, as the group is not only formed in affinity to the second theme of Rhapsody I but also in character and mood would seem to point to such a "contrasting second subject." Yet he did not follow through: this group did not become a "second subject." It seems that the urge of the work's over-all architecture was the stronger factor. This demanded that he proceed as quickly and effectively as possible to the last decisive group, which became the work's resolution (example 226). Thus the group in question became a kind of bridging preparation for that decisive utterance. It is a harmonic preparation by being an emphatic expression of the dominant, and it is a thematic preparation as its characteristic auftakt is taken over as the constant figuration in the concluding group.

The whole feature is a striking instance of how outer construction is influenced by a governing idea of thematic evolution. The very fact that the group in question was prevented by its architectural-dramatic function from developing to a full thematic section (as a "second subject") was probably the determining factor which produced a piece of "freer" proportions, for which Brahms then chose the title Rhapsody.

---

[1] At least it does so up to the point where the second theme is heard. In this first Rhapsody the difference from a true "sonata" lies merely in the fact that the development section and recapitulation of the first part elaborate only on the first subject and omit the second. Of course, to make up for this "omission" the Interlude section is interpolated, which in turn elaborates on the second subject alone.

An interesting interrelationship between the inner and outer form-building forces will also be seen in our next example.

Schubert: Impromptu, opus 90, No. 4

The opening section of this piece, so well known to every pianist, reads:

Ex. 230

By extracting from the opening figuration the underlying melodic line, a contour results (*a* in the following example), which by further abbreviation may be notated as the simple phrase shown in *b*. And by continuing to extract the essence in this way, the whole opening section (bars 1 to 30), omitting all repetitions, can be drawn in an outline given as *c*:

Ex. 231

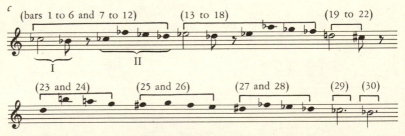

It becomes apparent that the idea upon which this engaging theme was built is in essence symmetric and simple. The theme opens with a figure (motif I) formed by a stepwise chromatic progression (C-flat, B-flat), which is followed by a phrase rising in a fourth (motif II), constituting the theme's melodic center (C-flat,

F-flat, E-flat, D-flat). This basic group is repeated literally and in transposition till the climax in bar 23 is reached, when the rise to the fourth is replaced, "intensified," by a rise to the sixth (D, B). These bars (23 and 24) are expanded by sequences to a wider melodic arc (23 to 30), of which the last phrase (29 and 30) is formed by the same notes with which the theme started.

Thus we witness a thematic evolution *within this opening section itself:* a shape centered on a rise to a fourth is developed and finally transformed into a shape culminating in a rise to a sixth, the whole process producing, in fact, one long theme.

The figurations from the beginning are now continued over a few bars, this time in major, whereupon a further incisive and most effective transformation introduces a new theme, rising in the lower voices:

Ex. 232

This is structurally and melodically a persuasive thought. But it is certainly remarkable that this theme shows itself on closer examination to be an extract of the essential idea expressed by the whole preceding section. The two decisive shapes of the opening section,

Ex. 233

are linked together to produce the new theme.

This theme is also developed, through sequence and modulation, to a wider arc. It is later reiterated, first slightly varied and subdued to a charming pianissimo,

Ex. 234

and is later repeated literally, which brings the principal part of the piece to an end.

After a sort of lyric middle part, a "trio," has been inserted, this principal part is repeated in full, the whole thus forming a perfect example of complete ternary construction. We must now turn to the Trio, because from the point of view of our subject the paramount question is whether and how this middle part is connected with the work's whole. Its opening reads:

Ex. 235

This design looks at first very dissimilar to that of the principal part. No motivic link between the two seems discernible. The incisive change of key and the entirely different figuration create a completely new picture. Thus it is particularly surprising that a closer examination reveals that not only is a connection traceable but that the theme of the Impromptu's principal part is, in fact, continued almost literally and even at identical pitch in the Trio. Schubert notated the trio in a sharp key (C-sharp minor), and this at first somewhat obscures the identity. But as soon as we restore the notation to flats, the thematic origin of the Trio theme becomes apparent:

Line of trio theme notated in flats

Ex. 236

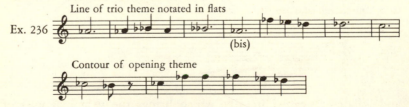

(bis)

Contour of opening theme

It is astounding what wonders an enharmonic change can perform. An entirely new conception of the Impromptu's plan arises. And although the Trio theme takes over the opening theme in the form to which it had developed at the height of its climax, that is, rising to a sixth instead of a fourth, the theme nevertheless sounds at the same pitch as at the beginning of the work.

From here on the thematic course of the Trio needs little comment, for the rise to the emphatic F-flat, E-flat, D-flat, remains its main and almost sole content. Considering this, it is remarkable how impressive and variegated the whole Trio appears. After the group quoted, the Trio part continues thus,

Ex. 237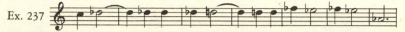

showing the line, now in chromatic progression, rising again to the F-flat, E-flat. Then, after a repetition mark, a group follows which (once more transferred to a notation in flats) reads:

Ex. 238

which again leads to the culmination on the F-flat, E-flat, D-flat. In between there are two little phrases (brackets in the example above) forming open triads. These phrases express exactly the melodic idea heard from the opening bars of the Impromptu. We must only imagine these open triads with the figuration of sixteenth notes instead of eighths to realize that the second triad is, even in pitch, identical with the opening of the piece. Following this recollection of the work's beginning, the opening section of the Trio reappears in recapitulation, now in major. Almost the whole of the recapitulation is a literal repetition of the Trio's opening section; only toward its close does the line rise to a higher peak. This changed part of the recapitulation reads:

Ex. 239

Thus the Trio, with a return in fortissimo to the very notes from which it started (B-double-flat, A-flat), has for the second time brought about the rise to the sixth. In brief, therefore, the thematic plan of the whole piece can be summarized as follows: The melodic extract of the principal part was a rise to the fourth intensified by a following rise to the sixth (*a* in the following example). Now the extract of the Trio presents itself as a twofold rise to the sixth, an "intensified intensification," as it were (*b*):

Ex. 240

Schubert's Impromptu thus furnishes another illustration of the important interrelationship between the two forces forming a work's outer construction and its inner thematic design. In essence the Impromptu represents a thematic evolution from one initial thought. There is, from the viewpoint of the inner thematic idea, no division between a principal and a middle part; but to endow his piece with the necessary differentiation, the composer let the first evolution of his thematic thought (the principal part) be followed by another part (the Trio), for which he chose quite different patterns of figuration. In this way the Trio became an almost separate section within the piece, though it, too, was in essence but a paraphrase of the original thought. Hence we realize that the creation of the Trio originated from the desire to render the outer construction of the piece effective, since a too obvious reiteration of the initial thought would have caused monotony. Here the "outer" form-building force, the idea of grouping, was the determining factor.

When the Trio is ended, the principal part is repeated literally, without any change or even the annexation of a coda. And we wonder whether this may indicate lack of thematic evolution. But, as we have seen, thematic evolution was still the decisive force shaping this piece. Of course an impromptu is not a sonata or a symphony of which the structural and dramatic course is one constant intensification. Although no final climax was reached, nevertheless intensification did take place within this simpler work—and this, too, is resolution.

As "resolution" gradually becomes one of the main points of interest in this inquiry, some further remarks may be added to clarify its sense and concept. We called "thematic resolution" those specific transformations through which a theme in the course of its structural evolution becomes the decisive, the culminating expression into which the idea of the work finally "resolves." However, as are almost all musical terms, so this one too is entirely appropriate only in certain instances. Yet, for the sake of simplification we include in it the whole sphere of phenomena which produces the effect in question. For naturally the evolution and transformation of a theme into the work's decisive utterance may be accomplished in an almost infinite number of different ways, and the difficulty in describing these features is owing to the fact that here, by their very nature, musical and dramatic phenomena melt into an inseparable unit. Thus the spirit and function of this sometimes subtle structural process will probably best be understood through further examples. We may start with Beethoven.

Beethoven's "thematic resolutions" have almost invariably one characteristic in common: structurally they transform a shape which has a quality of discord into an expression of perfect harmony. For instance, a line centered around a chord of the seventh is resolved into a triad, or a complex chordal progression into one rooted in the tonic-dominant relation. Correspondingly, in the dramatic-emotional sense Beethoven's resolutions lead from tension to release, from compulsion to liberation, from the tragic to the joyous. For these transformations on which Beethoven's architectural plans are centered, "resolution" is therefore a fitting expression.

In almost all of his symphonies we see the opening Allegro theme at the end of the movement changed into a shape of resolved discord, of released tension. The following examples demonstrate this phenomenon as realized in the opening movements of his first three symphonies. In these examples the form in which the themes appear at the beginnings of the movements, in the expositions, are juxtaposed to the form in which they appear at the movements' conclusions, in the codas.

Symphony III (coda)

Invariably the discords heard in the beginnings are in the codas transfigured into straight triads or scales. The example from the Third Symphony is of particular illustrative strength. Above are quoted two of the first movement's main themes. At the end of the movement these two themes appear together in contrapuntal simultaneity, in fact, as is proved by the continuation of the group (see score), in double counterpoint. With both themes resolved into perfect triads, with all edges and corners smoothed away, the dissonance and drama of the beginning have become an apotheosis of harmony and jubilation.

A similar spirit and idea lies at the bottom of all Beethoven's thematic plans. Within single movements the phenomenon is easily traceable, as it is brought about by simply resolving the themes into more harmonious variants, as was seen in the examples just quoted. In the frame of a whole work, however, the idea is materialized in a more complex manner, not merely by varying but by transforming an initial theme in the following movements into a new theme, until a shape is reached which represents the resolution of the work's architectural and programmatic content, its denouement. The technical handling of this process need not necessarily consist of exactly this particular method of resolving discords. In the Ninth Symphony, for instance, as demonstrated at the beginning of this study, the idea of the first theme, centered on its opening triad and reappearing in the following movements in constant metamorphosis, is in the last movement transformed into a continuous melodic line, thus "resolving" the rigid "theme" into an elastic tune, the "Ode to Joy." When in addition to this the second theme of the first movement, by appearing in inversion, has become the second theme of the Finale (the "Hymn"), and when finally "Ode" and "Hymn" are heard in fascinating contrapuntal unification as a double fugue—then the structural and spiritual plan of this great work is brought to its solution. In this case "thematic synthesis" rather than resolution would probably be the appropriate term. However, terms are not important. What should be emphasized above all is that the compositional course of a work is led to its fulfillment by a *thematic* process and not merely by linking sections together.

In the two instances just described ("Eroica" and Ninth Symphony), the final resolution is not brought about merely by transforming themes but also by combining themes in contrapuntal simultaneity. The "resolving" effect is greatly intensified by this procedure. Indeed, this is the highest and most profound role to which *counterpoint as an architectural phenomenon* can rise in music. For counterpoint in itself, that is, the mere simultaneity of musical lines, is not more than a technical device. Such simultaneity becomes a compositional life force only if applied to *thematic* shapes. The more familiar and meaningful the musical shapes have become in the course of a composition, the more powerfully—often with the impact of a revelation—will their contrapuntal combination strike the listener. Therefore we see such combination applied as an ever recurring effect throughout the ages, both in the contrapuntal and in the thematic styles.

Nevertheless, in the specific function as a final thematic resolution, great composers make use of this effect only in certain limited instances. The double fugue in the Finale of the Ninth Symphony, mentioned above, is no contradiction to this. For here the fugue themes are themselves "resolved" transformations of themes from previous movements and the fugal counterpoint merely leads the idea to a climax. Similarly, the contrapuntal unification quoted from the first movement of the "Eroica" represents only a final intensification of the structural idea involved, the core of which, as shown above, is that the thematic shapes themselves appear resolved into flowing triads of the tonic-dominant type. However, without such combining of counterpoint with true transformation (that is, if the only way by which the composer could lead his work to a climax consisted of a mere contrapuntal linking of its themes), the whole feature would sink to a lower artistic level and even assume a touch of the potpourri style.

To return to the question of "resolution," it is obvious that a clear description or definition of the technical procedure can hardly be given, as it differs in each case. Contrapuntal combination may often be included as an impressive or even crowning effect, but genuine resolution in the sense described must always consist of the transformation of the thematic shapes themselves. Characteristic examples of this type were seen in the resolutions demonstrated in Mozart's G-minor Symphony or in Brahms's Two Rhapsodies. In the Rhapsodies (example 228) the lowering of a theme's intervallic structure, together with other minor alterations, not only transforms the themes but carries the stream of the work itself into a new direction which leads it finally to a solution and goal.

Yet, be it repeated, the technical procedure through which such thematic fulfillment is brought about differs in almost every work with the specific dramatic-emotional idea to be expressed.

In **Mozart's Symphony in C major** ("Jupiter") for instance, the thematic figure of its opening (*a*) is in the last movement transformed into the serenely floating Finale theme (*b*):

Ex. 242

The feeling of being lifted to a lighter, higher sphere is increased when the Finale theme appears as the so-called "fugue." But to understand the full meaning of this shaping, we must compare the fugue (*a*) with the second theme of the first movement (*b*):

Ex. 243

Second **Allegro** theme (transposed)

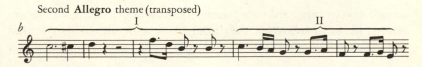

As has already been indicated, the fugue theme is itself a transformation of the first theme of the symphony's opening movement.
Now it becomes apparent that it is also a transformed reiteration of
the second theme. And by this process of thematic merging, the
original themes become entirely weightless musical lines, dancing
through space. Again the dramatic resolution of the work is focused
on thematic transformation.

But "resolutions" need not necessarily express an advance to a
happier, more positive state of mind. Even in the Brahms Rhapsodies, when toward the end of the work the decisive jubilant shape is
reached (examples 226 and 229), a few bars follow which, though
they merely express the concluding tonic enlivened by thematic
figuration,

almost reverse the hard-won triumph. However, triumph or melancholy, the main fact from the point of view of our subject is that
the spiritual-dramatic content of the work was brought about

through these technical-thematic changes. As for Brahms in particular, perhaps the magic of his music is in this very blending of jubilation and melancholy. In his **Second Symphony,** of which the thematic scheme of the first movement was outlined on a previous occasion (see example 113 and following), the opening shape of this movement (*a* in the following example) is taken over as the first Finale theme in a transformed version (*b*).

Ex. 245

The initial notes of this, the D, C-sharp, D, form one of the characteristic figures in all movements of the work. But then, in the Finale, the D, C-sharp, D, changes to its inversion, through which the second Finale theme is announced, which commences thus:

Ex. 246

This is a fascinating structural feature, for so ingeniously is this inversion carried out that the same notes, D and C-sharp, upon which the original shape was centered still form the basis for the inverted shape, although the key has been changed.

Besides, not only the first theme of the opening movement but also its second theme sounds through this Finale theme. Compare the two beginnings:

Ex. 247

One could actually say: The second Finale theme is simply the second Allegro theme in which the first Allegro theme is interwoven.

That the second Finale theme is actually a more intense, more concentrated expression of the idea personified in the second Allegro theme becomes clear by examining its full shape. In the following example the group quoted under *a* represents the melodic scheme of the second Allegro theme (omitting interwoven figurations), while the second Finale theme is given in *b*:

Ex. 248

It is obvious that the threefold rise to the sixth in the second Allegro theme is almost literally mirrored in the second Finale theme:

Ex. 249   *a* Second **Allegro**   *b* Second Finale

However, the climax which in the Allegro was formed by a rather complex line, constantly interrupted by intermediary phrases in the winds, appears now as one straightforward melodic arc. Moreover, by examining the full score, we see that the decisive thematic figures of all preceding movements are reflected in the secondary voices of the theme. (Even the second movement's opening shape is echoed in the viola part):

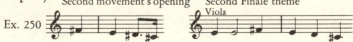

Ex. 250   Second movement's opening   Second Finale theme

Thus this Finale theme is indeed a synthesis of all the thematic impulses of the symphony. And in this synthesis the contemplative rhythm of the preceding themes changes to a jubilant march—a jubilation which here too has a touch of the tragic.

As for Beethoven's resolutions, they almost always convey the impression of a victorious rise after a tragic struggle, while Mozart's thematic plans often seem to resolve into an ethereal domain, beyond the tragic or victorious. Naturally, the final idea expressed by these "resolutions" is different with every composer according to his temperament, indeed, according to his whole outlook upon art and the world.

Beethoven: Fifth Symphony

The parallelism between a work's thematic mechanism and its spiritual-allegoric content becomes particularly transparent in Beethoven's Fifth Symphony. We will devote the remaining part of this chapter to a detailed examination of its course.

The symphony opens with the well-known historic call, which, by being repeated a tone lower, produces the following figure:

Ex. 251

This shape is referred to in some commentaries as the symphony's "motto," and as it seems rather fitting we may also use this expression. Symbolically and structurally these bars appear, as will be seen, as the directive from which the course of the whole work is developed. Apart from their structural role, we should remember that although we of today may take these bars for granted—since after Beethoven composers repeatedly applied similar effects—at Beethoven's time it must have appeared truly revolutionary to open a work with such small isolated phrases, not rounded to any group or period. Therefore, to call these bars the "opening theme," as has often been done, is somewhat misleading. Of course these introductory bars are "thematic" in their function, but they do not form a "theme." The melodic line of the actual first Allegro theme which follows immediately after the "motto" reads:

Turning to the other movements, it will readily be seen that all the themes of the work are formed from the same kernel and on the same pattern as is this opening theme. Here we beg the reader to be patient. Through the next paragraphs this analysis may seem somewhat repetitious in confining itself to pointing out affinities between the movements, as has been done with numerous other works in our study. In the present instance the demonstration serves as a necessary point of departure for an examination of the thematic process from which the architectural and dramatic content of this great work was developed.

In order to obtain a better insight into the structural mechanism of the first Allegro theme, we divide the thematic line quoted in the last example into *three segments*. Let us first look at segment I, as shown in the last example. According to the two peaks to which this shape rises, one on E-flat, the second on F, a contour (*a* in the following example) can be drawn from its course. Comparing this contour with the work's opening exclamation, the "motto" (*b*),

Ex. 253

it becomes apparent that the idea of the first Allegro theme is derived from a pattern expressing an inversion (or contrary motion) of the motto, now expanded and enriched by figuration to a full thematic line.

Since segment II (see example 252) is in essence a shape formed by a pair of thirds, one falling, the other rising, we can draw the structural extract of the whole theme (formed by all three segments) as follows:

Ex. 254

The second movement, the Andante con moto, is in A-flat major. Transposing a part of our last example to this key (*a* in the following example) and comparing it with the Andante theme, quoted below as *b,*

Ex. 255

we see that the beginning and the ending in the Andante theme clearly reflect segments I and III of the Allegro pattern. But segment II, the falling and rising thirds, also appears in the Andante theme, interwoven into segment I. Since segments I and II are thus already integrated in the first three bars, the resulting theme would have seemed too short had the composer immediately annexed segment III. Therefore he prolonged the theme by inserting bars 4 and 5. This prolongation is not a new thought (which would have constituted a "break" in the analogy to the Allegro theme) but a mere repetition of the preceding bars, varied by a different harmonization. This becomes easily recognizable in the following example, wherein the opening bars of the Andante theme (*a*) are compared with the "inserted" bars (*b*):

Ex. 256

Thus if we recognize these "inserted" bars as a mere varied reiteration of the opening bars and the theme as a summation of the three segments, the analogy in kernel between the themes of the first and second movement appears complete.

The analogy becomes even more obvious in the third movement, the Scherzo. As the Scherzo is again in C-minor, we need not transpose the Allegro pattern (*a* in the following example) but may simply compare it with the Scherzo theme (*b*):

Ex. 257

Clearly the two wings of segment I form the kernel of the Scherzo theme too. After this group has been repeated in a slightly varied version, the Scherzo theme continues thus:

Ex. 258

The melodic essence of the first part of this group is formed by the rising and falling thirds; but any indication of segment III, which we would have expected at the conclusion, is missing. However, though Beethoven replaced segment III by a different phrase, it can be proved that he nevertheless did conceive segment III as the fitting ending for the Scherzo theme. The proof is furnished in the Finale. The Finale of the Fifth Symphony constitutes one of those rare instances where Beethoven let part of a theme from one movement (in this case the Scherzo theme) reappear in verbal reiteration in another movement. And in this reintroduction of the Scherzo theme in the Finale, the ending of the Scherzo theme reads as follows:

Ex. 259

Here the missing link emerges: segment III clearly sounds as the conclusion of the Scherzo theme.

To make our search complete, we should not forget the Trio. Even this charming fugato, which succeeds the Scherzo as its Trio, indubitably mirrors the line of the Allegro theme, as the following comparison ascertains:

Thus there remains only the Finale. It must be stated that not the opening theme but only one of the later Finale themes reiterates the idea of the Allegro theme. With regard to this later theme, however, the identity is striking, though the shape is now transferred to major:

Why the *first* Finale theme does not seem to bear any direct affinity to the Allegro theme shall be explained. Having demonstrated the inner identities of the symphony's basic themes, the groundwork for our coming analysis has been laid. From here we may proceed to the actual object of our inquiry.

Beethoven is often quoted as having said about the opening bars of the Fifth Symphony, "Thus Fate knocks at the door." This was reported by Anton Schindler, friend and first biographer of Beethoven. There are those who question the reliability of Schindler's accounts, though his reports, when they could be traced through other sources, have in general been verified. Be this as it may, this particular utterance does not sound as if it had been invented. It has rather the typical Beethovenian flavor in its conciseness and inimitable mixture of transcendency and reality. *In referring to a structural detail it points to a spiritual allegory.* Thus it does not run contrary to the direction in which, according to all historical facts, Beethoven's artistic conceptions tended.[2] To picture Beethoven, as it has often been done, as the "absolute composer," who would have been the first to resent any affiliation of his music to the spiritual or allegoric sphere, is of course absurd. The "Eroica," the "Pastorale" with its subtitles, the "Grave Decision" in opus 135, the "Holy Song of Thanksgiving by a Convalescent," these and numerous other examples are sufficient proof to the contrary.

Therefore, it may well seem worth while to try to discover whether by using Beethoven's own words as a starting point, the structure of his symphony may yield more of its hidden symbols. In entering upon such an examination, two characteristic motivic features of obviously decisive significance for the architectural plan of the work must first be discussed. They are both apparent in the work's first bars, the "motto."

One of these features consists of a motif of note repetition with which the symphony opens, ♩♩♩ , and which subsequently, save for some sections, hardly ever disappears entirely. (The constant use of this little phrase of note repetition in the Fifth is a thematic feature that has become common knowledge in the musical world. However, unless integrated into the wider thematic concept of the work, it remains an interesting trait rather than a functional element in the symphony's thematic plan.) This motif runs through the whole section of the first Allegro theme, forming these almost uninterrupted characteristic figurations:

---

[2] To ridicule Schindler's credibility by pointing to a different utterance of Beethoven, who told another friend that it was the call of the yellow-hammer which provided the impulse for the first bar of the Fifth, does not carry much weight. For the two reports are not in the least contradictory. A bird's call might easily have created the first version of the phrase; the allegoric meaning, however, which the phrase later assumed is quite different. There might even be a deeper meaning in this twofold account. For bird calls have been regarded as omens throughout the ages—this was especially true in the Austrian mountain countries—so that Beethoven, in a mood of despair over his approaching deafness, might quite logically have been led to this specific interpretation.

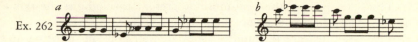

Ex. 262

Then, in the section of the second Allegro theme, it disappears from the thematic line itself, to reemerge, perhaps all the more impressively, in the bass:

Ex. 263

As said before, the motif then reappears throughout the other movements. For the sake of abbreviation, we will call this motif the *"beat-motif."* This threefold repetition of a note permeates the work, not only in its literal form, but also as an idea. The threefold utterance of a thought rather than simple repetition becomes a characteristic, recurrent feature in the Fifth Symphony. A few examples may follow, to which numerous others could be added:

Ex. 264

Thus the spirit of the beat-motif is present throughout the symphony even where the actual shape is not visible.

The other feature demanding special attention, in addition to the beat-motif, we will call the *hook*. It is also apparent in the "motto." This motto consists of a pair of falling thirds:

Ex. 265

However, this pairwise shaping does not produce one smooth melodic arc. Phrasing and accentuation rather create an effect of two interlocked hooks: ⌐⌐ .

And this hook form, *this shape and spirit of interlocking,* together with the beat-motif, pervades the symphony as one of its most striking motivic ideas. Thus, if the symbol of "Fate knocking at the door" is the one which Beethoven really had in mind, the beat-motif and the hook must certainly prove to be parts of this allegory; to pursue the working of these motifs in the further course of the symphony may yield interesting results.

Both motifs, the beat-motif and the hook, are immediately taken over from the opening shape, the motto, into the first Allegro theme. Not only does this first Allegro theme express an inversion of the hooked motto in the contour of its first eight bars (see example 252), but the theme's detail also points in the same direction. The theme begins with the "hook idea in the beat-motif figuration" (bars 6 to 8, *a* in the following example) to which bars 10 to 12 correspond (*b*),

Ex. 266

whereby the two shapes together echo the motto almost literally, even in pitch.

Previously we analyzed the course of the Allegro theme in its three segments. Now that we consider the theme not merely as a technical but as a musico-spiritual enunciation, it must appear as a very different idea from most of Beethoven's opening themes.

The above-quoted openings of the first three symphonies, for instance, all present lines which, although beginning either from triads or, in general, from harmonious shapes, soon move into areas of discord and tension. In contrast to this, the opening theme of the Fifth Symphony commences with a rather heavy utterance, characterized through the ominous beat-motif and hook, yet soon rises over the pair of thirds to an almost triumphant conclusion on the dominant triad. Such a quick evolution from tension to resolution within the first few bars is an unusual feature in the opening of a Beethoven work. As a rule *Beethoven introduces his resolutions at the end, not at the beginning of the movement or the work.*

If one wishes to pursue the allegory, the present shaping could only mean that the hero, in search of his destiny, turns swiftly and audaciously to where happiness and success seem to beckon.

However, if this interpretation is true, hope must soon have been succeeded by the realization that, in art as in life, there is no short cut to victory. For the chord which seemed to signify the cheerful goal (bar 21 in example 252) is immediately followed by a fortissimo shape which annuls all that has been gained—the grip of the hook is felt again. By connecting the end of the theme with the ensuing bars, as seen in the following example, an inversion of the motto emerges. Compare:

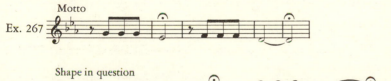

Ex. 267

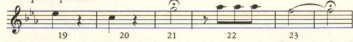

The interlocking thirds, supported by the two fermatas in both examples, a short one followed by a longer one, make the intentional analogy unquestionably clear.

And this feature, the attempt to build a straight, optimistic course —an attempt which, however, is invariably threatened by some inexorable grim reality—remains the basic idea of formation throughout the whole movement.

After the fortissimo phrase quoted in the last example is taken over in piano,

Ex. 268

the line soon soars, once more in an exuberant mood, to a peak, only to arrive again at a "call of Fate," mirroring the opening motto.

However, it is worth while to examine the "exuberant shape soaring to a peak" more closely. For this marchlike group, rising in interlocking thirds, is "optimistic" only in the rhythmical dynamism of the strings (see following example). But sforzando chords in the winds accompany the strings and make the whole group an utterance of intense discord:

It seems that the idea of the "hook" has even become alive in the *harmonic* sphere.[3] And only in the ensuing bars (quoted as *a* in the following example) is a truly optimistic state reached (thus corresponding to bars 19 to 21), whereupon, in continuance of the analogy, the above-mentioned "shape mirroring the opening motto" enters (*b*):

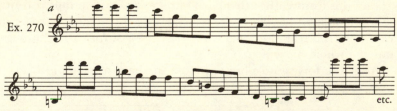

---

[3] Since in a Beethoven performance the strings in our modern orchestras greatly outweigh the winds, this feature seldom becomes audible in present-day performances, especially as few conductors ever attempt to bring these discords to the fore. However, a performer striving to realize Beethoven's intentions should not fail to make these collisions audible.

This shape, this "second motto," is a variant of the work's opening, formed by a pair of interlocking intervals which now are fifths instead of thirds. And just as the opening exclamation, sounded by the strings, preceded the first Allegro theme as its motto, so this call of the horns, as a new motto, announces the second Allegro theme. Consequently, just as the first motto reappeared in the contour of the first Allegro theme, the second motto is reflected in the second Allegro theme:

Ex. 271

Apart from this specific feature, the second Allegro theme also reiterates the pattern, or at least the idea, of the first Allegro theme. The openings of both themes are in essence identical, as the following juxtaposition shows:

Ex. 272

From this opening the second theme is developed to a shape of two interlocking phrases rising to two peaks, on E-flat and F (example 271), just as did the first theme. From here the second theme completes a further long ascent, in constantly rising and falling thirds,

Ex. 273

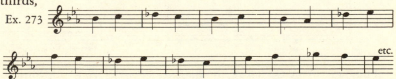

to a jubilant climax. Thus, though all this is now expanded and differently phrased, the three segments here too form the underlying essence. Especially the conclusion of the section clearly corresponds to segment III, now lifted to E-flat major:

Ex. 274

With an annexed concluding phrase, followed by two bars rest and a repetition mark, this wonderfully concise and concentrated exposition is brought to a close.

However, whether the exposition is repeated or not, in either case the shape immediately following is, significantly enough, again the motto, the call of Fate.

In this sense the development first elaborates on groups reiterating the first Allegro theme. Whereupon a new theme emerges within the development section, first in the violas and cellos as a sort of accompanying line to the "falling thirds" in the upper voices, as quoted in example 275a, then, by means of a "double counterpoint" appearing as the main voice, the soprano (b):

Ex. 275

This new thematic figure, in its direct course from the tonic to the dominant, has a quality of release, of resolution, somewhat similar to segment III from the first Allegro theme. We may call it the *development theme,* as not only is it first heard in the development section but it is also destined to play an important role in this section's further course. Indeed, it becomes the basic feature through which many of the following utterances are held together.

This ensuing part of the development section presents rather a unique picture in symphonic literature, although we have become so accustomed to it that we may not always be conscious of its full splendor and impact. There is, in this part, first a group storming to massed blocks of eruptive fortissimo chords, separated by abrupt rests:

Ex. 276

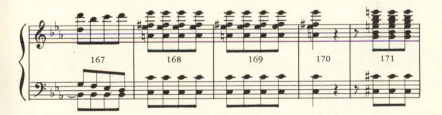

With regard to the figurate detail from which this design is formed, there can be little doubt as to its thematic meaning: this figuration symbolizes the beat-motif, the warning of Fate. But whether, apart from the detail, the wider musical lines in which these volcanic explosions are heard also form true thematic utterances would, if it could be verified, prove much more significant from an architectural point of view. And, indeed, the bass line discloses itself as the development theme just described. By drawing a contour from the bass of the last example, Ex. 277

the idea becomes evident to the last note.

This is certainly a striking feature, telling us much about Beethoven's structural way of thinking. This massed group is not merely a dynamic outburst of fortissimo chords but is focused on a bass which reiterates in a wide arc the lovely shape (termed the development theme, example 275) that characterized the preceding section.

Examining the other voices in example 276, we see that these too are entirely thematic utterances. The soprano, for instance, apart from indicating in its small phrases the same theme in diminution (see bar 164 and following), rises in parallel thirds with the bass, thus also sounding the wider contour of the theme. Although, therefore, the last note of this soprano should have been F, it suddenly turns back to D: Ex. 278

D "instead of F"

The "optimistic" theme was thus not allowed to run its full course —the hook motif is at work again.

The following part of the development section is developed from the second motto, as the preceding part was developed from the first. Three times the second motto is heard, together with which phrases echoing bars 25 and following from the first Allegro section (example 268) appear as contrapuntal lines:

Ex. 279

In the ensuing part a mysterious picture unfolds itself; magic colors set to music rather than definite "shapes" seem to shine through this score:

Ex. 280

Yet, part by part, this design also reveals itself as an organic expression of some of the work's basic thematic features. Three groups can be unraveled from the above example: a group comprising bars 196 to 205, a further group comprising bars 205 to 213, and finally the group from bars 213 on. By notating the first group as a line in which the difference in octaves is equalized, the shape given in the following example as *a* emerges, which is easily identifiable as mirroring a group from the second Allegro theme (example 273).

In turn, the ensuing group (bars 205 to 213) no less clearly mirrors the development theme, as can be heard through the contour given as *b:*

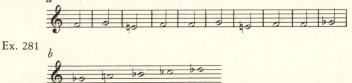

Ex. 281

The thematic meaning of the remaining part (bars 213 and following) is readily deciphered. These chord repetitions are none other than the beat-motif, which originally appeared as quick rattling drums and now is changed to slow mystic bells.

Any musical mind desiring an insight into the core of the compositional process cannot fail to be deeply impressed by what he discovers here. For the impact of all these eerie effects, this apparently purely emotional outpouring, is in fact brought about exclusively by the composer's *treatment* of his compositional lines, the essence of which is not new but simply the familiar thematic figures of the work.

But there is still one more feature in the group just quoted which requires special attention. There is a mysterious *rhythmical* unrest in these bars, in spite of their being an uninterrupted series of regular half-notes. The thematic meaning of bars 213 and following in example 280 has already been indicated. They express the beat-motif, now shaped in intense augmentation, which slows their original tempo no less than eight times:

Ex. 282

However, the rhythmic accentuation in which the composer wishes the four notes to be understood may be questioned, as both motivic interpretations ♫ | ♩ and | ♪♫ | appear in the score. Perhaps the preceding bars will offer a clue to this question. To bring this rhythmical problem into focus, we will notate the whole group at half of its rhythmical value and once again ignore the difference in register. In this accelerated tempo the melodic line of the whole part would read:

Ex. 283

Whatever phrasing we apply to this example—the ligatures are merely suggestions of the analyst—there emerges *a gap in the rhythmical symmetry,* as pointed out through the 1/4 bar in the example.

But simply to ignore the gap, that is, to interpret these shapes by continuing the 2/4 rhythm, would create this impossible result:

Ex. 284

impossible—since especially the last two bars (note the strong beat
on the C in the last bar) appear in entire contradiction to the
rhythmical role which they assume in all their other occurrences in
the work.

Therefore, there remains nothing but to accept the gap. Yet we
should probe into this problem and ask ourselves: What kind of a
"gap" is this actually? Is it not merely a gap according to an academic conception of rhythmical symmetry, which an equally
academic rule claims is unbreakable? But in the light of such an
example we have to admit that it is breakable. For in the score of
the Fifth Symphony, if anywhere, lies musical reality, Beethoven's
reality, proving that in living composition there is no such uncon-
ditional symmetry. Had this group been notated by the composer
in the quicker tempo of our fictitious example, its "asymmetric"
nature would have become obvious. However, in the slackened
tempo which the score presents, the surface seems smooth, yet the
asymmetry still exists. And this is exactly what Beethoven intended.
He wished this state of uncertainty, of unbalanced indefiniteness,
where one does not know when one phrase ends and the next begins.
It conforms entirely with the allegoric scheme; yet we would not
have gone into such detail about this feature were it not an exquisite illustration of how spiritual-symbolic effects are brought
about by technical means, just as the meaning of many technical
features can often be understood only from the symbolic idea they
personify.

When now the recapitulation enters, the motto and the opening
theme are repeated, but at the opening theme's conclusion a small
oboe phrase of inimitable tenderness is inserted. And it is both
touching and symbolic that even in this oboe ornament of tender
woe the motto, the call of Fate, is included:

Ex. 285

From here on the recapitulation repeats the exposition almost
literally, until the entrance of the coda. In the coda a new theme is
sounded, or, to be correct, a new version of a part of the second

Allegro theme (example 273) now shaped in the jubilant, symmetric accents of a victory march:

Ex. 286

etc.

Nevertheless, the victory, as will be seen, is quickly reversed. Again we are faced with the very phenomenon which we recognized as the essence of the structural and allegoric impulse throughout the whole movement: *the compositional course strives to an earlier resolution than the law of symphonic logic allows—wherefore it must fail.* Solutions are not reached in the first act of a drama.

This victorious coda-march and its fateful outcome represent a central point in the work's dramatic-symbolic evolution. This evolution set out from an emphatic opening shape, the motto, which was characterized by two motivic features: the beat-motif and the hook-motif. Whenever the compositional design tried to emancipate itself from these dominating forces, these features reappeared, like a reminder, restoring the inherent law.

The two motivic features constituting the core of the motto, also, as we remember, form the beginning of the Allegro theme:

Ex. 287

In this example the A-flat and G are the very notes through which the actual collision forming the hook-motif is brought about. Subsequently this A-flat to G becomes in itself a motif and symbol throughout the movement. Therefore when the march of the coda, as described above, intonates its jubilant rhythm, it is precisely through this A-flat to G that its course is interrupted. In an emphatic eightfold repetition (marked by asterisks in the following example) this A-flat to G sounds forth, blocking the optimistic march and compelling it to vibrate on the same repeated G's with which the work opened. For a few bars (bracketed in the following example) the line again attempts to break into the victorious march, but the attempt is immediately frustrated; the constant G's, the beat-motif, are stronger, and the motto, the call of Fate, appears on the scene in all its grandeur:

Ex. 288

At this point an indication of the opening theme shyly reappears; but its power has faded, its dynamic vigor changed to pianissimo, the instrumentation thinned, and the optimistic parts (segments II and III), to which the theme soared in the beginning of the work, have vanished. What remains are the first few bars of the theme, sounded twice, above which, in the woeful piano of the oboe, floats the ominous A-flat to G, the symbol of the hook:

Ex. 289

With an annex of a few chords of the dominant and tonic, hammering out the beat-motif, the movement concludes in grim fortissimo.

The ensuing movements continue to develop the ideas and problems introduced in the opening movement. The theme of the second movement, as was shown previously, reiterates the essence of the first Allegro theme entirely, though in appearance and character it naturally represents quite a different shape. In the melodious lines of the second movement, the striving toward a quick solution seems again to be expressed, now perhaps transferred to the realm of dreams, of beauty or art—or whatever simile may seem appropriate. In fact the whole idea is even intensified in this movement. For the resolving shape soon tries to become the leading thematic thought, and in the following bars it even outdoes itself, as it were, by progressing still a third higher. An ominous feeling seems to have accompanied this step, as the sudden pianissimo proves. Indeed, at this point something uncanny happens: the beat-motif is heard again (the following example being quoted from the second occurrence of this passage, as the idea becomes here more transparent):

Ex. 290

It seems that even in the seclusion of a dream there is no escape from inborn law and destiny.

But the following Scherzo seems to be a turning point. In the Scherzo theme (see examples 257 and 258) the hook-motif and the beat-motif have not disappeared; they are almost emphasized. Yet this theme is an enunciation of utter optimism, of almost unbounded joy of life. The allegoric conclusion is not to be mistaken: though we cannot "conquer" Fate, nor evade its predestined law, we can build the course of our life upon it *and thus triumph, not in spite of fate, but through fate.*

In this sense the Scherzo actually represents a huge auftakt to the last movement—note the oft-described, infinite crescendo pedal of the drum on C. Of course the unique effect of this pedal does not lie in the giant crescendo as such, which in the commentaries usually forms the point of emphasis, but in the fact that it remains on the C and does not change to the G—as ten out of ten composers before Beethoven, and nine out of ten even after him, would have done it. For this rocklike C, the tonic, which persists while the other instruments proceed over different harmonies to prepare for the Finale forms the focus on which the structural and symbolic idea of this pedal phenomenon centers. The violins and violas first sound in unison with the pianissimo drum, but gradually they swerve away while the drum, hammering out its crescendo on the tonic, remains immovable—like one who has finally become aware of his goal and whom nothing can divert. No other instrument or combination of instruments could have expressed or impersonated this idea as convincingly:

Ex. 291

With the entrance of the Finale, a new instrument appears that has not been heard in the work before: the trombone. And these trombones certainly mean more than merely the inclusion of a means of increased sound in the last movement. For the trombones coincide with and emphasize the moment when the real resolution is brought about, when the very thought which from the beginning seemed to be the goal emerges at last as the decisive theme of the symphony. Starting from the wonderful high C of the trombone, the first Finale theme reads:

Ex. 292

Now at last we understand the thematic meaning of the Finale theme. In the Finale theme the optimistic shape, the decisive segment III, with which the first Allegro theme *ended*, now constitutes the *beginning*. Indeed, as the contour set under the theme in the last example shows, segment III, the resolving motif, opens the Finale theme as C, E, G, and leads over segment II, the falling and rising thirds, to an even more emphatic repetition and confirmation of its own shape on a higher pitch, F, A, C. Three times this F, A, C, is heard in jubilant figuration, whereupon the line is continued in a long arc of motivic variation until it arrives at,

Ex. 293

In this shape segment I thus reappears also in the Finale, through which the complete identity of substance is extended also into the last movement. However, this segment, too, has now become an optimistic feature. For though technically the hook-motif still forms the essence of this shape, to which the beat-motif adds the vibrating tremolo accompaniment, the thematic line itself now expresses that same spirited rhythm that characterizes the whole movement. The hook-motif and the beat-motif, these symbols of "Fate," are still present in the Finale, but they now enrich and no longer hinder its jubilant pulse.

This spirit of resolved tension continues throughout the whole Finale. It reaches a climax in the last theme, which appears in the concluding section of this movement's exposition and later in its coda. This *coda theme,* as we may call it, commences thus:

Ex. 294

Apart from the three D's, which might point to the beat-motif, we wonder what is the connection of this shape with any other theme of the work. There must be a connection, for this shape is not a casual phrase but the main thematic idea into which the whole course of the work finally leads. In the search for some previous thematic utterance to which this theme may be linked, it strikes us that, save for changed accidentals due to the major key, these are exactly the same notes from which the motto, the work's opening exclamation, was formed. *This coda theme thus would represent the "resolved motto,"* the symphony's opening shape made straight —a direct line, free of any corners or hooks. And although this interpretation may at first seem surprising, especially to one unaccustomed to thematic concepts, it is the one to which the structural and symbolic idea of the whole work finally evolves: the symphony's opening shape, the ominous motto of Fate, is resolved to a victorious conclusion. This conception is confirmed by the further course of the coda theme itself, which in contour conforms astoundingly with the opening theme of the Allegro:

Ex. 295

Then, through a last feature, this idea is lifted to a peak. For this "resolving theme," consisting of the transformed opening exclamation, the "straightened" motto, appears finally interwoven with another shape of a similar resolving spirit; namely, with the opening theme of the Finale. Yes, the Finale theme sounds as a jubilant contour from the coda theme:

Ex. 296

This is indeed the great resolution of the Fifth Symphony. At last, the idea to which the work strove from its beginning has become reality in this triumphant thematic combination. In the following group the first Finale theme itself reappears in a canonically shaped apotheosis:

Ex. 297

Orthodox minds may be puzzled by some collisions in this contrapuntal design (see asterisk in the example). However, this open fourth on a strong beat is not a shortcoming but is of magic power, as for a final thrilling instant it holds the line in suspense before the all-resolving unison.

As the last melodic utterance, or perhaps only melodic indication, of the whole work, a reminiscence of the hook-motif reappears in the following group, now of course not a contrasting but a resolving feature, harmonized as an emphatic tonic-dominant progression:

Ex. 298

After this a lengthy C-major triad concludes the work. One has almost the feeling that with this endlessly prolonged triad the work reaches a state beyond mere conclusion. All melodic nuance which in this realm might symbolize a residue of the material world is here avoided. Even at the one point (brace in the following example) where almost every composer would not have missed the opportunity of intimating once more the triumphant motif C, E, G, Beethoven—whose motifs at other times sound in every voice—abstains

from it and returns from the E to the concluding C. Only the unbelievably high E of the trombone is heard as a last flaming accent:

Ex. 299

All allegoric interpretation becomes superfluous. It was never the
purpose of this analysis to explain the content of the symphony
through any programmatic commentary. What was intended was
to show *that a work of musical art is determined by laws so strict,
logical, and organic that it becomes in itself an allegory of all creation.* And it is through this *inherent* allegory that an eternal bond
between musical shapes and the human world is sustained. Owing
to this bond, almost any symbolic interpretation can be applied to

a musical work and the equation will still remain balanced. If the symbol is given by the composer himself in a title, text, or any other form, this can often illuminate the whole structural horizon and help us to understand the most profound connections. For in the deepest sense music appears not only as a symbol for human ideas and emotions, but these ideas and emotions themselves may perhaps become symbols for a higher reality of which music is one expression.

7

SPECIFIC TYPES
OF STRUCTURAL CONSISTENCY

One fact emerging from the preceding part of our study must be particularly realized for the proper pursuit of our investigation. It is the fact that the interconnections shown to be at the basis of the architectural plans in the works analyzed so far, almost invariably proved to be interconnections centered not merely on affinities between small motivic particles *but on affinities between full "themes"* —that is, shapes of considerable length and weight forming in themselves complete musical statements. That our presentation is mainly centered on thematic rather than on motivic connection is one of the fundamentals in this whole inquiry. Of course motivic particles constantly play an important role in a work's structure. Themes are built from motifs, and motivic features in general account in great part for a work's structural consistency. Yet the deeper architectural unity of a work is usually centered on the transformation and evolution of the actual themes, as was shown in the preceding chapters.

However, of exactly what length a shape must be in order to function as a "theme" cannot be defined even approximately. And composers may in some compositions, or in parts of them, reduce to some extent the size and significance of the themes. If the composer then wishes to maintain his work's structural consistency, his technique has to be centered largely on motivic transformation rather than transformation of themes. By such treatment a compositional design will emerge different in some respects from the usual structural picture. It may be instructive to include some types of this technique in our analysis.

Claude Debussy, "La Cathédrale engloutie" [1]

As a first example we may turn to Claude Debussy's prelude for piano "La Cathédrale engloutie" (number 10 in his first volume of piano preludes).

This work is chosen not only as an impressive illustration of this type of structural formation but also for certain of its psychological and historical aspects.

This great French composer was said by some contemporary critics to be, and has since generally been regarded as, the creator and representative of impressionism in music—a term borrowed from the fine arts, where, toward the close of the nineteenth century, it indeed referred to a new style and technique. However, whether this term denotes any artistic reality in music may be debatable. Be this as it may, the opinion has been cherished that Debussy's music, apart from its new style and individual character, of which there can be no doubt, has in addition abandoned the whole idea and technique of thematic consistency through which the preceding period shaped its compositional products. Besides, this belief was nurtured by Debussy's personal and oft-uttered aversion to the "formalistic" concept of nineteenth century music, denouncing even Beethoven and Brahms. Misjudgment of the achievements of other composers and other styles is said to be a privilege of geniuses, but the conclusion drawn in this instance, that Debussy's music lacks structural consistency in the classical sense, is certainly erroneous, as seen in the following analysis of "La Cathédrale." Though utilizing a completely new idiom of melodic-harmonic expression and tone color, and though, according to our preceding explanation, the work's consistency is based more on the evolution of its motivic particles than its themes, its final structural unity and logic are as strict and transparent as those of any classical work.

Two little fragments, henceforth called motif I and motif II, form the motivic basis of "La Cathédrale." In the course of the composition motif I releases two variants, one with a fourth instead of a fifth (we may term it I*a*), another with a third (I*b*). In the following example these motifs are set forth:

---

[1] In this chapter all musical quotations from Claude Debussy's *La Cathédrale engloutie* are published with the permission of A. Durand et Cie, Copyright Editors (publisher), Paris.

Ex. 300

From these few small particles and, naturally, their transpositions and inversions, the whole piece in all its complexity and originality is shaped.

Ex. 301

The above is the first section of "La Cathédrale."

The piece opens with a harmony on G, from which a melodic line rises in "chordal unison." As readily seen, the motivic essence of this bar is an expression of motif I. In fact, it is a multiple expression of this basic motif. For by connecting in bar 1 the G of the opening chord to the following D (as shown in example 302*a*), the (transposed) motif in inversion is heard at the very beginning.

Then the motif, now at its "true" pitch, as D, E, B, sounds from the chord series (example 302*b*).

Thereupon the first two chords of this figure are repeated an octave higher, as though the motivic line were to continue, with the continuation having become inaudible, as it were, in this utter pianissimo (example 302*c*),

Ex. 302

a feature which most effectively expresses the work's programmatic idea (the legend of the lost island). In this connection it is interesting to note the ties on the last chord of bar 1 (example 301) pointing to—what? If the meaning were: to nothing, to silence, there would be a rest in bar 2. But there is no rest. The right-hand part in bar 2 (and bar 4) presents the amazing picture of a bar without either notes or rests. Thus the ties on the last chord in bar 1 can only point to the unperceivable, the infinite.

When bar 2 follows, a bass figure shines out that at first would appear to be merely an open version of the opening chord. But linking these notes to the F in bar 3, the inversion of motif I is again heard through D, G, F (see brace):

Ex. 303

And the same feature is repeated a tone lower in bars 4 and 5. As meanwhile in the upper voices the phrase from bar 1 is also constantly reiterated, all parts converge finally to a unison on an E (bar 5). On this E the melodic course is halted and the introductory group (bars 1 to 6) ended. As seen, this whole group represents but an uninterrupted series of versions of motif I. However, from the contour of the bass line another melodic figure sounds, and we recognize motif II, the falling third:

Ex. 304

After these bars of introductory improvisation, a group emerges which seems to represent in itself a complete musical utterance, which we may therefore call a theme (bars 7 to 13). The line of this *first theme* is continuously permeated by a kind of pedal on the E. Unraveling this texture (compare example 301), its actual melodic course reads:

Ex. 305

The structural idea and motivic source of this shaping is so transparent that it needs little comment. The substance of its opening bars is built from a summation of the basic motifs: II, I*a*, II. Then the highest note of this group, the G-sharp, is taken over an octave lower to begin the next group, which repeats the combination of the same motifs. The line finally revolves between D-sharp and C-sharp (bar 12) before it closes in the B (through motif II). This last phrasing almost seems to indicate an intention of a renewed expression of motif I*a* (indicated through the G-sharp in small print in bar 13 of the last example), through which the theme could have been further extended. But the composer preferred to return to B and thus close the group.

The last bars (13 to 15 in example 301) of this section recall the opening bars. In fact, their shaping is a confirmation that our interpretation of the opening bars was not arbitrary but taken from the composition itself. For the inversion of motif I, pointed out through a connection of bar 2 with the F in bar 3, here appears (as E, B, D) clearly within one bar (13), while by including the C from the following bar (14), motif II sounds at the same time from the bass line:

Ex. 306

Besides, the upper line in bars 14 and 15 also shows the validity of our conception, according to which the motivic series was prolonged from the last note of bar 1 to an "inaudible" B. For here, in bar 15, this B really sounds. Also, this B and, in addition, the slight difference in harmonization between bars 14 and 15 and bar 1 provide the composer with the opportunity to render the other voices also "motivic," so that, in fact, three independent motivic courses result:

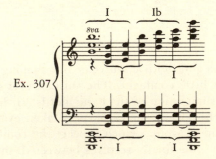

Ex. 307

Having thus demonstrated the thematic quality of every note in this design, we must still refer to one more structural feature, one of the most impressive of all. The reader may once more turn to example 301 and follow the course of the soprano throughout this whole section in order to discover whether or not an *over-all* thematic idea unites these sixteen bars.

From bars 1 to 5, a sustained D sounds as the towering musical landmark, as it were. The next group, the theme (bars 6 to 13), projects a throbbing E through the long extended E-pedal. This D–E immediately recalls the work's main motif, D, E, B (example 300*a*), with which the piece opened.

Does this motif also really determine the larger sectional shaping?

If so, the melodic pivot of the following group would have to be B. Indeed, a glance at bars 14 and 15 shows the B sounding from the summit of these bars. Thus a huge motivic contour (example 308*a*), almost anticipated through thematic logic, proves to be in fact the composition's plan. (Check the validity of the following example by comparison with example 301.)

In addition the line of the bass descends (over two falling thirds, G, F, E, and E, D, C) from G to C. Linking this falling fifth, G–C, to the B which forms the foundation of the next section, again the same constant motif (here in inversion) emerges (example 308*b*).

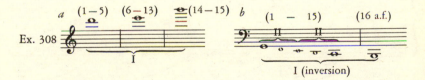

Thus the astounding fact presents itself that the contours of the soprano and bass of the whole section each constitute a giant expression of the basic motif. The contour of the soprano utters the motif in its direct form and at original pitch, while the bass denotes the motif's inversion, corresponding exactly to what the opening bars express in small phrases.

Continuing our analysis of minute detail, we turn to the following section, which reads:

Ex. 309

Already aware of the structural pattern on which the piece is centered, we will quickly recognize the basic combinations in this part also. In particular, the analogy of this section's first bar (16) to the work's opening bar is striking:

Ex. 310

For in spite of all differences in appearance, the inner design of both these shapes is brought about through exactly the same overlapping of two expressions of motif I:

Ex. 311

This pattern is continued through three bars until in the beginning of bar 19 the last note of the ceaselessly repeated motivic phrase (F-sharp, G-sharp, D-sharp) appears with the D-sharp enharmonically changed to E-flat. In the following bars the pattern continues, now in the key of E-flat and enriched by a repeated alteration of motif I with its variant Ia (as indicated by the braces in example 312).

In the left hand, meanwhile, as a contrapuntal embellishment, motif II, the falling third, appears. Corresponding to the motivic alteration in the right hand, this motif also is heard in two variants: as a falling third or a falling fourth (motif II and II*a*):

Ex. 312

Once the shaping of motif II as a scale fragment has thus been introduced, this feature gradually becomes a motif in itself (bars 23 and following). However, what must be emphasized is that these "scales" are merely motivic figurations, while the original motif still remains the underlying structural basis, as shown in the following example:

Ex. 313

The group that follows (bars 28 to 40) has again this quality of a melodic utterance complete in itself, which we may therefore register as the work's *second theme:*

Ex. 314

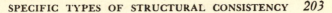

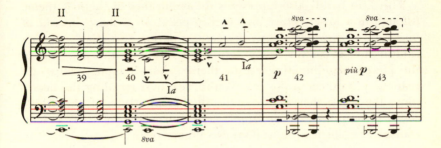

The motivic connection of this theme to the first theme and, in general, to the preceding part of the piece, is evident (as shown by the braces).[2] However, this theme, the thematic line as a melodic

---

[2] Attentive readers may, perhaps with some irritation, have noted that our motivic tabulation in the above example does not always correspond to the division of the theme as phrased by the composer in the score. (Similar observations may have occurred in previous examples throughout our analysis.) However, this does not contradict the validity of our

utterance, is not actually a transformation of the idea of the first theme, such as we have seen in most previous examples in this book. The affinity of the two themes—a very close affinity—lies more in the identity of their motifs. And in the bridging group (40 to 46) immediately following, these motifs are continued without change, the bass delineating motif II in a large arc, while the soprano commences with motif I*a*. It is also noteworthy that by linking the E in bar 47 (though it appears here three octaves lower) to the constant G–D in the preceding bars, again the motif (G, D, E) is sounded, even over the barrier of the bar rest (46).

This E in bar 47 also represents the reentrance of the first theme (though in a lower octave and with a pedal on G-sharp instead of on E), through which the work's recapitulation is reached. The recapitulation is completed by a full reiteration of the first half of the piece, including the second theme, though some groups are reduced and others prolonged. With a few bars recalling the beginning, the work then closes. Thus the architecture of the whole composition presents, even from a traditional point of view, a clear, transparent scheme, the well-known binary form.

Apart from this question of outer form, the point that interests us most is that the rich and variegated design of "La Cathédrale" is shaped entirely from the two motivic particles quoted; actually not a

---

motivic interpretation; it rather confirms our oft-advanced explanations of structural formation. *For the conscious phrasing and grouping of a work's shapes, as they finally appear in the score, need not necessarily conform in every detail with the mold in which these shapes first grew in the composer's mind from his motivic ideas.* The truth of this can be shown through an abundance of examples. Even the opening bar of the piece proves it. In this opening bar the first three chords must have arisen in the composer's mind as an expression of the melodic particle G, D, E, which then became a motif. Yet, owing to the phrasing in the score, the first chord (as similarly the first chords in bars 3 and 5) appears somewhat divorced from the following chords (see example 301). To be sure, the composer intended this separation of the chords from their original motivic meaning in order to produce the wonderful effect, as of distant bells, on which the piece so impressively centers.

The frequent discrepancy between the manner in which shapes seem to be divided if one follows the phrasing marks given by the composer, or if one traces the motivic elements, is the reason that the phrasing marks are often omitted in the musical examples quoted in this study.

single note is excluded from this structural unity. Indeed, two full themes of great melodic breadth were developed from these two minute particles.

However, a decisive fact here becomes apparent. These two themes, though they shine out as the central melodic lines in the work's design, have nevertheless, with regard to the structural evolution of the whole, a somewhat static quality. Each theme is repeated, but, save for some annexed prolongations, almost literally repeated, not transformed; the thematic idea does not really move. Here the distinction between the two principles, namely, "outer form through grouping" and "inner form through thematic evolution," becomes strikingly visible. In fact we recognize *two separate conceptions of a "theme."* From the point of view of the outer proportions of a composition, a theme is that shape around which a section is centered. But from the point of view of thematic development, a theme is that basic musical thought from which the further utterances of the work are derived in constant transformation and evolution, possibly leading to final resolution.

The themes of "La Cathédrale" are themes in the first, outer sense of the term. But here a realization of particular interest presents itself; namely, that the fact that the themes themselves lack evolutional impulse does not seem, in this work, to constitute any weakness from an artistic angle. For evolution is very much at work in "La Cathédrale" within the *motivic* realm. The different motivic variants, the ever changing combinations of the given motifs, the fact that the contours of large sections are formed from motifs—all this endows the piece with a sufficiency, indeed, an abundance, both of structural and of dramatic life. And when as the work's concluding phrase, motif II, which as E, C-sharp, opened the first theme, now is changed to E, C-natural, then by this minute change even a kind of "thematic resolution" is accomplished.

How unimaginably deep the motivic penetration goes may be realized through a last feature to which attention should be drawn; namely, the *harmonic* shaping of the piece. For the harmonies and chord combinations of "La Cathédrale" are a magnificent illustration of how in modern music even the harmonic sphere can become a full part of the thematic unity. In classical music, with its limited range of harmonies, comparatively few, though sometimes very impressive, thematic expressions through harmonization are possible. Here, in Debussy's work, the thematic permeation of the harmonic domain becomes complete. From the very first bar, the chords and their series are but additional utterances of the basic motifs. By cross-connecting voices of adjacent chords, as for instance in the group quoted as *a* in the following example, versions of motif I invariably become apparent, as shown in *b*. Later in the work this thematic permeation becomes more and more outspoken and is even manifest in the single chords (*c*):

Ex. 315

Beethoven: Quartet, opus 135

Leaving Debussy's serene melancholy and turning to the austerity of Beethoven's last quartet, opus 135, we feel indeed as if we were entering a different world. Nevertheless, contrasting in their style and artistic intentions as these two works may be, we will discover that the idea of evolving a full compositional picture from one or two short motivic particles appears in both as the structural ferment. As will be seen in the forthcoming analysis, this idea is particularly apparent in the first movement of the quartet. In fact this movement presents the interesting and unusual picture of having no actual "themes" in the full sense of the word at all, though it is distinctly divided into thematic groups and sections. Or, to use a different terminology, the composer chose in this first movement a thematic thought which is so short and concise that it is difficult to differentiate this small phrase from a motif. From this thematic-motivic particle, however, he developed the intricate design of the whole movement in utter consistency.

In the following, the opening group of the quartet is shown (the notation reduced to two staves):

Ex. 316

At first glance it might seem questionable whether in this complex design of multiple phrases an idea of a unifying pattern is to be discovered at all. The structural shaping of the first bars is symmetric and clear. However, the next little group, reading,

Ex. 317

seems rather aloof in character from the opening bars. One would assume that the composer wished here to introduce some new motivic material. Yet if we resolve these shapes from their figurate appearance, they turn out to be mere inversions of a part of the opening bar. We must simply notate the group without the C-pedal which is interwoven into the phrasing. Then it reads:

Ex. 318

The first of these particles is obviously formed as a transformation (even at identical pitch) of the characteristic figure from the quartet's opening:

Ex. 319

We called such transformation, interversion. Moreover, as this particle is twice repeated in transposition, the contour of the group as a whole expresses the G, A, B-flat, which is the minute opening particle of the work, as formed through the grace notes:

Ex. 320

But we may still probe more deeply into this design. For not only the opening particle but, at the same time, the very core of the opening bar seems interwoven into the group's shaping. In the example below, *a* shows the kernel of the opening bar. By lifting some notes of the present group into relief, as indicated in *b*, we see that the work's opening thought factually appears in reversion:

Ex. 321

The following example charts briefly the motivic course of the quartet's opening bars:

Ex. 322

However, the final validity of this interpretation can only be proved or disproved by the further course of the work. If this opening exclamation really is the basic motivic brick from which the quartet's architecture is developed, then it must—hidden perhaps, yet unmistakably—appear continually in the following groups. The next group reads:

Ex. 323

At first glance it would seem doubtful that this design would strengthen our point. Nevertheless, merely equalizing the difference in octaves, the following shapes appear in relief:

Ex. 324

This time no doubt is possible. For these are clearly two utterances of the opening thought.

Let us dwell on this for a moment. Bars that in the score present a picture, such as,

Ex. 325

once the difference in instruments and octaves is leveled, reveal themselves as none other than a twofold repetition of the very opening of the work:

However, anyone who still questions the inner identity need only look at the following bars. For here the last group is repeated—but repeated with a minute yet significant alteration, the interpolation of some thirty-second rests. And through these rests not only the melodic line but also the rhythm of the opening bars now reappears with irresistible clarity:

Besides, to make the analogy complete, the ascending third (motif II) both introduces and concludes the group, just as it does in the opening bars:

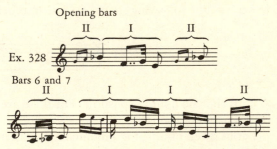

Thus we see that once we pierce the surface, these shapes which seem to bear no resemblance to each other reveal themselves in substance as fully identical.

The following four bars present an entirely new picture. Their full thematic meaning will be shown in a few moments. But the fact that these bars, though in detail formed by different motifs, are also permeated by a contour expressing motif I becomes apparent in the following outline:

Ex. 329

The subsequent conclusion of the quartet's first section reiterates the opening thought in two new shapings:

Ex. 330

To make the idea of the preceding dissection more transparent, a kind of thematic chart may be added, showing that the course of the quartet's opening section *in its entirety* consists of but a succession of the basic motifs. The main motif is marked I, the second II, while the little particle forming the second half of motif I is marked *a*, as it sometimes appears independently.

Ex. 331

Thus an astounding picture emerges. As has already been indicated, the section just analyzed actually contains no "theme" but merely two short motivic phrases from which the whole design is developed. However, owing to this lack of actual themes, these short motivic phrases do not function here as "motifs"; that is, they do not appear as common particles uniting different themes. These motivic phrases appear rather with the peculiar function *of substituting themes.* They are used and treated in a "thematic" manner.

However, this omission of real themes and their replacement by motifs imposes a certain strain on the listener. For it is more difficult to follow a structural design built by constant reiteration and transformation of short motivic phrases than one centered on easily discernible full-sized themes. Here we have the reason for that oft-voiced, erroneous opinion which holds the last quartets to be almost without "form." Our analytic description of opus 135 shows how unfounded such a contention is.

Moreover, although no actual themes are to be heard, the movement is clearly grouped into *thematic sections*—a first and a second thematic section (the latter commencing with the group quoted below in example 337).

What therefore is to be demonstrated is the possibility and principle of a structural method based on motivic rather than on thematic consistency. However, significantly enough, this specific method of forming is sustained only in parts of the works quoted. In Debussy's "La Cathédrale" the purely motivic sections are interrupted and held together by two distinct themes; in Beethoven's last quartet, as will be seen, the initial "motif themes" are in the following movements replaced by outspokenly "thematic" structure. In fact, the very dramatic-allegoric idea of the work is based on this differentiation and transformation from a motivic to a thematic concept of forming.

To fully complete our "grammatical" demonstration, we must here too glance at the bass line. The opening notes of the following example show the first shape emerging. (We begin with the B-flat of the viola as, naturally, in a thematic examination one must consider what *sounds* as bass, not merely what is played by the lowest instrument):

Ex. 332

What we hear and, accordingly, what will probably turn out to be a motif is the falling seventh B-flat–C, within which a descending second, D-flat–C, is interwoven. And we see that this falling seventh (B-flat–C) is indeed the main feature forming the subgroups, while the descending second (transposed) furnishes the detailed figuration.

This pattern of a falling seventh and second, by the way, forms also the actual content of the previously quoted soprano bars 10 to 14:

Ex. 333

We return to the bass line. This summation of a seventh and second constitutes, as we must now understand, merely the *obvious* phrasing of the bass. For digging deeper into its shaping, we become aware that the work's main motif is also integrated into this seemingly so different design. The motif appears first in bars 4 and 5:

Ex. 334

though here merely as an indication, whereby a G (notated in small print) has to be added to make the feature transparent. In the following bars, however, the bass clearly expresses an inversion of the prime motif, even at original pitch, moreover with the ascending third annexed, just as in the opening bar:

Ex. 335

A few words more to indicate the continuation of the thematic homogeneity in this movement. The first section is followed by a kind of fugato, formed through a series of variants of the main motif:

Ex. 336

With the last note of this, the movement's second thematic section enters, opening thus:

Ex. 337

Again, as demonstrated through the notes in bold print, the overall motif is easily discernible.

This whole scheme of almost replacing thematic by motivic consistency is completely changed in the following movements of the quartet. Naturally, in these following movements the motivic affinity continues. At the same time, however, themes reappear as the principal actors and lead the drama to its fulfillment. In fact, it is particularly impressive to observe how the final transformation of the small opening particle into a full theme is used to personify the programmatic idea of the work.

As for the next two movements, the Vivace and the Adagio, we need only point briefly to the way in which their opening shapes vary the original motif. Compare:

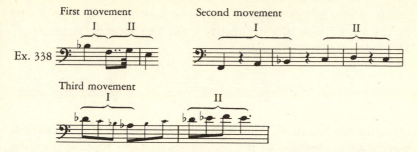

First movement   Second movement

Ex. 338

Third movement

But after the close of the third movement, the Adagio, the score presents a rather unusual picture. Before the Finale the composer interpolates a *title* followed by some notes with a text, representing a *question* (Grave) and an *answer* (Allegro).

The title reads: "Der schwergefasste Entschluss" (The Grave Decision). The question and answer read: "Muss es sein? Es muss sein!" (Must it be? It must be!).

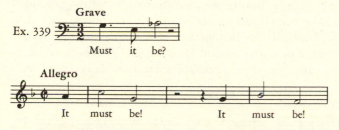

Ex. 339

These notes are not, of course, supposed to be played or sung: they obviously represent a kind of motto to the Finale. In these bars Beethoven offers us a rare glimpse into his inner creative domain. First, these lines prove irrefutably that in Beethoven's mind his musical utterances were linked to spiritual, even perhaps to intellectual ideas, though some orthodox commentators may angrily repudiate such a conception. They also prove that Beethoven does not achieve this linking by a musical description of happenings, as in the case of the so-called "program music," but rather *by conceiving the structural essence of a work as a spiritual allegory.*

This becomes amazingly clear in this instance. For neither Beethoven nor any other composer searching for a melody, a "song" for these words, would have set them to music in this way. These notes are not a tune. They are structural bricks connected to a spiritual allegory. The clue to their structural meaning is presented by the second part of the "answer." For this second "It must be" and the work's opening shape:

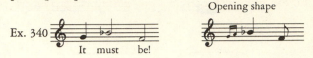

are obviously identical. And while the first part of the "answer" is merely a transposition of the second—both parts together forming a shape which later appears as the first theme of the Finale—the "question," the G, E, A-flat (example 339), is the inversion of the same shape.

Thus we see the work's basic structural thought emerging in the composer's mind as an allegory, a symbol of that eternal question which everyone must face at the end of his earthly span.

Beethoven obviously answered this question first in a mood of grim or almost grimly humorous determination, with a sudden Allegro forte after the Grave pianissimo of the preceding introduction. However, beneath this humor lies woe, as the wonderful, dissonant harmonization of the second "It must be" proves (asterisk in the following example), whereupon the forte itself is replaced by a *piano subito:*

Combinations of this shape form the main content of the Finale. However, finally a new tune arises. It is first introduced rather inconspicuously, only to be superseded by the "It must be." But toward the conclusion of the work this new tune sings its way into the foreground, sounding from the high register of the cello:

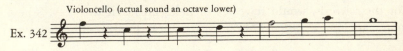

This shape, too, is of course formed from the work's opening motif. But the phrase that originally was, in all its brevity, an expression of somber woe has now become an utterance of light and almost dancelike cheer:

Ex. 343

In the transfiguration of the somber opening *motif* to the serene *theme* of the Finale, the thematic resolution and the innermost content of the quartet come to fulfillment. How touching in its folksong-like simplicity is this last theme in Beethoven's last work— reminding one of a man who, returning to God, speaks again with the voice of a child.

This spirit of transcendent simplicity is intensified by the subsequent repetition of the theme in pizzicato pianissimo, which, in turn, is repeated, now contrapuntally linked to a new soprano in the first violin. These lines produce the most ethereal dissonances ever heard in music—dissonances which are clearly audible (see asterisks in following example) and yet have not the slightest quality of discords, as the whole group is immovably embedded in the tonic:

Ex. 344

It is significant that this soprano, though itself a motivic imitation of the theme, clearly echoes the "Ode to Joy" from the Ninth Symphony. The programmatic idea of including this ray of joy in music announcing the approach of death is tremendously persuasive.

When this stage is reached, the "It must be" concludes the work, now no longer as the "grave decision," but, in fortissimo unison, as final triumph:

Ex. 345

Thus the theme itself ends the quartet. Beethoven completely avoids those meaningless chord repetitions with which composers from time immemorial have concluded their works. His last utterance is his last thought.

8

THEMATIC KEY RELATIONS

This chapter, which advances some observations on the thematic nature of key relations between the different sections and movements of a musical work, should be regarded as a kind of annex to the main body of our inquiry. The phenomena brought about by these relations, interesting as they may appear in many respects, nevertheless, as a whole, lack the binding, lawlike quality which otherwise makes the thematic principle the structural backbone of so many great works of musical literature.

A number of such key relationships have already been quoted. Now we may expand our examination to a more general picture. However, as has just been indicated, some reservations must be kept in mind from the outset. Above all, we should keep in mind that the possibilities of expressing thematic thoughts through keys are limited. For instance, according to the conception valid in Mozart's or Beethoven's time, there was only a comparatively small choice of key relations between movements from which to draw. One scheme was to stay in the same key throughout the whole work, merely changing from major to minor, or vice versa. Apart from this, the middle movement could be in the key of the third, either the major or minor third, or for that matter in its inversion, the sixth; [1] furthermore, it could be in the key of the fourth or its inversion, the fifth.

As these few keys represent almost the whole available list, it is

---

[1] Logically, if for example two movements are in the keys of C and E, we cannot know whether the composer had an interval of a third or a sixth in mind. However, we may come to find that in certain instances the thematic interpretation may serve as a clue.

219

understandable that the idea of "thematic keys" cannot be regarded as a principle universally valid throughout compositional literature. Great composers would hardly have enforced key relations which they considered artificial in order to express motivic thoughts between movements. In such cases they would abstain from expressing any thematic ideas through their key relations.

Yet the abundance of striking, even fascinating examples of thematic key relationships to be found in classical music is astounding. Moreover, even when no actual motif is expressed through the keys, we may see the spirit and principle of such a relationship at work in determining the keys of the movements and sections. Let us take, for example, the key relationships within Beethoven's First Symphony and those within his piano sonata, opus 13, the so-called "Pathétique."

The motivic nucleus from which all the themes of the First Symphony are derived is centered on a fourth (*a* in the following example; compare also example 129 and following), while the "Pathétique's" central motivic idea is based on a third (*b*):

Ex. 346

Consequently, the key scheme formed by the movements of the First Symphony (C, F, C, C) is focused on a fourth, whereas that of the "Pathétique" (C, A-flat, C) is based on a third.

Of course, C *down* to A-flat is a third, but why did Beethoven not prefer the direct way C–E-flat?

Because had he chosen E-flat as the key of the second movement, he would have forfeited another equally important thematic effect; namely, to have the theme of the second movement reappear at original pitch as a transformation of the work's opening theme:

Ex. 347

1st movement (**Grave**)   2nd movement (**Andante**)

Thus instead of C–E-flat (as the keys of the first two movements) he decided in favor of the contrary motion, C–A-flat.

Not only the key relationships of the movements but also those of the single sections are centered in the sonata on a third and in the symphony on a fourth (or its inversion, a fifth). The fact that this also corresponds to the traditional modulations (to the dominant in a piece in major, and to the relative major in a piece in minor) does not lessen the thematic importance of this feature.

In the symphony, both in the first and last movements, the key schemes between the first and second themes are C–G. In the second movement the key scheme between the two sections is F–C, and since this is C-minor, it cannot even be said to have been chosen as representing the traditional dominant. Moreover, the second section progresses over A-flat to D-flat, thus expressing even in the modulation the work's basic motif (in transposed interversion as C, A-flat, D-flat). The development section of the first movement modulates similarly over constant fourths to (intermediary) dominants: A, D, G, C, F, B-flat, E-flat.

In the sonata, on the other hand, the keys in the first movement read: C (Grave), C (first Allegro theme), E-flat (second Allegro theme and end of exposition), G (second Grave), E-natural (development section), thus forming an uninterrupted series of thirds.

In the second movement of the "Pathétique" the three themes are in the following keys: first theme, A-flat; second theme, F; third theme, beginning in A-flat and modulating to E, enharmonic substitute for F-flat.

Therefore, ignoring the small second Grave, the sectional keys in the first movement read as shown in example 348a,[2] to which the keys of the second movement form precisely the contrary motion (b). The relation between the keys of the first and second movement, C–A-flat, is expressed by the keys of the three themes of the last movement (c):

Ex. 348

---

[2] This motivic key scheme (example 348a) recalls the abrupt change between major and minor in the Allegro theme's beginning:

Ex. 349

Whether or not one credits the composer with having consciously planned every detail in this scheme, it remains unquestionable that he chose thirds as basic key relations in the sonata, and fourths in the symphony.

To be precise, the second Finale theme of the "Pathétique" would probably be classified as being in the key of E-flat rather than in B-flat (although strict key designations imposed on small groups within a larger whole may, as such, often appear debatable). However, in this instance the dominating *pitch* (B-flat) of this second Finale theme replaces the key proper as the group's thematic symbol. In fact, the working of this principle can frequently be observed.

Accordingly thematic "key relationship" must not always be brought about by the keys themselves, but may occasionally be materialized *by pitches emerging within the keys.* Beethoven's opus 57, for example, the so-called "Appassionata," is in F-minor. Yet the thematic idea expressed by the work's key relations is not centered on the F itself, but on another tone of the F-minor harmony. The decisive motif of the sonata reads:

Ex. 350

This basic figure appears either as C, D-flat, C, or as C, D-natural, C (as in the work's opening group, example 351*a*). This opening group is then repeated half a tone higher (example 351*b*) and is thus centered on D-flat:

Ex. 351

Since in a third group the theme returns to the pitch of C, the three groups together express C, D-flat, C, in wide contour.

The same motif in transposition is heard as A-flat, B-flat, A-flat, from the beginnings both of the Andante and Finale theme:

Moreover, C, D-flat, C, constantly emerges at original pitch at decisive points in the work: for instance in the first movement, toward its close (*a* in the following example); in the second movement when the regular figuration *b* is significantly changed to *c;* or in the Finale in its most characteristic figure (*d*):

And it is this very motif C, D-flat, C, which as a giant motivic contour unites the whole work. Indeed, the whole sonata, through its key relationships, *becomes one great expression of its basic motif.* That this constituted the conscious architectural scheme of the work will now be demonstrated.

The first movement is in F-minor. However, it is not F but C (as a part of the F-minor harmony) that becomes the towering note in the movement's contour. With C the movement begins and ends. On C the opening theme (see example 351*a*) is centered, as is also the second great theme in A-flat:

Ex. 354

(This theme, by the way, expresses through its corner notes the basic motif in inversion: A-flat, G, A-flat [3]). In particular the idea of C as a thematic basis is emphasized by the infinitely long sustained C with which the movement closes:

Ex. 355

The second movement is the well known "theme with variations" in D-flat. The conclusion of its theme is quoted below as *a*. This theme reappears at the close of the last variation, but now its very last notes are omitted. Instead it concludes as shown in *b*:

Ex. 356

---

[3] The content of this theme, of course, also comprises other thematic features. The above, as must be understood, is not a thematic analysis, but merely an indication of certain points connected with the present question of key relations.

What has happened here?

The melodic line, having reached the D-flat, is arrested, for D-flat is the very note on which the work's basic motif (C, D-flat, C) is centered. The fermata on this pianissimo D-flat symbolizes a moment of contemplation at the end of this dreamlike movement. The Andante has fulfilled its course, and now the architectural idea of the work as a whole comes to the fore. The pianissimo D-flat is repeated fortissimo, with a second fermata forming the last chord of the Andante, and it is then repeated thirteen times in the pulsating tempo of the following Finale:

Ex. 357

A thirteenfold repetition such as this might appear somewhat questionable from a purely formalistic point of view. But endowed, as they are here, with thematic meaning, these accented D-flats acquire extraordinary power.

For since in this last movement the D-flat falls back to the C,

Ex. 358

all three movements are held together by this huge expression of the motif, as a great building might be held together by its central arch.

Thus the thematic force frequently becomes an important factor in determining the keys of a work's movements. Does not the key scheme of the "Moonlight" Sonata—all three movements being in C-sharp (though in the Allegretto notated as D-flat)—charmingly recall the characteristic figure of the sonata's opening theme?

Ex. 359

Even the rhythm of the motif might seem to be mirrored in the brevity of the second movement.

Similarly, the opening of Brahms's Second Symphony is indicated

Ex. 360

by the relationship between its first two movements, the first movement being in the key of D, while the second movement is characterized by its dominating pitch, F-sharp.

And in the Two Rhapsodies the contour of the work's opening theme, starting with F-sharp–D, echoes both in the opening notes (pitches) of the two pieces, which are F-sharp and D, and in their keys, which are B and G.

In Mozart's "Jupiter" Symphony the key scheme is C, F, C, C, thus mirroring the motivic fourth of its main theme (*a* in the following example), while in the G-minor Symphony the basic melodic sixth (*b*) resounds unmistakably from the movements' keys, which are G, E-flat, G, G.

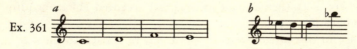

Ex. 361

There is also in this G-minor Symphony a specific effect pertaining to key relationship between the movements. The melodic line in the second movement of the symphony closes with the particle quoted as *a* in the following example, while the third movement, the minuet, opens with *b*:

Ex. 362

Linking these two phrases together, the symphony's opening theme (which appears in the minuet in transformation) reemerges in its original shape.

To be sure, we would not have quoted this feature, which, though an undeniable fact, might still be thought to have come about by chance, were it not that such thematic connections from the end of one movement to the beginning of the next are frequent and undoubtedly conscious effects in classical literature.

Schumann's *Kinderszenen* provide some impressive instances of this type. As was shown in a previous chapter, the themes of the first four pieces of the *Kinderszenen* are formed by different expressions of one basic pattern (see example 51). In the fifth piece ("Glückes genug") the theme is no longer a literal reiteration but a transposition of this pattern. However, it is interesting to see how Schumann compensates for this sudden change in thematic pitch. Number 4 ends with a chord of the seventh with a long sustained high G on the top; and since F-sharp, E, D, sound from the opening of number 5, our ear, accustomed to the familiar thought, instinctively links the two pieces together.

Ex. 363 — End of No. 4 / Beginning of No. 5

Thus the theme at original pitch sounds through, even when the actual thematic course temporarily follows a different path.

A somewhat similar device is to be seen in number 7, the "Träumerei." "Träumerei" opens with C, F, while the original thematic pattern transposed to this key would have been A, F, or A, C, F. In other words, to complete the full thematic pattern, an A is "missing" in the beginning of the "Träumerei" theme. However, the A does sound, not at the opening of "Träumerei" itself, but as the last note of the preceding piece, "Important Event."

Number 13, the concluding piece of *Kinderszenen,* "The Poet Speaks," presents an opening theme even more different from the basic pattern than that of "Träumerei." In our previous analysis we elaborated on the programmatic meaning of this particular opening theme, which reads F-sharp, G, C. However, here too, just as in

"Träumerei," if we link the concluding E of the preceding number 12 to the opening of number 13, the original theme sounds through (as demonstrated in *a* of the following example). And the repetition of this very effect in the piece's recapitulation renders the composer's intention unmistakable. For here again the E is the last note preceding the reappearance of the theme in the recapitulation. In fact, this whole preceding passage is one expression of this thematic E (example 364*b*).

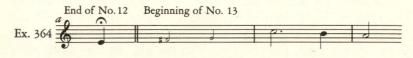

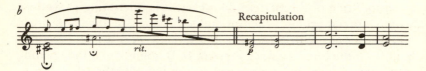

Thus, although in these pieces the actual themes are different from the basic pattern, the original idea is invariably restored *by creating connections over the barriers between the single pieces and sections.*

The key scheme of *Kinderszenen* confirms the idea of thematic unification through key relations. The keys of the thirteen pieces of *Kinderszenen* are listed in the following chart:

Ex. 365

This scheme obviously consists of three groups, each of which expresses the sixth on which the work's main theme is centered. The double role of the G-sharp and G-natural fully corresponds to the "twofold identical pitch" (sharpened and regular) as described in our previous analysis.

Examples, finally, that even skeptical minds may consider convincing are to be found in Beethoven's quartets opus 130 and 131.

The opening shape in the quartet opus 130 is quoted below under *a*, while *b* shows the succession of keys expressed by the work's respective movements:

Ex. 366

Naturally, the last movement must return to the key of the first. But apart from this, the corner notes of the opening theme, B-flat, G, E-flat, are indubitably reiterated in the key scheme. (And even the concluding D of the theme reappears as D-flat in the midst of the key scheme.) The choice of G-minor as the key of the fourth movement to follow the D-flat of the third movement is so unusual that we must assume that it was the composer's intention to express the theme through the keys.

In opus 131 a similar intention seems to have been at work. Here the first movement is in C-sharp, the second in D. The *Encyclopædia Britannica*,[4] in an analytic sketch on the harmonic relations of the quartet's movements, elaborates on this key succession, "surprising" in a work of Beethoven, without, however, attempting an explanation. But the explanation is to be found in the thematic sphere. For if we link the C-sharp of the first movement to the D of the second and to the A of the fourth (as the so-called "third movement" consists only of a few modulatory bars and establishes no actual key), the thematic meaning of the "surprising" key becomes evident. The opening theme is clearly mirrored in the keys [5] of the first movements of the work.

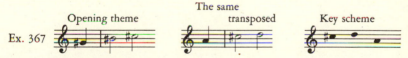

Ex. 367

The author is fully aware that the suggestions put forward in this chapter must remain somewhat fragmentary. Nevertheless, he is of the opinion that he would have deprived the reader of a whole vista of interesting ideas had he completely ignored this less manageable part of his subject. For though it may not always be possible

---

[4] See footnote on page 350.

[5] That the key scheme expresses the theme in transposition rather than at original pitch is explained by the fact that the first movement must naturally be in C-sharp, the basic key of the work. Since, however, the opening theme starts with G-sharp, the theme could be expressed by the key scheme only in transposition.

to furnish strict proof, the existence of a strong thematic impulse behind composers' choice of key for movements and sections is unmistakable.

Of course the question of thematic key relations is only part of a problem of much wider scope and more general significance; namely, the problem of interrelationship between the thematic and harmonic spheres in music. Reference to the thematic function of harmonies, harmonic progressions, and modulations was repeatedly made in this inquiry. But to pursue this topic in detail is somewhat beyond the range of this study.

Part Three

EVALUATION

AND

WIDER OUTLOOK

9

IS THE THEMATIC PROCESS
CONSCIOUS OR SUBCONSCIOUS?

In the introductory pages attention was drawn to the fact that thematic structure never formed a concrete part of our theoretical system. Some explanation for this fact may gradually have become apparent in the course of our study. One important reason is the nature of thematic structure itself. For the thematic phenomena are so manifold and complex that in a sense they evade academic tabulation. Though they can perhaps be described, they can hardly be comprised in an actual "system." They are too intimately connected with the creative process itself.

Once a realization of this intimate connection dawns on the intelligent musician, the question is almost bound to arise: Is thematic structure the result of a conscious or subconscious process?

It would be alluring to believe that it is subconscious. Such an assumption would open wide avenues of further speculation, and the author must confess that at the beginning of his search he, too, was inclined to lean in this direction. To be sure, even were we to accept the belief that this process was subconscious, this would in no wise affect the value of the findings set out in this analysis. However, confronted with an abundant variety of different and irrefutable proofs, the author is now convinced beyond a doubt that it was, at least in the representative works of great musical literature, essentially a *conscious* process. The great composers were fully aware both of the thematic principle and of the technique through which they materialized it. As this consciousness was supported and complemented by a thorough technical training, this constant transforming of musical ideas into different shapes finally became the composer's customary way of expressing himself, his natural musical language. As a consequence of this, however, the actual forming of many thematic features, especially smaller ones, may often in musical practice have come about instinctively, or even automatically.

There is no contradiction in this. We must ask ourselves: What, in the last analysis, is conscious and what instinctive? Where is the border line? For instance, our language, our speech—is it a conscious or a subconscious process? Obviously it is both. We are conscious of what we wish to say, yet we formulate our phrases and sentences almost automatically.

So also in music, do not the harmonic progressions take shape in this combined conscious-subconscious way? A composer who builds a little phrase as a series of harmonies (for instance, II, V, I, to quote an elementary example) is certainly aware of this fact. Yet the compositional procedure through which the harmonization is carried out is not calculated but is simply the result of his natural musical instinct. No one doubts this where *harmonic* progressions are concerned, as every musician's mind is trained to these conceptions by his theoretical education. Neither would one question a composer's inspirational impulse because he happens to be conscious of some basic principles according to which he accomplishes his harmonic shaping.

But as soon as features of this "hidden" *thematic* affinity are pointed out—hidden because no theory tabulated them—an air of puzzlement arises. "Is it possible," one is asked, "that this beautiful theme of Beethoven's came about through 'structural' [implying a conscious, calculated] shaping?" If so, many dreams of an Alice in Wonderland state in which a composer's mind is supposed to work would be destroyed. Yet a genuine composer's imagination is no more hampered by thematic than by harmonic principles.

In our preceding examples a profusion of thematic features of such outspoken, specific, and elaborate nature presented themselves that the attentive reader will scarcely harbor any further doubt as to the composer's conscious intention in producing them. Although no additional confirmation is perhaps necessary, it may nevertheless prove satisfactory to turn to an example in which *a proof of almost mathematical conclusiveness* becomes apparent. The example is from Beethoven's quartet, opus 130, in B-flat major. Some striking

affinities between the different themes of its first movement were
pointed out in an earlier chapter. Now we may examine its third
movement, the Andante con moto. It opens with these bars:

Ex. 368

As in many previous instances, upon comparing this whole picture to the first movement's opening group, one at first hardly under-
stands how an affinity could be traced at all. But examining the
first violin part in the third movement (henceforth called in brief
the Andante) more closely, we discover that it is an almost literal
repetition of the shape from the first movement's Introduction
(henceforth called the Adagio), though in an entirely different
rhythm and phrasing.

Ex. 369

Checking note for note, we recognize as identical in both movements B-flat, A. (The A is notated as B-double-flat in the Andante's first bar. As these notes are in the second bar of the Andante repeated, now the B-double-flat appears as A here too.) Then follow, always identical in both movements, A-flat, G. Now comes one note that is different: the E-flat of the Adagio is replaced in the Andante by a C, after which, however, the course is again literally identical: D and C.

Thus with the exception of one changed note (and the accidentals adjusted to the respective key) the whole Adagio reemerges literally in the Andante theme. Yet what different worlds are expressed by these two themes merely by altering the rhythmical value and function of individual notes.

Now we may follow the part of the second violin (see example 368). Let us for the moment skip the first bar, since, as easily seen, in this bar the part of the second violin must be connected to the viola part, which follows a different thematic course. But from bar 2 on, the second violin appears to progress in unison with the first violin; however, they are not in complete unison. Two sixteenth rests shine out in the fourth bar—and now we are at our "mathematical" proof. These sixteenth rests must on first consideration appear peculiar; they seem strange in a "grammatical" sense, particularly in relation to the first violin. It would have seemed so much more natural to have inserted an F instead of the first rest, and perhaps also an F (or another note) instead of the second rest, or otherwise to have changed the phrasing. The rests, at any rate, are almost an obstacle to the executant, as they interrupt the natural flow. Had the rests appeared likewise in the first violin, we could at least imagine that this was Beethoven's particular conception of the melodic course, which, even if we do not "understand" it, we have no right to question. But emerging as they do, in the part of the second violin alone, the rests are little perceivable, and we wonder why Beethoven inserted them at all.

The riddle's solution comes from the thematic side. *For only through these sixteenth rests do these bars of the third movement become a literal reiteration of the quartet's opening theme.*

Let us compare the two shapes again note for note (the opening theme is *a;* the shape in question, *b*):

Ex. 370

In both shapes we read: B-flat, A, A-flat, G. And it continues—almost unbelievably—E-flat, D-flat, C. The identity, save for the accidentals, is complete to the last dot. But this startling analogy would have been entirely obscured without the rests.

This is an example of almost uncanny power. Anyone who ever doubts that the different movements of a work of Beethoven's are thematically connected need only think of these rests. They prove with perfect exactness, first, the thematic affinity itself, and second, that this affinity is the result of the composer's full structural intention. It cannot even be suggested that these violin parts took shape in the composer's mind, half-consciously as it were, as a musical recollection of the Adagio theme. No one in whose ear an instinctive reminiscence of the Adagio theme is sounding would shape it in the form in which it appears in these violin parts. This particular shaping could have been brought about only by a conscious mind trained in this special technique of transformation.

We may dig further into the work's elaborate structure. Returning to the first bar of the second violin, already identified as part of a melodic course continued in the viola, we see that bar 2 of the viola repeats this bar 1 of the second violin literally. This thematic shape (beginning with bar 2 in the viola) is given under *a* in the following example (notated an octave higher). This viola shape has no affinity to that of the violin parts nor to the quartet's opening theme, with which the violin parts are identical. Rather it constitutes an independent counterpoint to them. However, the viola part is formed in clear affinity to another of the work's leading themes; namely, the theme of the second movement, the Presto, quoted below as *b*:

Ex. 371

It is obvious that in their melodic and rhythmical meaning, and even in pitch, these two themes have a common kernel, though they were necessarily shaped as different utterances, each adapted to the character of its respective movement.

Thus the familiar spectacle is repeated. The third movement of a work is shaped from the thematic thoughts of the two preceding movements. In some previous instances the same feature was brought about by blending two themes into *one* new shape. Now the themes are brought together *in a contrapuntal utterance* to form the new group: the violin parts of the third movement reiterate the first movement's opening, while, simultaneously, the viola plays a kind of replica of the second movement's theme.

Nevertheless, as indicated, the second movement's thematic "melody" itself shows no affinity to the quartet's opening theme. Try as we may to unravel a relationship, the two shapes bear no resemblance to each other whatsoever. This seems at complete variance with the conception of Beethovenian structure as we envision it. How can this contradiction be bridged? The answer is: We must simply consider not solely the Presto theme's first violin part but the full theme in its four voices. This Presto is quoted as *a* in the following example. Drawing a line from the bass of this theme to the upper voices, and comparing the contour thus formed (*b*) with the Adagio theme (*c*), we realize how clearly the Adagio theme is integrated in the Presto theme.

Ex. 372

b   Extract of **Presto** theme

c   **Adagio** theme

The only point where the identity is not obvious is when bar 3 of the Presto passes into bar 4 in a half-close. Had the composer concluded these bars through E-flat, D-flat, C, in the first violin (instead of E-flat, E-flat, F), the identity would have been complete. Nevertheless, an identity to the Adagio theme is still apparent in the second violin, as seen in the above example.

However, we must not forget the aforementioned fact that the Presto's thematic melody itself does not bear the slightest affinity to the quartet's opening theme and that such affinity can be traced only, as it were, indirectly. A shaping of this type is not entirely new in our investigation—readers may have noticed similar shapings in previous examples—and it should by no means be regarded as less effective than the usual method of establishing concrete, direct affinities. In a work of the length and austerity of this quartet, it is even an asset to feature essentially different thematic ideas. This produces the desired variety, the thematic wealth of the composition, especially if thematic consistency is still secured through the indirect relationship.

Yet it must be repeated that between the two thematic lines themselves no affinity can be discovered. This example leads us to a wider conception of thematic transformation. Full thematic consistency can be created among independent shapes if they are linked by contributory features.

In chapter three we distinguished between imitation, variation, and transformation as three stages of structural formation. Now we expand this list. The gamut between full identity and complete nonrelationship may be set up as follows:

1. *imitation,* that is, literal repetition of shapes, either directly or by inversion, reversion, and so forth;
2. *varying,* that is, changing of shapes in a slight, well traceable manner;
3. *transformation,* that is, creating essentially new shapes, though preserving the original substance;
4. *indirect affinity,* that is, producing an affinity between independent shapes through contributory features.

Between imitation and nonrelationship [1] lies a whole complex of features comprising all degrees of structural relationship. Varying, that is, altered repetition, is gradually intensified until it becomes transformation, which forms the central, the most concentrated expression of the thematic phenomenon.

But now a further category, number 4, is added, indirect affinity. Referring to our last example, the melodic line of the Presto theme presented itself as a shape completely independent from the opening theme of the first movement, the Adagio. Yet a relationship was easily established by including other voices in the picture. However, in this same Presto theme still another type of indirect affinity becomes audible. True, its thematic line shows no kinship to the quartet's opening theme. But there is another thematic shape *between* these two themes which is readily recognized as related to both. This shape is heard in the introduction of the first movement immediately after the opening group. The following example reveals both affinities. Under *a* the shape in question is compared to the Adagio theme (*b*); under *aa* the same shape is compared to the Presto theme (*c*):

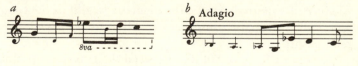

Ex. 373

The phenomenon is familiar: by singling out certain notes, one kinship becomes apparent; by singling out others, another. The

---

[1] It should be mentioned that truly unrelated shaping represents a type virtually unknown in great compositional literature.

result is important; namely, that two shapes which as such have nothing in common can none the less become organic parts of an architectual whole through a mediator, a third shape related to both.

However, number 4 on our list should not be confined to such indirect relationships. It should, in a wider sense, rather be understood as including any transformation wherein the affinities of the shapes in question seem less clear, less outspoken, than the usual ones. As the following examples demonstrate, even these somehow remote affinities, which analysis often has difficulty in making credible, occasionally produce strong musical effects.

One important relationship has not yet been tested in our analysis of the quartet, namely, the relationship between the theme of the Introduction and the first theme of the following Allegro. Knowing that in a work by Beethoven an affinity usually exists, notwithstanding a seemingly utter dissimilarity, we detect the pattern of the opening group incorporated several times into the Allegro theme. The composer's intention becomes all the more clear if we start the quotation of the Allegro theme with the last notes of the preceding Adagio-Introduction. The opening theme is given below as *a*, the Allegro theme (preceded by the last bars of the Adagio) as *b*:

The Adagio motives (a plus b) can be traced four times within the line of the Allegro theme. Of course, looking at these cascading G-minor passages in the Allegro theme, one would be inclined to argue that the introductory group may be shown to be included in the Allegro, but that this is a theoretical, an "analytical" rather than a musical affinity. Now even if we were to accept this opinion as valid, it would at least assure us of the composer's conscious intention in producing the feature. For, if it did not come about through a natural musical impulse, Beethoven must obviously have felt an urge to incorporate the "analytical" affinity for structural reasons.

However, pursuing the affinity further, we become strongly aware that it has also, after all, a decisive musical effect. It was pointed out earlier that features of such a specific and intricate nature could scarcely have come about as the result of mere instinctive recollection. Yet "instinctive recollection" certainly plays an important role here—however, not the composer's recollection but the recollection of the listener.

Let us first take the second bar from the Allegro singly, and compare it with the introductory shape:

Ex. 375

Introductory shape   Second bar from **Allegro** theme

The listener, with the first shape embedded in his ear, could not help hearing it resounding from the Allegro bar, even though no awareness of the technical relationship may have entered his mind; especially since Beethoven's striking dynamic gradation intensifies this effect. The unusually abrupt change from forte in the Allegro's beginning to a sudden piano and again to a sudden forte in the midst of a passage, *precisely at the moments when the motifs enter*, makes it almost impossible not to hear in the Allegro an image of the Introduction. In fact, without such thematic purpose these constant dynamic changes must appear puzzling.

Moreover, let us also glance at the second violin part of the theme. Its line from B-flat to E-flat, then from C to F (see example 374b), manifestly conforms with the contour of the Introduction's shape, the full course of which (a repetition omitted) reads:

Ex. 376

etc.

Thus, even if no direct awareness, either "theoretical" or "musical," of the affinity between the two themes were felt by the listener, his ear, constantly exposed to identical phrases, would willingly accept the Allegro as a logical continuation of the Introduction. Indeed, if we listen to the Allegro theme by itself, it hardly appears as an impressive musical utterance. These étudelike passages, we must admit, lack the beauty and originality we expect from a theme of Beethoven's. Only because they enter after the expressive Adagio, *and because the Adagio's recollection magically resounds through them,* do they exert a stimulating effect on a susceptible listener and prepare his mind for the quartet's further manifestations.

Indeed, the idea here involved should be thought through to its innermost meaning. For much of the purpose and function of the thematic process reveals itself in the last examples. And though we have seen in our analysis an abundance of examples in which a shape reappeared in the contour of a following theme in "direct" transparency, we have also seen others where the thematic idea became apparent only by "rearranging" the design, as for instance in Mozart's G-minor Symphony, by exchanging the octaves in which some phrases were notated in the score. Similar "liberties" were taken in our analysis on several other occasions. Though the continuous logic of our subject itself must sufficiently have proved the structural validity of the phenomena described, there may still have remained a slight inhibition in the minds of some readers. "Even granting the structural affinity," it might be said, "we can still not *hear* a sixth as a predominant feature, if, by exchanging octaves, this 'sixth' is notated as a third." The solution is that the composer may not even have wanted to impress the sixth on the listener. As previously said, composing is not providing examples for the sake of thematic identity. Whether or not the inner identity is *demonstrable* is a matter of entire indifference to the composer. The fact that he did build the whole piece on one common thematic basis is important, as it assures him that the listener, by this same process of "subconscious recollection," will accept the seemingly different utterances as one consistent whole. This, and nothing else, is the final purpose of the thematic technique.

Returning to our point, it is evident that examples like the ones in question represent further irrefutable proof that this whole phenomenon of "thematic identity beneath outer variety" was materialized in full consciousness.

But it is for more fundamental reasons that this whole subject was here treated so copiously. This differentiation between "conscious" and "subconscious" is far more than just an interesting psychological problem. It represents an important, indeed, a decisive factor both from a musical and from a historical point of view. Again we have reached one of the focal points in our discussion; one against the background of which many of our preceding deductions may gain added meaning; one that may also determine the future trend and final idea of this investigation. For the full meaning of the classical technique, the true greatness of its structural achievement can be apprehended only if we realize that the thematic phenomenon constituted a conscious, a systematic principle. Classical music would never have become what it is if this principle had not been applied consciously. And it will be seen in the forthcoming investigation that the direction which the musical evolution has taken up to our very day was in many respects influenced by the fact that this conscious, systematic application changed or, may we say, declined into a subconscious and occasional one.

Before going into detail on this problem, we may extend our examination to one other part of the quartet opus 130; namely, its fourth movement, Alla Danza Tedesca. As usual we must start with a description of the movement's opening theme and its relation to the work's whole, though it is actually a feature emerging in the movement's later course which at present is of particular interest to us. The movement opens with a theme (a in the following example) in which the eye is caught by the meticulous dynamic shading. The crescendo and decrescendo in the very first bar seem rather unusual, as they almost contradict the natural rhythmical flow. At any rate, this nuance makes the B the most accented note in the first bar. But taking this B as the starting point, suddenly this theme also becomes a transparent image of the work's opening (b):

Ex. 377

We recognize how, in both themes, the line falls from B to G, then soars to E. And the analogy in the phrasing continues, though D–C in the first movement is changed to G–F-sharp in the fourth movement. To realize the full analogy, one has but to notice the symmetry in the endings of each of the two halves of the themes.

However, he who searches for literal analogy will find it by including other voices: for then D–C and A–B, the group endings of the first movement, appear verbally in the fourth (see score). It would, of course, be pedantic at this stage to elaborate at any length on such a feature. We must finally come to understand that the core of the thematic idea lies in creating compositional oneness from manifold appearances, not in producing "startling" similarities. More impressive than any literal identity in the themes quoted are the analogous dynamic marks. These striking crescendos followed by sudden pianos (bars 2 and 4 in the theme of the first movement and bars 3 and 7 in the fourth) at precisely corresponding points in the thematic course should alone suffice to assure one that when the composer formed the Danza Tedesca, the call of the work's Introduction was still alive in his mind.

And now we may turn to the feature for which actually this movement was included in our examination. Near the movement's conclusion eight bars appear which represent a unique picture in string-quartet writing. The shapes of this group recall strikingly the movement's opening theme, though the whole design seems somewhat shuffled. To clarify this, compare the movement's opening theme (*a* in the following example) with the present group (*b*) and follow their course:

It turns out that bar 8 of the opening theme is now bar 1 and bar 7 now bar 2, while 6 becomes 3 and 5 becomes 4. In the second half, however, the bars are no longer shuffled; bars 1 to 4 simply become bars 5 to 8 of the new group.

The whole feature is, of course, a perfect example of transformation; interversion, reversion, repetition, as well as a change of instruments are here combined. Now it is clear that a transformation of such a particular, eye-catching quality could not escape the attention of the commentators. This shaping is most obvious; the particles of the theme, though exchanged, are literally preserved; also, throughout the whole group only one instrument plays at a time. In such transparency they could not fail to recognize the idea.

Yet the analysts, while they acknowledged the fact, felt rather bewildered by it. For since the current theory is unaware that such severing and interchanging of shapes constitute the regular principle of compositional formation, they were at a loss to classify and justify this particular and cheerful application. Even Beethoven's foremost admirers evaluate this scrambling of thematic bits into "a kind of musical crossword puzzle" as a whim, a not too fortunate example of an all too witty, eccentric way of writing.

Now on one point the analysts are right. This group is a manifestation of musical humor. But it is neither out of character with the rest of the movements nor with Beethoven's whole idea of structural formation. The mood of buoyant lucidity and speed (Allegro assai) which the composer wished for the movement leads quite logically to this gentle explosion of wit at its conclusion. Above all, however, the witty effect is not based on any unusual method of formation, but merely on the fact that the otherwise hidden mechanism of thematic structure is here for once brought out into the open: the "secret" is here exposed. A falling coulisse produces a comical effect not only on the theatrical stage but in any domain of art. And though used in the above example—intentionally and ingeniously— to crack a musical joke, the method itself—that is, treating melodic shapes as a sculptor would, molding, tempering, and rearranging them—is the very technique through which the works of our great musical literature are formed. The technique as such cannot produce great art. But this is the technique through which the great composers manifested their thoughts.

The last example, apart from its individual interest, must also impress us from a wider aspect. For we suddenly see in thematic technique and as a truly thematic feature, shapes and ideas which we might rather have expected to find in a work of the contrapuntal era. Adding this observation to realizations fostered by the examination of the quartet's other movements and, in fact, by the whole trend of the recent part of our analysis, the direction in which our subject originally pointed may be affected. Our conception of the function of the thematic phenomenon itself and its role in the evolution of occidental music may undergo a complete change. Even the distinction between the "contrapuntal" and the "thematic" principle, introduced at the beginning of our inquiry, pales in the light of this changed and increased insight.

Of course the specifically technical aspect of structural forming in the contrapuntal era was entirely changed in the classical period. But behind this changed technique *one common underlying idea of structural thinking*, which spread through the ages and became the backbone of our musical evolution, becomes visible.

The ensuing chapters will lead us over some of the main points of this evolution up to the present time. Through this we may come to realize that not only the basic spirit of this compositional thinking, but even many concrete features and the manner of their application were miraculously retained throughout all these periods, apparently so different in style and technique.

10

ROOT AND GROWTH
OF THE THEMATIC PRINCIPLE

Seen from a higher spiral of observation, the development of the thematic technique appears in a new light and becomes an inseparable part of a continuous evolutional whole.[1] Let us begin this new phase of discussion with a quotation from a work by **Guillaume Dufay,** the great musical figure of the fifteenth century. On the Gregorian melody quoted below in *a,* Dufay wrote a three-part composition of which the opening groups are given in our example *b* (reprinted by Alfred Orel in Adler's *Musikgeschichte,* 2nd ed., Vol. 1, p. 300):

Ex. 379

Discant

Contratenor

Tenor

---

[1] In order to avoid misunderstanding with regard to the oft used terms "evolution" and "evolutional", the author wishes to state that he is well aware that evolution in the sense of "progress" constitutes a conception which scholars do not like to see applied to the sphere of art. However,

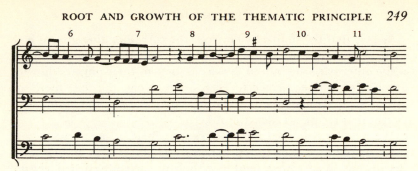

Before proceeding to our specific point of interest, we may investigate the method of structural forming which this design reveals.

The example consists of two corresponding halves, the second of which represents a varied reiteration of the first. In the discant the first half stretches over a full seven bars,[2] while in the lower voices (the contratenor and tenor) the D and G in the second half of bar 7 already form the beginning of the second group. (To be exact, the G in the tenor line of bar 7 represents both the end of the first half and the beginning of the second group.) It is interesting to see how each of the corresponding halves of the voices resembles the other. To this purpose we put the two halves of the contratenor one beside the other and likewise the two halves of the tenor:

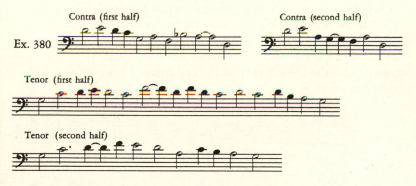

Ex. 380

without entering into any discussion regarding this contention, it must be emphasized that in the survey of the following chapters, as in our whole presentation, the idea of evolution is meant to refer essentially to the development of structural formation, especially of the thematic technique.

[2] In the following we refer to bar numbers, though it must be understood that the modern conception of bars as divisions which regulate the basic accentuation was foreign to Dufay's time.

We see that the similarity between the corresponding groups is in some parts very close, several little phrases being even truly identical, while other parts are indeed "varied," some of their phrases showing absolutely no resemblance to each other. None the less, there are always some corner notes, at the opening, at the close, and in between, that secure an identity of kernel.

We now may proceed to the question whether any relation, and if so what kind, can be traced *between* the voices. The upper voice, the discant, is of course merely a slightly varied, enriched version of the Gregorian melody. But if we follow the course of the tenor attentively, we discover that it too is but a varied version of the Gregorian tune, though varying is here carried much further than it was in the discant. Compare:

Ex. 381

It is obvious that there is a common contour underlying these two shapes. In addition to this, the contratenor turns out to be a free yet indubitable inversion of the tenor. In the following example compare the first part of the contratenor (*a*) with the first part of the tenor (*b*), and the second part of the contratenor (*c*) with the second part of the tenor (*d*):

Ex. 382

Thus we recognize as prevalent throughout the whole of this example a method of formation to which attention was drawn in Chapter 3, namely, *thematic varying*. Indeed, at Dufay's time it represented the foremost structural agent, while imitation, save for specifically canonic compositions, was only occasionally used for smaller parts. In fact, in the present example thematic variation works in both directions: it forms the successive groups and also the three voices which are, directly or indirectly, derived from one basic idea, the cantus.

Studying the detail of the compositional procedure here involved, we come to some startling realizations. Although in this typical example of fifteenth century music, the idiom and form seem vastly different from the music of our epoch, there is nevertheless a far-reaching similarity in the spirit and method through which a thematic bond is established.

Let us take, for instance, the second themes in the Allegro and Finale of Mozart's G-minor Symphony, as quoted in Chapter 5:

Is not *the manner and degree* in which each of these themes resembles and differs from the other very similar to that pointed out in the example from Dufay?

Comparing in the Dufay example the discant to the tenor (or for that matter any shape of the first half to its corresponding second half), the following characteristics can be pointed out:

1. the two shapes have a common kernel;

2. important parts of one shape are missing in the other;

3. rhythm, accent, position, and function of even the melodically similar parts are changed;

4. in spite of these differences, the common kernel still sounds at original pitch.

Point by point these are the very features which in the Mozart example characterize the transformation of the Allegro theme into the Finale theme.

There is still another consideration of interest. Glancing at the harmonic picture in the Dufay example, we see that most of its harmonies consist of chords of the sixth, or chords of the fifth plus octave $\binom{8}{5}$, all enlivened by occasional suspensions. Such shaping in a series of sixths, which developed from the technique of the faux-bourdon, was extensively applied in the polyphonic art music of this period. Therefore to modern observers, who are perhaps less "thematically" minded, this piece of Dufay's might easily appear as a compositional utterance wherein merely "a melodic discant is accompanied by two lower voices," that is, a piece built upon the harmonic principle of the faux-bourdon. But by thus not realizing the *thematic* interconnections between the voices, and simply acknowledging that the composer managed to add impressively suitable chords to his melody, they would completely ignore Dufay's true intention and achievement; namely, the combining of harmonic and thematic ideas, or, in other words, producing a faux-bourdon *by means of a thematic counterpoint.* Perhaps even in Dufay's time many looked at this music from such a purely "harmonic," non-thematic point of view, though they would have used a different terminology to express themselves.

Today, too, there is a tendency to conceive large parts both of classic and of modern music in this superficial way, as "harmonized melodies." The example from Dufay's work, however, shows clearly that if so viewed, the whole range of expression emanating from the thematic content escapes comprehension.

The Gregorian melody used by Dufay is, by the way, one of the most frequently recurring and oldest melodic types of the chant. It is revealing to study the different forms which this melody assumes in the **Gregorian psalmody.** Peter Wagner (again in an example from Adler's *Musikgeschichte,* page 109) quotes the following forms, the first *(a)* representing a choir version from the ordinary Officium, the second *(b)* a choir version from the Mass, and the third *(c)* a version from the solo-psalmody: [3]

Ex. 384

---

[3] The sustained notes in the example are the so-called "recitative-tones," on which the psalm-recitative is centered.

No comment is necessary. This is like a textbook example of thematic varying. Carried over from the first centuries of Christianity, these shapes clearly exemplify the roots of compositional formation as growing from an impulse *to enrich and finally to change a given musical thought*. The history of music is in one of its most essential respects a huge elaboration of this principal impulse.

However, as for Dufay and the music of the contrapuntal period in general, since the whole origin and theory of the cantus firmus confirms it so strongly, the basic thematic identity between such seemingly different shapes is generally accepted as a fact. Historians outdo each other in praising the exquisite manner in which these composers managed to have their melodies reemerge in numerous varied appearances and disguises. Then should we not trust that what Dunstable, Dufay, or Okeghem achieved, Mozart, Beethoven, and Brahms were equally capable of accomplishing? But here, as theory has not prepared us otherwise, we are often inclined to regard these thematic identities, if we notice them at all, as incidental. Yet comparison with older music proves conclusively that to demonstrate these identities between seemingly unrelated shapes in the music of the classic or romantic era is not to reveal some mysterious, incredible phenomena outside any authorized grooves of musical thinking. On the contrary, in the light of historical evolution these affinities must appear as perfectly organic, legitimate components of musical formation.

A century after Dufay, **Palestrina** wrote his great works. It should prove interesting to investigate whether the structural ideas pointed out in the foregoing are still at work in his time and style, or whether these ideas have changed and perhaps advanced toward actual transformation. As an example we may choose the Palestrina Mass *Iste confessor,* the name of which is taken over from the Gregorian hymn on which the work is based. The version of the hymn tune which seems to have served as Palestrina's model reads:

Ex. 385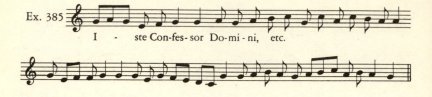

I - ste Con-fes-sor Do-mi-ni, etc.

The opening phrase of this tune forms the beginning of all the parts of the Mass, such as Kyrie, Gloria, Credo, and so forth, with the exception of the short Hosanna, which is an elaboration on the hymn's concluding phrase. A glance at the opening of the Kyrie for instance (example 386a), shows that "varying" is no longer the only and main structural force, though it still plays an important part, but that we are now in the heart of "contrapuntal imitation." In fact, in the shaping of the Kyrie simple imitation is increased to "imitation in pairs," as the two upper voices (as a unit) are imitated by the two lower ones, a feature which, already in use before Palestrina, was gradually developed to one of the strongest effects in choral writing.

The following parts of the Mass display a collection of almost all possible contrapuntal combinations of the figure used in the opening of the Kyrie. For instance, in the beginning of the Gloria (example 386b) this thematic figure appears in jubilant chordal unison. In the Credo (example 386c) the contrapuntal idea of the Kyrie is reversed: the melodic lines remain, but the superius ("soprano") is now the opening voice and the alto enters after it.

Ex. 386

Similar yet always different contrapuntal variants open all the other pieces.

Returning to the opening movement, the Kyrie is, as customary, divided into three sections, Kyrie eleison, Christe eleison, and again Kyrie. The beginnings of these three sections read as follows:

Ex. 387

and we see that linked together these three sectional beginnings produce the Gregorian hymn, or at least its first half (see example 385).

However, not the beginnings alone are derived from the hymn. To understand the elaborate complexity in which this music is formed, we must realize that every "bar" in every voice of the Mass is either a direct repetition, an inversion, a reversion, or a varied version of a hymn part. Yet what a firm unified architectural whole we see emerging from the "accumulation of motivic particles."

If such subtle motivic integration is, at least for this old music, a generally acknowledged fact, there are still other, perhaps even more impressive, thematic ideas hidden in the web of this exquisite work that seem much less noticed and to which none of the numerous commentaries points. For in some particularly emphatic movements of the Mass, as in the Gloria or in the Credo, not only motivic parts but the continuous line of the full hymn tune sounds through. To demonstrate this striking feature the entire opening section of the Gloria is quoted in the following:

Ex. 388

How can the hymn tune be here deciphered? True, parts of it shine out strikingly, yet the full course of the melody hardly seems present. However, linking different parts of the soprano and tenor, the following line is easily unraveled:

Ex. 389

* This one note, G, is taken from the bass, while the tenor has a rest.

This is indeed the complete uninterrupted hymn (example 385) at its true pitch. (Follow this course also in example 388.) Only the last few notes swerve to a different final (tonic)—a very usual procedure during this whole period, when a gradual shift from the conception of Church modes to that of modern tonality was already in the making.

From a structural angle, the most impressive fact in this remarkable shaping is that the hymn did not emerge from a random crossing of voices, but the parts of the soprano and tenor were linked into one line *by regular, systematic alternation.* A strong and intentional architectural effect, indeed, a divination of the future phenomenon of transformation speaks from this structure. It is the same impulse that led Beethoven and other composers to produce their startling contours, these "hidden" reappearances of one shape in a later theme of the same work; to produce them, moreover, at original pitch and in a new design and key, thus assuming quite a new harmonic function.

In all the music of the period quoted in this chapter, a further point of interest to our subject becomes visible. It is the principle, to which reference was made on several occasions in the course of our analysis, that the accidentals pertaining to a melodic line are frequently changed in a later reintroduction of the same shape. Though our general knowledge of the practical application of accidentals in old music is still incomplete, we notice that in the performance of both the Dufay and Palestrina examples some accidentals must have been used, of which we can say that they did not appear, and could not have appeared, in the Gregorian model. That throughout the contrapuntal period some laws regulating the use of accidentals have been practiced is certain. In this sense accidentals were not essentials but indeed "accidentals" if not of the design, then at least of the notation (*musica ficta*). An ingenious compositional experiment of the great fifteenth century composer Jean Okeghem demonstrates the idea here involved very lucidly. Okeghem's *Missa cujusvis toni* presents the noteworthy case of a composition that, by changing the accidentals, can be sung in any of the four authentic Church modes, which means, with ever changed accidentals, according to each specific mode.

In all these effects characteristic symptoms of the later technique of transformation become apparent. If in the course of our analysis, "thematic identities" (in works of Beethoven and others) were demonstrated whereby the melodic structure often seemed entirely changed due to the addition or omission of accidentals, it must be realized that here too not an arbitrary conception of the analyst is presented but an age-old way of structural thinking manifested.

Advancing from Palestrina to **Bach,** we find ourselves in the midst of a world of structural ideas which, viewed from the past, seem but a renewed and intensified expression of the thematic mechanism shown in the examples from Dufay and Palestrina; yet seen in the light of the following development, these ideas at the same time appear as the beginning of the very structural impulse from which the works of our great classical and even romantic composers are formed.

To demonstrate this, we turn to one of the most magnificent creations in musical literature, Bach's High Mass, known as the B-minor.[4]

_____

[4] The universally accepted title of B-minor Mass is not a fortunate one. Bach himself called his work simply Missa. The Mass begins in B-minor

In its tremendous compass this work displays an almost unimaginable wealth of diverse forms and characters which are, nevertheless, *all bound together by one basic thematic root.*

The work opens with an Adagio group of four bars. Though these bars form the opening group of the first "movement" of the Mass, the Kyrie, they are at the same time somewhat separated from the Kyrie's course, which actually begins only after them. For had this introductory group really been meant as an integral part of the Kyrie's architecture, then, in one form or another, it would have to reemerge in the Kyrie—which it does not. In the way it appears in the work, this cosmic cry for divine mercy has two architectural functions: it represents an introduction to the Kyrie as well as a solemn programmatic and structural motto to the whole of the Mass:

Ex. 390

but concludes in D-major. Moreover, the whole harmonic scheme proves that this conclusion in D-major was a well prepared, intentional concept. The keys of the last eight pieces of the Mass read: D-major, A-major, F-sharp minor (with a second part in D-major), D-major, D-major, B-minor, G-minor, D-major.

The main contour of the soprano is obviously a line stretching from D over E and F-sharp to G, then returning, in contrary motion, over F-sharp and E to the initial D, before it concludes on F-sharp in a finishing clause. In brief extract the melodic core of this shape can therefore be described as a rising plus a falling fourth (D to G and back to D), which we may call *motif I*.

However, in the last bar the first violins take the lead and sound above the choir in a passage of sixteenth notes. Thus the original rise to G (the fourth) is enlarged through a further rise to B (a sixth), which we may call *motif Ia*. In this sense the full contour of the introductory group should read as quoted in example 391*a*. This melodic basis is enriched by an additional figure, heard by connecting some lower voices to the soprano. We may call this new figure *motif II*. It appears, as seen in the following example, in several versions, most of which, though not all, are characterized by a diminished fifth. By including this motif II, the actual melody of the opening bars assumes the form shown in example 391*b*.

Ex. 391

The other voices of the introductory group are built and combined from the three motifs just described (I, I*a*, and II). For instance, the bass in its first half forms a rising fourth (B to E) and in its second half a falling fourth (B to F-sharp), while the interval separating the two halves is a diminished fifth, thus indicating motif II, reminiscent of bar 1 even in pitch.

No. 1. Kyrie eleison

Since in a narrower sense the opening group is the introduction of the first piece of the Mass, the Kyrie proper, the theme of this Kyrie is a very close reflection of the melodic line expressed in the Introduction.

All the themes of the Mass are quoted in example 392. The Kyrie theme is given as No. 1 in example 392.

No. 7 Domine Deus

No. 7a

Soprano

Do - mi - ne   Fi - li

Tenor

Do - mi - ne De - - us

No. 8 Qui tollis

Qui tol - lis pec - ca - ta mun - di

No. 9 Qui sedes

Qui se - - - - - - des ad -

No. 10 Quoniam

Corno da caccia

Bassoon   *tr*

etc.

No. 11 Cum Sancto Spiritu

Cum Sanc - to Spi - ri - tu in glo - ri - a De - i

No. 15 Et incarnatus est

No. 17 Et resurrexit

Et re-sur-rex - it,

Orchestra

No. 18 Et in Spiritum Sanctum

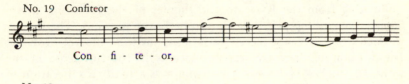

Bass Et in Spi - ri - tum Sanc - tum

No. 19 Confiteor

Con - fi - te - or,

No. 19a

Alto   Tenor

Ex - pec - - to re - sur-rec-ti - o -

No. 20 Sanctus

Sanc - tus, Sanc - - - tus,

No. 21 Hosanna

Ho - san - - - na,

No. 22 Benedictus

Be - ne - dic - tus, be - - ne - dic -

No. 23 Agnus Dei

The melody that was heard in the Introduction by connecting voices has in the Kyrie proper become a continuous line forming the theme of the fugue into which the Kyrie develops. This Kyrie theme, rising from B over C-sharp and D-sharp to E, is a transposition of the introductory line, which rises from D over E and F-sharp to G. Yet we see here a powerful example of the phenomenon of identical pitch. For the second half of the Kyrie theme, reaching its culmination on G, the sixth, and followed by a finishing clause on F-sharp, thus becomes identical even in pitch with the second half of the Introduction (compare the soprano in example 390), though there these same notes represented only a rise to the fourth. In other words, although actually a transposition, the Kyrie theme sounds in its decisive part as a reiteration of the Introduction at original pitch.

Turning from the Kyrie to the themes of the following movements, one guiding principle should be borne in mind. The themes of Bach's Mass are not mere "variations," as were the voices in the Dufay example; they are transformations in the full sense of the word. In Dufay's "Salva nos" the tenor was actually a reiteration of the discant, though a distinctly changed one, with some phrases added, others omitted. But in the Bach Mass any new theme, though developed from the old idea, is an entirely new musical thought. Only a common contour is identical, and it, moreover, often sounds merely from a part of the new theme. However, at this stage of our analysis the difference between themes built from common material may sometimes be of even more interest than their similarity. And we consider it as one of the composer's most admirable structural achievements that he managed to link these themes of the twenty-four pieces of the Mass not merely into architectural unity, but that he was able to produce from this unity such a variety of completely different shapes.

No. 2. Christe eleison

The Christe eleison is a vocal duet accompanied by strings. The movement opens with a theme in the violins (No. 2 in example 392). We see that this shape, though as a whole a totally new utterance, is nevertheless framed by a figure that expresses the contour of the work's opening group: motif I at original pitch (beginning with D and ending with G, F-sharp, E, D). In fact, several times is the ascent to, and the descent from, the G indicated. Upon examining the content within the "frame," we discover that it consists of phrases molded in the shape of motif II.

However, the example shows only one of the thematic groups of the Christe eleison, namely, that of its orchestral introduction. And when the vocal part enters, another theme is heard. This vocal theme, too, features familiar motifs. This may be demonstrated most impressively by comparing the theme (*a* in the following example) with a group from the preceding Kyrie (*b*). Only the voices necessary to show the affinity are quoted:

Ex. 393

Thus the idea according to which the composer formed the Christe is clear: he invented two new themes, one orchestral and one vocal. (In the course of the work they are joined contrapuntally.) Of these two themes, the orchestral theme is embedded in the initial thought, while the forming of the vocal theme must have been directed by a recollection of some shapes from the first piece.

No. 3. Kyrie eleison (second Kyrie)

The theme of the second Kyrie is given as No. 3 in example 392.

This shape needs no comment; it is a clear replica of the original idea in its rise to, and fall from, the fourth. In addition, when in the fugal development the next voice, the tenor, enters (beginning with C-sharp, D), the "increased" rise, the rise to the sixth, also becomes audible.

Of course, the second Kyrie theme is a transposed version of the initial thought. Nevertheless, the original pitch also comes into its own, even in this piece in F-sharp (example 392, No. 3a). As indicated by the braces, the initial thought is here heard in two utterances, which appear side by side: first at the pitch of the Introduction and then at that of the (first) Kyrie proper.

No. 4. Gloria in excelsis

The Gloria reiterates the thematic type of the Christe. This is a significant feature. For the work's architectural logic is greatly strengthened by the fact that, in addition to being built on a common thematic basis, there are also some specific thematic categories that constantly recur.

No. 4 in example 392 gives the theme of the Gloria as it first enters in the alto, developing motif I*a*, the sixth, whereupon the bass enters, expressing motif I, the fourth. Both are heard at original pitch.

No. 5. Laudamus Te

The Laudamus introduces a new type (No. 5 in example 392).

If we ignore the first and last notes of this shape, which are partly necessitated by the text, this theme features in its first half the rise to the fourth. (The contour is emphasized through the charming trills—notice that the E in the following bar does not bear a trill.) In its second half, it features the descent from the fourth. The rise is transposed to the key of the movement; the descent, however, sounds, even in the new key, at original pitch.

No. 6. Gratias agimus

The Gratias is architectonically one of the most significant parts, as its theme represents the simplest, the most concise expression of the original thought. The contour has now become the theme itself (example 392, No. 6).

No. 7. Domine Deus

Here the theme (example 392, No. 7) appears as a shape in which the first half of the original thought, the rise, is cut off so that only the descent remains. But the bass features the full thought with an interwoven indication of motif II. The abrupt, emphatic entrance at the high point is heard three times within the three opening bars of the orchestral introduction. And when the solo voices enter, it is of particular effect that the tenor also starts with the high G. Then by including the B of the soprano, motif I*a,* the sixth, becomes audible in addition, by a combination of the tenor and soprano, as demonstrated through No. 7*a* in example 392.

No. 8. Qui tollis

The theme is quoted as example 392, No. 8.

The integration of the initial thought at original pitch is transparent. In the curve from the F-sharp down to the B and up to the G, motif II also seems indicated. Of course, this theme deviates strongly in character from the previous ones. Nevertheless, are not the nature and degree of this deviation quite similar to the manner in which, in earlier periods, a figural discant differed from the original chant?

No. 9. Qui sedes

Here still another entirely new figuration appears (example 392, No. 9).

The pitch of motif I (see notes in bold print) is that of the first Kyrie, while motif II is again interwoven.

No. 10. Quoniam Tu

In this theme (example 392, No. 10) the prime thought, again at original pitch (fourth and sixth together), sounds from the bassoons, to which the corno di caccia provides an effective discant. This discant, by the way, is a kind of augmentation of the theme of the preceding piece. (Compare the phrases in braces with the theme in Qui sedes.)

No. 11. Cum Sancto Spiritu

This movement is one of the most extensive and most emphatic of the Mass. Accordingly, the outline of the prime thought assumes huge proportions (example 392, No. 11).

The giant thematic arc in the choir, from D to E to F-sharp to G and back, while the orchestra sounds the same idea in shorter groups formed by different instruments, is of tremendous effect. Anyone who has a feeling for choral and orchestral writing must shiver under the impact of these sustained fortissimo notes from the choir, which release the work's ever recurring prime thought at original pitch, while the orchestra continues its course of whirling and blaring winds.

No. 12. Credo in unum Deum

After the most ecstatic comes the most solemn of the work's utterances. As Bach took the traditional Church melody for the theme of his Credo (example 392, No. 12) it might at first seem that here, for once, he relinquished the idea of having his initial thought integrated in the theme of this movement [5] and that he contented himself with letting it sound from some secondary shapes, for instance, from the variant into which the theme develops in the alto (example 392, No. 12a).

However, the prime thought does appear in a most emphatic expression in the Credo also. When the Credo-fugue concludes, its theme is heard in augmentation. And in this powerful augmentation of the liturgic melody, Bach manages to integrate the prime thought of his own Mass, at first transposed and finally with a part of it even at original pitch (see example 392, No. 12b).

No. 13. Patrem omnipotentem

The theme enters in the bass (example 392, No. 13). If one doubts the integration of the initial shape in this voice, he may look at the tenor, which takes it over in a more transparent variant, returning to original pitch (example 392, No. 13a).

---

[5] As for the fact, and its implications for our subject, that the Credo was the first part of the Mass to be written, compare the footnote on page 274.

No. 14. Et in unum Dominum

A duet for soprano and alto. We quote the theme (example 392, No. 14) from the alto, as there the prime thought appears at original pitch, rising first to the fourth, then through transpositions of its own shape to the sixth. The small phrase marked by braces is a characteristic particle that was first indicated in the theme of the Christe eleison and by being subsequently several times repeated, itself became a motif. We will encounter it as a motivic figure in some of the following movements.

No. 15. Et incarnatus est

Every piece brings new images within which the old thought reemerges (example 392, No. 15). The basic shape sounds from the upper voice of these chords as from gentle bells. Figures recalling motif II are inserted.

No. 16. Crucifixus

The Crucifixus is centered on a basso ostinato, consisting of a group of four bars which express a falling fourth (example 392, No. 16). Continuously repeated, from the beginning to the end of the movement, these bars form an impressively mournful base to the idea of the Crucifixus.

Over the orchestral accompaniment the chorus enters. This choral design, though a contrapuntally elaborate setting, seems at first to bear little resemblance to any familiar thematic shape. In fact, these echoing whispers appear too fragmentary to represent a theme. However, by linking these choral fragments together, it becomes apparent that they form a new pattern of the old thematic idea. The rise to the fourth and sixth (motifs I and Ia), and also motif II, then sound through. To make this transparent, only the octaves have to be changed, as demonstrated in example 392, No. 16a. This is certainly an illustration of exquisite transformation. And that the composer must have meant it this way is proved by the fact that, after the group has been repeated, the same initial thought which was first effected by joining voices is now heard sounding from a single voice (as for instance from the soprano, in example 392, No. 16b).

No. 17. Et resurrexit

The theme is quoted as example 392, No. 17. The initial thought at original pitch (motif I) clearly forms the content of the soprano, which is merely framed by the two A's. The violins intensify the idea by a simultaneous rise to the sixth (motif I*a*).

No. 18. Et in Spiritum Sanctum

Though carried up to the E, which is only an unaccented, though melodically important, passing note between the two D's, the initial idea appears transparently integrated here too (example 392, No. 18).

No. 19. Confiteor

Again the contour of the theme is formed by a rise to the fourth and the sixth (example 392, No. 19). Though the last bars seem an octave too low (as necessitated by vocal limitations), the justification for the above interpretation is furnished by Bach himself. For when, in the five-voice fugue of this Confiteor, the bass enters, the theme is repeated literally, but with the last part now climbing to its natural position in the higher register.

The Confiteor is the most extended movement of the Mass. Its second section, rejoicing in the thought of the Resurrection of the Dead—therefore, like the Et resurrexit, of the same jubilant character as the Gloria—returns quite logically to the old thematic utterance at original pitch (example 392, No. 19*a*).

No. 20. Sanctus

See No. 20 in the example, to which no additional comment is necessary.

No. 21. Hosanna

The Hosanna is for two choruses and is similar in type to the Gloria. After an introductory choral fanfare, followed by a few orchestral bars, the choruses enter with the thematic utterance. The tenor of the first choir heralds the prime thought at original pitch (example 392, No. 21).

No. 22. Benedictus

How charmingly the initial thought is here entwined!

No. 23. Agnus Dei

The original thought again frames this beautiful theme, while versions of motif II form its melodic substance.

No. 24. Dona nobis pacem

With this movement we have reached the work's conclusion. Dona nobis pacem is a literal repetition of the Gratias agimus (No. 6), with a changed text. We remember the theme of the Gratias, which we called the simplest and most concise expression of the thematic thought, "the work's contour having become the theme itself." As Bach closes his gigantic creation with this supplication for peace, choosing the same music which he first used as a solemn manifestation of thanks, the inference in a structural and programmatic sense cannot be mistaken.

It should be stressed that the foregoing description was by no means intended as an analysis or even an outline of the work's structural and dramatic content (not to mention the metaphysical symbolism which may be integrated in this creation and by which even its architecture may to some extent have been influenced). Our sketch points out only a few characteristic thematic elements, and its main purpose was to show how the technique of thematic varying, which, with imitation, for centuries has been the foremost agent of structural formation, was now changed and intensified into real transformation. This process of change and intensification can actually be seen at work in the beginnings of Bach's High Mass. Among the work's twenty-four movements we find a few that indeed simply reiterate in slightly varied form the thought of the Introduction. In others the ornamentation, embellishment, and variation are so much increased that the resemblance to the original idea is less obvious, though it is still unmistakable. But in a third group the differentiation, the "contourization" has reached such a degree that on the surface the affinity is difficult to trace, and a deeper analytic examination, based on an understanding of the whole technique of transformation, is necessary to unravel it.[6]

---

[6] Readers familiar with historical data concerning the Mass may have wondered how to reconcile certain facts with the basic idea advanced in this analytic sketch. Bach's High Mass was, as we know, written over a period of years. The Credo was supposedly the first to be finished, followed by the Kyrie and the Gloria. But, what is more, several of its movements were "borrowed" from Bach's earlier compositions, mostly from his cantatas. This is obviously the reason that in all current commentaries the work is described more or less as a collection of diverse "numbers," without any unity binding the whole work together. Apparently, the critics knowing the historical facts refuted even the possibility that a composition of which some parts were originally meant to build another work could yield architectural unity.

Yet examining the "borrowings" and how they were effectuated, they not only do not contradict our conception, but indeed form one of its most brilliant confirmations. With irresistible clarity they show that Bach simply could not imagine any theme for his Mass from which the work's basic shape did not resound in one form or another; in fact, we are here once more at one of our "mathematical" proofs of the consciousness of this endeavor.

There is, for instance, Patrem omnipotentem, No. 13 of the Mass. Its theme is borrowed from the opening chorus of the cantata *Gott wie Dein Name*. The cantata's theme is quoted in the following example as *a*. This shape does not reflect in any sense the thematic prime thought of the Mass. Bach, however, did not simply "borrow" the cantata's theme. For the "loan," when it appears in the Mass, reads in the form given below as *b:*

Ex. 394

But through this slight change, inconspicuous as it is, the theme has become an entirely new musical idea, which in its rise from D to G and back, *expresses exactly the main thematic shape of the Mass*. And although the outer course of the cantata is strikingly maintained throughout the Patrem omnipotentem, often even to the minutest detail of its polyphonic web, the change of the basic thematic shape is also carried out thoroughly and intensely throughout the whole piece, so that the Patrem omnipotentem finally becomes a completely new musical work. Once again, with

Thus an intriguing question arises: In what, if at all, does this state differ from that of full transformation, described as the principal structural phenomenon of the classic, the "thematic" period, centered on Haydn, Mozart, Beethoven, and their successors?

---

almost irrefutable conclusiveness, a proof is given of the reality and consciousness with which the thematic principle is applied by the great composers.

Bach sometimes achieves a result similar to that in the last example by a mere transposition.

In the following the theme of Cantata 46 is quoted as *a*. But in the Mass it appears as given in *b*:

Ex. 395

Again through this simple but ingenious procedure suddenly the initial thought of the Mass at original pitch is heard from this borrowed design.

These or similar methods of assimilation are to be seen in all parallel cases. A shape is "borrowed" or inserted only if either the shape itself bears a resemblance to the basic thematic contour of the work—as for instance the liturgic melody of the Confiteor:

Ex. 396

—or if Bach thought it possible to adjust and transform the shape to become an organic part of the architectural whole. No composer with an inherent thematic sense can react in any other way.

The implications of this are not always understood. Even Beethoven's Ninth Symphony, that pinnacle of structural consistency and perfection, was not safe from the absurd insinuation that its architecture is not truly organic, because it was built from material originally meant for two or even three different works. Such intimations are pure nonsense. For a composition's architectural content, its strength or weakness can be judged only by what is expressed in its own final score. A genuine composer always manages to make his score a manifestation of oneness, no matter from where he may have secured the original material.

The answer is that it differs not so much in nature as in its *architectural function*.

Bach used this technique of transformation only to create the necessary unity between the *beginnings* of his twenty-four movements. But *within* each single piece of the Mass the old devices of imitation and variation are still the only structural forces at work. The great innovation brought about in the classic, the thematic period, is that transformation became a structural agent within one piece, within one movement.

This is a tremendous fact in an evolutionary sense. As a result, music was set on a new path. For the idea of a large musical unit was inconceivable before this.

Naturally, there were large, even gigantic forms in the old style, such as Masses. Yet they were but accumulations of many pieces, even though they were held together by affinity of material. But musical entities of the size and range of a symphonic allegro by Beethoven, Brahms, or Tchaikovsky were unknown in those earlier days. The change took place when Haydn and Mozart filled the new architectural patterns which had sprung up in the works of some Italian and German ("Mannheim") composers with the polyphonic profundity that was the great heritage of Bach and his predecessors.

This heritage, however, was not presented to them on a silver platter. True, it is confirmed that Haydn, Mozart, and Beethoven knew some of Bach's music. But Bach was at that time almost a forgotten man; in fact, most of his best works, for instance, the High Mass itself, had remained until then next to unknown. Thus Haydn and Mozart had to discover anew these wonders of thematic variation and permeation: they had to recreate them for themselves.

Haydn intimates in a letter to Prince Öttingen-Wallerstein in 1781, introducing his new string quartets (known as the Russian quartets from their dedication to Prince Paul of Russia) that he has entered upon a new phase in his compositional activity. After having refrained for ten years from composing quartets, he says that he wrote these works "in quite a new, particular manner" (*auf eine ganz neue, besondere Art*). There is no doubt that he was referring to the thematic and contrapuntal intensification of his style. The liking and capacity for contrapuntal writing had at this time greatly diminished; in fact, any attempt to introduce in the lower voices figurate ornaments that echoed the upper voice contrapuntally was then (only a few decades after Bach's death!) regarded as unforgivably old-fashioned, except perhaps for some sections in a sonata's development or the like. Haydn, as we said, reconquered this polyphonic spirit for his own music, using it in his own way. From his immediate predecessors, the above-mentioned Italian, "Mannheim," and earlier Viennese composers, he had taken over the outer patterns for his quartets and symphonies—patterns which his genius had enriched and endowed with that crystalline strength and splendor that made them the architectural models for the whole following period. He filled these patterns with thematic and contrapuntal depth, with this "new, particular manner" of structural formation.

Whether he was also the first to introduce, or rather to reintroduce, in a new, definitive form, the idea of *thematic transformation,* the crowning phenomenon in the thematic technique, is difficult to decide.

One thing should be remembered. A great part of Haydn's more important works, in fact, most of what today we consider his real creative achievement, in which his new technique was actually unfolded, originated in the last two decades of his life, that is, at a time when Mozart had already died and Beethoven was well on his way to developing his own style. Influenced by the fact that Haydn was in years the eldest, and that Beethoven happened to have had some lessons from him, we are often inclined to accept Haydn as the "father" in all respects. There is no doubt that both Mozart and Beethoven learned much from Haydn, but it is no less true that Haydn learned much from Mozart and Beethoven.

Be this as it may, in the works of Mozart, Beethoven, and even in the last works of Haydn we see the all-decisive phenomenon of thematic transformation in full bloom. It is indeed the decisive phenomenon, as in it is incorporated the very principle from which grew the structural message of the ensuing epoch. When Bach's structural idea of developing an abundant variety of beginnings from one basic thought was applied as a forming principle within one uninterrupted piece (a symphonic movement), and when this principle of "oneness in variety" was finally expanded to bind different movements together, then the door to a new era was opened. For the birth of the symphony is in the last analysis not to be dated from the appearance of its outer architectural pattern, not even from

the inclusion of second themes into this pattern, but from the day
when, in a Haydn or Mozart symphony, types of formation like the
following one came to life. The first Allegro theme and the first
Finale theme from Haydn's Symphony in E-flat (1789) are given
below:

Ex. 397

Two themes sound here, different in melody, rhythm, tempo, and
appeal—different in every way. But transpose the Finale theme a
third up, place the two themes in juxtaposition, and a miracle comes
to pass:

Ex. 398

A structural spirit that found its primeval expression in the
Gregorian chant; that evolved to richer and subtler application in
the works of Dunstable, Dufay, Okeghem, Josquin, and Palestrina;
that was further intensified in the almost mystic differentiation

among the twenty-four themes of Bach's Mass, now comes to fulfillment in a technique which is both natural and complex, and as
simple as it is profound. The ground was laid for the magnificent
edifices of the modern symphony and the modern music drama—
architectural constructions of a scope, the like of which the world
had never known before.

To understand the impact of this revolution, we must reconsider
its sober technical aspects. For the technique of thematic transformation was applied not merely in forming the themes of the different
movements or the first and second themes of one movement. In the
fully developed phase of this technique, every group, every "bridge"
or transitory passage, indeed, every voice becomes a separate, a new
musical utterance based on a kernel identical to, or derived from,
the initial thought. Had transformation not become an inherent
part of musical thinking, no symphony by Mozart, Beethoven, or
Brahms, no song by Schubert or Schumann, no opera by Verdi or
Wagner could have come to life in its present form.

In the music of Beethoven this principle was brought to its utmost
concentration and widest expansion. In the next chapter we shall
see the part it played after Beethoven and to what degree it is discernible in the musical evolution up to our time.

11

BLOOM AND DISSOLUTION
OF THE THEMATIC PRINCIPLE

The musical development from Haydn on, until the latter part of the nineteenth century, is, in historical presentation, usually described as the classic-romantic movement, the actual classical period comprising mainly Haydn, Mozart, Beethoven, and perhaps Schubert; the romantic period includes the whole gallery of notable composers following them. As in all historical classification it is difficult, though perhaps unimportant, to set up clear boundaries and to define the exact content of these terms. Thus the last part of this development, until almost the turn of the century, is not regarded as belonging to the romantic era proper but, lacking a specific term, is usually called the postromantic period; while another (though also not distinctly demarcated) evolution, preceding the actual classics, is often termed the preclassical period.

One quality that, in addition to other traits, characterizes and distinguishes this whole epoch is its particularly expressive, personal way of melodic shaping. And within this whole, the romantic period shows an intensification of the same trend; to this we shall return later. But taken in its entirety and viewed from a wider aspect, we must realize that with regard to melodic expression there is a fundamental difference between all music, roughly speaking, before Bach and after him.

Such personal, expressive melody, which to us is almost synonymous with music itself, is an invention of the most recent centuries, unknown in previous times. In the contrapuntal age composing was centered more on what the composer produced from his melodies

280

than on the expressiveness or originality of the melodies themselves, which were often not even invented by the composer but were taken from a wide inheritance of essentially religious music. Even the melodic lines that the composer invented and, in general, the melodies of secular and even popular musical production, which were certainly less strict and less bound to "objective" patterns than were the orthodox Church melodies, are still far from the freedom, color, and individual sensitiveness of the melodies of Mozart or Beethoven, let alone those of Schumann, Chopin, or Tchaikovsky.

This is, of course, a summary presentation. There were of old, repeatedly, periods which showed a strong trend toward "personalized" melodic shaping. They appeared, for instance as early as the fourteenth century, with the forerunners of the madrigal and related forms in Italy and France and, in general, whenever art music was inspired by folk music. Nevertheless, viewed as a whole, the distinction made above, though no clear demarcation in time can be set up, stands as a fact.

An important characteristic through which this classic-romantic melody of the last centuries is distinguished from that of the older periods is the rhythmical elaboration and rhythmical differentiation of its shapes. In the contrapuntal era rhythm, accent, and even tempo were, so to speak, not essentials but almost rather attributes of a melody. It is for this reason that the whole technique of the cantus firmus could be developed to such a tremendous extent. For it seemed quite natural to use a Gregorian shape as a basis for a new composition, though in this process its rhythmical delineation often had to be entirely changed. But if on a melody of Beethoven, Schubert, or Chopin only comparatively slight rhythmical changes are imposed, it becomes a completely different musical utterance.

However, it is through this very fact that the phenomenon of transformation became possible or, at least, developed to such an important part of musical forming. For a "contrapuntal" shape that is altered rhythmically remains easily recognizable as a variant of the original, wherefore we called such change "varying." But a melody of the classic-romantic type, even through a minor alteration of accent, often changes its whole character and becomes an entirely new musical being; it is transformed.

Of course in this respect rhythm is not the only element but merely a very characteristic one. What has been said with regard to rhythmical alteration likewise holds true with regard to other changes. The melodic shapes of the classic-romantic period are so clearly characterized that the slightest change in the harmonic meaning, a shift in tempo, an omission, interpolation or variation of particles, immediately creates a new musical utterance, a transformation.

To sum up: personal melody, with its distinctive rhythmical, harmonic, and other individual meanings in each instance, now emerged in music and became a powerful factor in composition. And together with this change, and through it, another no less important development took place: the technique of thematic transformation became the foremost structural agent. As described in the foregoing chapter, it was the extraordinary achievement of the great classical composers to unite these two forces; namely, the new personal melody and a technique of forming (that is, the technique of transformation), equal in structural strength to the highest examples of the past and even surpassing them in its greater freedom, wider range, and form-building power.

And here we come to the point to which at present we wish particularly to direct attention. It is the fact that the process just described did not come to an end with the classics *but was continued, and in a certain sense even amplified, in the following romantic period.* This fact must above all become clear to us if we wish to obtain a real understanding of the musical evolution of the last century. It was an evolution of almost unimaginable range in its overwhelming richness, splendor, and variety; yet it was also somewhat problematic in the exaggeration, ambiguity, and dissolution of its expressive power.

Historical evaluation is of late inclined to overemphasize the negative side of the picture. This, however, leads to a misconception of a most important period in musical history, and we may endeavor, in the following, to clarify this matter.

As indicated, in the long period before the advent of the musical spirit of which the classics became the crowning embodiment, it was structure rather than melodic expression that constituted the foremost creative factor in music. Whenever in preclassical times the melodic element tried to establish itself as a sovereign force, this was, significantly enough, accompanied by an often brusque departure from the structural concept in music—a departure that sometimes led to an almost complete, if temporary, abandonment of the polyphonic idea itself. Not until in the classical evolution, when the old contrapuntal technique of imitation and variation was complemented and enriched through thematic transformation, did music succeed in bringing an intense melodic impulse into complete unity with the age-old standards of structure and polyphony.

It is this unification, this blending of the two elemental musical phenomena, melody and structure, that was the decisive force from which arose the fascinating evolution which we call the classic-romantic period. In the music of the early classics, and especially of Beethoven, a balance and synthesis of unimaginable perfection was reached between these two forces. But in the period after Beethoven a slight preponderance of melodic emphasis and dramatization gradually made itself felt. Once more the eternal play of action and reaction was at work. Since for long periods structure and form had been, perhaps too exclusively, the main objects of compositional endeavor, now the interest was, often somewhat violently, shifted toward melody, color, and the expression of personal emotion. Thus there grew a tendency to judge the strength of a composition by its melody and flavor rather than by its structural shaping. To "understand" music frequently meant to translate it into poetic symbolism, almost with a reluctance to touch technical ground. The consequences of this whole trend were enormous, and we are not yet fully aware how decisively it changed our entire musical outlook. Indeed, its influence is felt up to the present time. Many people, even today, when thinking of a Beethoven, Schumann, or Tchaikovsky symphony, a Verdi or Wagner opera, recall mainly some characteristic melodies and orchestral effects, while the whole thematic and contrapuntal web of the work, through which alone these melodies become the very message which the composer wanted to convey, remains a vague, amorphous mass in their minds.

Now it must be understood that the advent of personal melody [1] does constitute a tremendous phenomenon in music history. A whole new world was thereby included in the palette of the composer. But the real significance of the inclusion lies in the fact that these new

---

[1] According to the explanations previously advanced, the term "melody" should be understood as comprising a melodic utterance in, and together with, its specific harmonic, rhythmical, and in every respect individual shaping.

melodic shapes, capable of expressing an almost infinite range of human experience, were uttered by means of a structural mechanism of timeless validity and enduring power.

Only on the basis of this realization can we fully understand the gigantic, indeed, the unique achievement not only of the classical period but also that of its romantic and postromantic aftermath.

With regard to this romantic and postromantic period, however, such an understanding is by no means general. Since our theoretical perception is not trained to a full comprehension of the technique of thematic transformation on which this period too is centered, our conception of the structural depth of these compositions is necessarily incomplete. Especially in comparison with the music of the contrapuntal age, into which we gained deeper insight during recent decades, historians and aestheticians are inclined to see in the music of the romantic era mainly the sensitiveness, beauty, and emotional strength that emanate from its characteristic melodic lines, often missing the elaborate structural complexity by which these lines are manifested and through which they are unified to artistic entities of the highest order. Indeed, from the structural point of view the works of the classics and their romantic and postromantic successors form one uninterrupted evolutional growth, one continuous embodiment of the thematic principle.

In the application of the principle, certain changes gradually become visible. For the further the "personalization" of the melodic lines progresses, the more numerous the shades of expression and mood the composer attempts to include in his work, the more difficult becomes the task of integrating his utterances into one thematic mechanism. *Thus in the music of the latter part of the nineteenth century, we see these two forces, thematic expansion and thematic unification, in a constant struggle.* Whether this conflict must be called a decline is open to discussion.

Also, it should not be forgotten that in the music of Bach, Mozart, or Beethoven almost every work is in a sense a fulfillment of their creative capacity and intention—a situation almost unique in musical history—while in the ensuing period the creative output of even the greatest composers shows valleys as well as peaks, and much that is in between. Certainly this is to a great extent due to the struggle and dilemma just described. Yet should we not judge a composer according to his highest achievements?

True, compared to the two or three classic giants, the romantic period meant a lessening. Both spiritually and structurally, the musical ethos of the classical age was somewhat weakened in the romantic period. Nevertheless, taken as a whole and according to its best achievements, this period, too, carried forward our great occidental heritage. The essence of the classical endeavor, to manifest personal musical expression in structural objectivity, was continued and even enriched in its scope, although the strictness of formulation may have been slackened. There is hardly one shade of human emotion which does not resound from these vibrating lines, which in spite of their kaleidoscopic diversity never entirely break loose from the structural whole in which they are unmistakably entrenched. In imaginative wealth and abundance this classic-romantic evolution is without parallel in history. How otherwise could this music have conquered the earth and remain victoriously alive today when even its latest enunciations are close to their centenary. That our contemporary music, fascinating in many of its aspects though it is, still struggles desperately for recognition is in no small measure due to the fact that it is inevitably locked in an unequal fight with music of a preceding period which is unique. At this music future ages will look, just as our world now looks at Renaissance art, Greek drama, and the Egyptian Pyramids.

The first part of this evolution, the specifically "classical" period culminating in Beethoven, has, with regard to the phases through which the thematic idea passed, already been described in considerable detail. In the following we will try to show some of the various forms and guises which the same idea assumed in the period after Beethoven and up to our own time.

Schumann in his analysis of Berlioz's *Symphonie fantastique*, after outlining the "form" of the work in the traditional way, continues: "Thus far, we have been concerned with the garment, but now we turn to the fabric from which it was woven—to the musical composition." And, significantly, he proceeds, over a quotation of some effective harmonic progressions, to the description of the work's thematic structure. In touching upon the thematic unity throughout the symphony's five movements, he follows Berlioz's own program guide as given in the preface with which the composer introduced the first performance of his work in Paris in 1830 (three years after Beethoven's death!). But it is noteworthy that Schumann does not seem to consider such unity between the movements as an exceptional case unexpected in a symphonic work. In like manner Schumann deals with the thematic homogeneity of the movements in another symphonic work of his time, Mendelssohn's A-minor Symphony. Here he says: "The melodic courses of the principal themes in the four different movements are akin; this will be detected even upon cursory comparison"—a wording which certainly implies that there must be many instances where such thematic identity exists, though it may not always be as easily detectable. Again, in a general discourse on contemporary composition, he deplores the lack of true understanding of the symphonic form in his time. "Frequently," he exclaims, "the slow movements are there only because they are not supposed to be missing; the scherzos are scherzos in name only; and *the last movements no longer know what the preceding ones contained.*"

What does all this reveal? It tells us that the idea of complete thematic unity in a symphonic work, as realized so admirably in Mozart's or Beethoven's symphonies, was still firmly alive in the minds of the great composers of Schumann's time. But it also tells us that such consciousness was not common knowledge among average musicians. Indeed, it seems as though a full awareness of the elaborate nature of the, so to speak, partly hidden thematic structure of the great masterworks had not spread beyond the limited circle of a few select musical minds.

Berlioz: *Symphonie fantastique*

Hector Berlioz, to be sure, was one of the initiate; and, returning to his *Symphonie fantastique,* we may try to unravel the deeper strata of its thematic design. Berlioz centers the "program" of his work on an artist's unbounded love for a beautiful woman, the vision of whom, as he says, always emerges in his mind in connection with, or symbolized by, a musical thought. "This is the reason," he continues, "why the melody with which the first Allegro opens, reappears in each movement of the symphony."

This opening group of the symphony's principal theme is given under *a* in example 399. And its reappearance in the following movements is easily traceable. It is sounded in the midst of the dancelike second movement, "The Ball" (*b*). A reminder of it returns toward the end of the third movement, "Country Scene" (*c*). At the close of the fourth movement, the "March to the Gallows," it reemerges, here again in its full shape, in the pianissimo of the clarinet (*d*). And in the Finale, the "Witches Sabbath," it reenters directly after the introductory bars. Here it is heard at original pitch, though rhythmically altered (*e*); through this alteration, as the composer stresses, the "noble melody has become a cheap, sensual dance tune," in accordance with the programmatic idea.

Ex. 399

These are the occurrences of the principal theme throughout the movements. But the point of real interest with regard to the structural idea of this symphonic work lies elsewhere.

In the *Symphonie fantastique* there are *two layers through which the thematic unity of the work is expressed*. The one, the outer layer, consists of this literal, or almost literal, reappearance of the principal theme at decisive moments, to which in his program Berlioz specifically draws attention. But beneath these obvious thematic reiterations there is a second structural layer, brought about through the thematic homogeneity of all the other themes in all the movements, indeed, of the work's whole material. This second, inner thematic unity is naturally not as conspicuous as the first, since the core of it is not repetition but transformation. Berlioz is very conscious of the two principles and makes a clear distinction between them. He indicates this distinction in the program, saying that in the symphony "the reflection of his idol and the idol itself endlessly haunt him like a *double idée fixe.*" In these words the twofold nature both of the work's programmatic and of its thematic content is admirably comprehended.

In the examples quoted hitherto, the first, the outer layer of the work's design was shown, namely, the literal recurrences of the symphony's prime thought. The composer sharply defines this thought in his program as "the melody which opens the first Allegro." Through this wording confusion is avoided with any transformation of the same theme that may emerge in the course of the work. But to these transformations our analysis must now turn, as they form the second, inner strata of thematic affinity connecting the symphony to one structural whole. As a point of departure we must again choose the opening of the Allegro, for naturally in this initial theme, in this programmatic *and* thematic *idée fixe,* both the inner and the outer architectural contents of the work converge as in a focal point.

This central shape, already quoted in example 399a, and which may henceforth be called *motif I,* forms of course only the opening of the Allegro's first theme, the full course of which may be sketched as follows:

Ex. 400

It is interesting to unravel the actual musical content of this rather lengthy thematic shape. The core and essence of its opening group, the structural expression of our *idée fixe* (bars 1 to 8 in the above example) is a melodic rise to an F (which is emphasized by a sforzando), from which the line falls back to the E, and beyond. On this towering F–E the melodic as well as the emotional tension of the whole utterance is focused. In fact, the entire theme is but a constant paraphrase around this one particle F–E. All the following groups (bars 8 to 15, 15 to 19, 19 to 23), in ever higher arcs, land on this F–E. Only the group which now follows (23 to 27) leads, through a still higher transposition, to F-sharp instead of F. But the very next group (27 to 32) again returns to F-natural–E. And the then following concluding group of the theme (32 to 40) likewise returns to the F–E, the arrival on the F being especially emphasized by a fermata (bar 38). In this last somewhat lengthy group a new melodic phrase (32 to 35) is interpolated which we may call *motif II*.

We elaborated on the course of this theme in some detail, for it discloses a construction quite different from the type to which we have become accustomed in the preceding examples of Mozart, Beethoven, or Brahms, yet it is a construction of convincing logic. True, Beethoven's themes show more cogent proportions, a stricter method of grouping and periodization. Nevertheless, the structure of this theme, too, is in its own right convincing, and the connection between the musical and emotional impulse is impressively transparent.

However, the full scope of Berlioz's thematic strength is not exhausted with the structure of the thematic melody alone; we must also listen to the "accompaniment" of the theme. This accompaniment is grouped on these bass particles:

Ex. 401

and these figures are not chosen at random. They, too, mirror the two first groups of the thematic melody, the first of which opens with G–C, the second with D–G (see example 400).

But now follow the upper line of the accompaniment (again example 400). It reads, D, E, F, E (bars 7 to 23), or in other words, it, too, expresses the work's prime thought, the *idée fixe*, literally, even in pitch. This is followed by some transpositions of the same thought, whereupon the line concludes (bars 38 to 40) again with F (D), E.

Features like these and many more of the same kind, though they form important elements in vitalizing the compositional design, easily escape the notice of one unaccustomed to piercing the thematic surface. Yet the romantic style is replete with such *counterpoint that does not sound in contrapuntal lines* but is charmingly submerged beneath figurate patchwork. The consequence is that romantic music in general, and Berlioz's in particular, is often decried as virtually homophonic. The common view holds that Berlioz's melodic lines, his scintillating orchestral colors and effects spring from a pro-grammatic and emotional impetus, from a strong romantic bent, but scarcely from a truly musical, structural impulse. Yet the deeper we delve into his compositional fabric, the more we come to realize that such a view is entirely without justification.

The section following the theme reads:

Ex. 402

of which the first part (40 to 47) may on first glance appear to be one of those typical "bridges" made up of impetuous but hollow passages and merely inserted to lead to the second subject (48 to 54); that is, if we can call this soft, short phrase a "subject." Yet un-raveling the core and inner contour of this shaping, the whole group, including the "second subject," appears as but a transformed and, so understood, very impressive and logical reutterance of the main melodic ideas of the first theme. First motif I is heard twice: first at original pitch, culminating on the E, F, E (42 to 44), then on D-flat, C (47 to 48), whereupon in the "second subject" a blending of motif II and I is effectuated. Here the appearance of motif I, the *idée fixe*, F–E (51 to 52), is underlined through the entrance of the horn, ac-companying the melody in sixths (see score). If a composer turns for his emotional tensions to lines like these, we must concede that the innate form of his self-expression is genuinely thematic.

Accordingly, the whole movement is but a chain of transformations of the same basic idea. Logically, this ever recurring prime thought is thus already heard in the Largo-Introduction with which the symphony opens, though here disguised in a minor key and therefore sounding as F–E-flat instead of F–E-natural (quoted as example 403*a*). In the following movements the thematic metamorphosis increases in degree and scope. The dance tune of the second movement in its new key and shaping (example 403*b*) cannot deceive us as to the basic identity of this melodic arc to the Allegro theme's main thought. While F appears here as F-sharp (on which Berlioz imposed a significant sforzando), the exact pitch is restored in the next, the third movement, the lovely theme of which is quoted as *c*. Again note the sforzando on the F. Then, shifted to G-minor, the F–E sounds as F–E-flat (again an accent on the F!) in the marchlike theme of the fourth movement (*d*):

Ex. 403

a Largo

b Valse

c Adagio

d Allegretto

In the fifth movement, then, the Finale, no real transformation is introduced as the movement's first theme, but instead merely a rhythmically changed variant of the Allegro theme, expressly so described by the composer (example 399*e*).

However, this Finale carries also a second theme which is really a new thought, a theme which, one would think, cannot show any affinity to the work's material, as it is taken from quite a different musical realm, namely, the liturgical melody of the *Dies Irae*.

Yet here we have reached the climax of the work's deeply conscious thematic planning. For the same great spectacle which we encountered when Bach took the granite lines of the Gregorian Credo into his Mass is repeated in this work of the romanticist Berlioz. Indeed, be it Bach, Beethoven, or any composer of thematic responsibility, such inclusions are made only if they can be integrated into the work as fully organic parts of the thematic whole. Thus we hear the tubas of the Last Judgment roar their apocalyptic message,

Ex. 404

culminating on the same rise to F–E (here E-flat) that was the core of the symphony's prime theme. To the hero of the *Symphonie fantastique,* his *idée fixe* must resound even from the last trumpet. In a towering contrapuntal elaboration of this *Dies Irae* theme and the first Finale theme, the work is led to its conclusion.

There is one fact in Berlioz's life stressed by all his biographers: his unbounded adoration for Beethoven. Usually, however, this is considered as the touching enthusiasm of a young genius rather than the expression of any spiritual or technical kinship. Berlioz's musical idiom, style, and taste, his whole concept of artistic and human values, seem remote, if not opposed, to those of the great classicist. Could Berlioz's devotion, then, have found no concrete, no specific fuel to kindle his interest as a musician?

Indeed, the kindred force to which Berlioz felt himself so attracted was Beethoven's *thematic* mastery. It was the magic spell that fascinated Berlioz, and he endeavored to revive it, and to a certain degree succeeded in doing so, in his own so different style and idiom. Of course, since the common view, though certainly acknowledging Beethoven's wondrous thematic complexity as a fact, has nevertheless not yet unraveled its full nature and ramifications, it is only natural that the scantier, less ponderous thematic achievement of his disciple did not reap the appreciation it deserved. Thus Berlioz's strength and interest in thematic formation came into complete disrepute, the undeniable appeal and charm of his compositions being ascribed, almost exclusively, to their emotional and programmatic power. Often his creations are even labeled as springing essentially from a literary rather than a musical impulse.

However, such a view entirely misconstrues the innermost endeavor of Berlioz's art. Were it not for their musical qualities, these works could hardly have held their own for more than twenty years. Yet the best of Berlioz's compositions still sound as fresh today as at the time when they were written, though a great part of their literary adornment strikes us as obsolete if not childish. In fact, on thinking through this matter soberly, the connection between the programmatic and musical course often becomes surprisingly loose, indeed, questionable; however, the music stands its ground, while the program evaporates into the void. The programmatic assertion, for instance, that the hero at the end of the first movement seeks refuge in religious consolation and thereupon immediately proceeds to a ball is, from a literary point of view, certainly a problematic feature. In all likelihood what happened was that the composer, having completed the musical course through which he had led his theme, sought for a satisfactory conclusion to the movement. But as his structural imagination did not encompass the classic idea of a crowning thematic resolution, he contented himself with letting the opening theme reemerge in a lento-pianissimo phrase, followed by a few sustained concluding chords. From a musical point of view this is, though perhaps not overwhelming, nevertheless a perfectly acceptable solution. However, the programmatic idea is brought to a standstill. To solve the dilemma, this ending was interpreted as religious consolation. But no musical mind trying to relive this process will doubt for a moment that the musical course came first and the programmatic, the literary, followed afterward.

Indeed, if we try to evaluate Berlioz's art as a whole, we cannot avoid coming to the conclusion that besides having enriched the orchestral palette with new enchantments and accents, his actual strength as a musician lies in the pronounced sense of thematic consistency, which as a pioneer he managed to transfer into an entirely different idiom and, in fact, into entirely different patterns. Thus he opened the door for the romantic way of thematic thinking —a thinking which is freer than that of the classics yet perhaps no less intense and penetrating.

Schumann: *Symphony in B-flat major*

In this evolution Robert Schumann was another leading force. Although usually considered the embodiment of the purest romanticism, Schumann's whole idea of compositional creation was rooted in structural conceptions. Certainly, his way of thematic forming and transforming is more akin to the classic pattern than that of Berlioz. The structural plan of two of Schumann's representative works has already been examined in our analysis. Now a brief description of the main thematic relationships on which the architecture of his First Symphony (opus 38) is centered, may be added.

In the following example the opening group of the symphony's Maestoso-Introduction is quoted as *a*, the melodic essence of which, omitting the repetition of the first two bars, is added in *b*, while the principal theme of the following Allegro is given in *c*:

We see that the Allegro theme is, in essence, a (transposed) replica of the introductory theme, all three motifs being easily discernible; even motif II (the rise to the octave), now aligned to the regular rhythm of the Allegro, reappears. And the third part of the Allegro clearly reflects motif III of the introductory theme, though in new figuration and with an added extension that leads the theme to a conclusion on F.

We may skip from the first movement to the Finale, the theme of which reads:

The inner identity of this theme to the themes of the first movement is, in spite of its dissimilar appearance, traceable in very impressive transformations. This Finale theme opens with motif II (the thirty-second-note passage from the Maestoso-Introduction), which appears here so augmented as to form, together with an added auftakt, a solemn intrada to the Finale. On the other hand, the second half of the Finale theme (motif III) is an image of the version in which this motif appears in the Allegro:

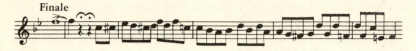

Finale

Thus the Finale theme is built by combining two halves: one from the Maestoso-Introduction of the first movement, the other from the Allegro theme, while motif I appears merely interwoven in the figuration of the second half.

This idea of developing a new theme from a combination of two thematic halves from other movements is the way in which all themes of this symphony are built. The startling thematic interconnections between the various halves of the themes of the different movements are seen in the following comparison:

Ex. 408

Allegro (transposed)   Larghetto (first half)

bis

Larghetto (transposed)   Scherzo (first half)

Maestoso (transposed)   Larghetto (second half)

Maestoso (transposed)   Scherzo (second half)

Once the thematic unity of the symphony has been affirmed through shapings like these, once the work has been, so to speak, socketed in such immovable yet elastic structural ball bearings, even occasional melodic detours, such as are inherent in Schumann's romantic way of expression, cannot disrupt the work's architecture. Though in style and idiom both Schumann and Berlioz are far removed from Beethoven, in a certain sphere of structural thinking they are nevertheless his disciples. Yet while each of these romanticists fully realized that a work's structural force depends on the strength of its thematic permeation, they strove toward their goal along widely separated paths.

In a quantitative sense Berlioz's thematic technique is much more thorough than Schumann's. He equips his design, quite apart from the frequent and, so to speak, scheduled recurrence of the programmatic *idée fixe,* with constant motivic reminiscences; he misses no opportunity to swerve from any melodic course in any voice, at least for a few moments, to a close and obvious similarity with the initial thought.

In contrast, the architectural unity of Schumann's symphony is anchored in its thematic depths and is, in this respect, much closer to the classical ideal. He eschews, as did the classics, verbal motivic repetitions, unless they are called for by the work's over-all plan. From the irrevocability of Beethoven's strictness, however, even he is separated by his specifically romantic desire for expansion. He invents the different themes in his work according to a conception of strong thematic unity; but once a theme is introduced, he lets it go its own way, concerned more with its individual expressiveness than with its function in furthering the structural and dramatic story of the whole.

Chopin: *Piano Sonata in B-flat minor*

Still another and highly impressive way of applying the thematic principle is seen in Chopin's music, for which we choose the B-flat minor sonata as an illustration. In fact, Chopin's method of developing thematic architecture is in many nuances very different from all forms to which we have become accustomed in our previous investigations. We may therefore examine some of the structural features of the B-flat minor sonata in detail.

The work begins with a weighty group of chords (*a* in the following example), which Chopin notated in a manner almost bizarre.[2]

---

[2] Chopin obviously was reluctant to notate the progression F-flat–F-natural and therefore chose E instead of F-flat. Through the E he was forced in the continuation to replace the D-flat harmony by a C-sharp-minor triad, and the resulting colorful notation must have appealed to his romantic sense.

Reduced to a notation enharmonically simpler (*b*), the interesting motivic content becomes easily readable:

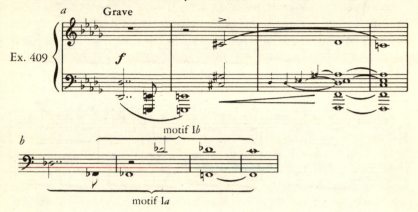

Ex. 409

It becomes clear that this is a contrapuntal overlapping of two versions (I*a* and I*b* in the above examples) of the same motivic thought, the one being the inversion of the other.

For a work of such power and dimensions as this sonata, these bars seem an unusual opening. Too short for a "Slow Introduction," and dwelling almost entirely on the D-flat, the shape is, from a purely melodic angle, not particularly impressive. But from a structural point of view, this brief Grave-Introduction is a decisive utterance, full of thematic dynamism. It prepares the listener's receptivity to the following Allegro, indeed, to the whole work, even though he may be unconscious of its influence. The variegated and fantastic thematic picture Chopin manages to evolve from this inconspicuous introductory shape is almost incredible.

The first Allegro theme opens with the characteristic agitato figure of bar 9 (see example 410). By lifting the B-flat an octave higher—a leap which is actually effectuated in bar 11—the identity to the introductory motif becomes apparent.

However, the theme thrives on more than merely this identity of particles. Actually, in its wider melodic contour the whole of the theme is an elaboration of the introductory phrase. The full theme reads (the bar numbers are those of the whole movement, not of the single example):

Ex. 410

Both groups, the first four bars (9 to 12) and the second four bars (13 to 16), express in their contour the introductory motif as quoted under *a* and *b* in the following example. However, a longer contour (from bars 9 to 16), forming a rising seventh instead of the original sixth, is also heard (*c* in the following example). This intensification of the initial sixth to a seventh later becomes one of the thematic features of the work. And if we include the next bar (17) in the line, a third contour becomes audible, rising from D-flat (bar 9) over E-flat and G-flat to D-flat (bar 17), which, together with the continuous A-natural in the accompaniment (11 to 15), produces a figure (*d* in the example below) that is, almost literally, the grace-note phrase (see example 409*a*) from the Grave-Introduction.

Ex. 411

In bar 17 the climax is reached and the second half of the theme, the melodic descent, begins. This whole second part is characterized by a phrase formed by a stepwise descent of four notes, which we may call *motif II*:

Ex. 412

However, to secure unity with the first half of the theme, Chopin not only continues the initial rhythm but also links the new motif II with a kind of inversion of motif I:

Ex. 413

Interestingly enough, the bass of the theme is formed by a line expressing inversions of motif I and motif II:

Ex. 414

What we wish above all to make transparent by the detailed description of this theme is the principle of Chopin's shaping. As is clearly seen, not only the motivic detail of the theme but also its wider melodic line are derived from the original thought of the Introduction, to which merely one new phrase (motif II) is added.

Having once been uttered, the first theme is repeated, whereupon the second theme enters. This second theme is one of these yearning cantilenas, the Chopinesque origin of which cannot be mistaken; and with it one of those small miracles with which the technique of thematic transformation often surprises us becomes apparent. For the beginning of this characteristic Chopin cantilena is actually a greatly slackened reiteration of the nervous, agitated first theme:

Ex. 415

The young composer of today may well be impressed by the discovery that these lines of Chopin, so often described as the archetype of purely emotional outpouring, are firmly rooted in structural ground.

The connection of the second theme to the work as a whole is not confined to its first three notes. For the varied repetition of the theme which follows, commences thus:

Ex. 416

And in this variant the affinity of the second theme to the work's initial thought (motif I*b* in example 409*b*) becomes transparent.

Hence the sonata's second theme, no less than the first, is simply a derivative of the introductory motif. The motivic change from the sixth to the seventh is here included as an ornament in the melodic line itself (the G-flat in the above example). With this we encounter a type of structural handling particularly characteristic of Chopin. Such *thematic ornamentation,* as it may be called, must not be confused with the usual interpolation of mere embellishments and fiorituras. Chopin's ornamentation goes to the marrow of the thematic organism, constantly enriching it with new variants.

After having concluded its first appearance, the second theme is repeated, again in an ornamentally expanded group. Near its climax and conclusion the following characteristic ornamentation is heard:

Ex. 417

This figure is destined to play a role in the work's further thematic development.

Then, forming the concluding section of the exposition, a third theme enters (see following example) which again recalls the idea of the Allegro theme (even identical in pitch), or, to be accurate, is a combination of the Allegro's first and second theme. (The affinity between the second and third theme is indicated by the braces.) Compare the three themes:

These three themes form the material from which the whole movement is built in constant ornamentation, yet with an almost rigid adherence to the basic idea. Once the unified structure of the first movement has thus become clear, the design of the following movements as the natural outgrowth of the first cannot be mistaken.

The next movement, the Scherzo, however, requires a few explanatory words. To understand the specific thematic pattern from which the Scherzo theme is built, we must for a moment return to the first movement. The last group of the first movement—let us call it the "Coda group"—forms, in its rise from D to B-flat–A, a most emphatic reutterance of the initial thought (to which in bars 237 to 241 a few concluding chords are added). Comparing this Coda group (quoted as *a* in the following example) with the Scherzo theme (*b*), which in the sonata enters as its immediate continuation, the similarity in outline is obvious:

A striking and highly effective way of interlacing movements here becomes apparent. Starting in the Coda group with the second note, D-sharp (in the Scherzo notated as E-flat), and embroidering the line with a different figuration, namely, the characteristic phrase quoted in example 417, the vivacious Scherzo theme stands before us. As Chopin apparently planned the Scherzo in E-flat, yet wished to carry over the essential pitch of the concluding group from the preceding movement, he had almost no alternative to omitting the opening D.

The "cutting off" of a first note is not an unusual device in the technique of transformation; we have seen it time and again in the works of other composers.

Moreover, the D is not really "cut off" here. Though not opening the Scherzo itself, it is heard as the last note of the preceding movement (see example 419*a*). Had this D not been felt by the composer as necessary to the thematic design, in all likelihood he would have closed the movement with B-flat, to which the whole group tends. That Chopin really had the initial thought in mind when he formed the Scherzo theme is borne out by the fact that in the following bars he immediately annexed a group expressing the motif in its full course from D to B-flat–A-flat:

Ex. 420

Of course, to complete the analogy to the first movement, motif II would now be due; and indeed it emerges in the next group, though the stepwise descent of four notes is here adjusted to the ¾ rhythm of the Scherzo:

Ex. 421

The Trio of the Scherzo follows: If the analogy continues, the Trio should reflect the Allegro's second subject. Comparing the two,

From second **Allegro** subject

Ex. 422

Trio theme

the similarity is obvious.

To lay bare the thematic essence of the third movement, the Marche funèbre, the opening group of which reads,

Ex. 423  etc.

we must, for the time being, ignore the constant note repetitions inserted to create a mood characteristic of a funeral march. By omitting these rhythmical repetitions, the full motivic contour of the Allegro theme at original pitch clearly emerges:

To this, motif II is again linked in a meaningful annex (see brace above).

To complete the analogy, the composer shapes the Trio of this movement, too, as a recollection of the ever recurring cantilena. Compare:

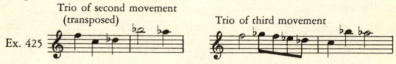

Thus we reach the Finale. The design of the Finale is so strikingly in accord with the idea of the Allegro theme that it really is surprising that at least *this* analogy was not noticed long ago. Both themes follow the same pattern,

while the ensuing parts are characterized by motif II:

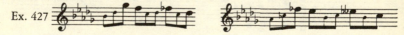

In this movement, with its fluttering character, the thought of a true cantilena as the second theme was out of the question. Nevertheless, the idea of such a melodious second theme is charmingly indicated in the second section of the Finale, that is, exactly when due, through figurations such as:

Ex. 428

Guided by these structural clues, the compositional process through which the work must have grown becomes strikingly transparent. We can imagine a musical thought, pregnant both with emotional impulse and with structural possibilities, revolving in the composer's mind. Visions flash up of the various configurations [3] and moods which this thought may assume, *and thus the different sections and movements take shape.*

The composer hears the figure of the Allegro agitato (*a* in the following example) become, in a new muffled rhythm, the drum of the funeral march (*b*), or a woeful chant (*c*). He conceives the chant itself in three different variants as a "second theme" (*d*) and as the trios of the Scherzo (*e*) and of the Marche (*f*):

Ex. 429

---

[3] Some of the melodious parts of the sonata (such as the trios of the second and third movement) are said to echo Polish folk songs. We do not know whether Chopin built his work from this source or whether these familiar melodies returned to his mind while he was composing, because they were so akin to the thematic pattern. At any rate, he certainly managed to fit them successfully into the sonata's unity.

In this creative process it is well-nigh impossible to separate the emotional and structural elements, as one element works through the other. But one thing is certain, and that is that Chopin's music, notwithstanding its melodic expressiveness and "romantic" subjectivity, is firmly entrenched in thematic homogeneity and thematic transformation. Moreover, these transformations are not only convincing in their musical and emotional variety, but ascend to the highest role which transformations can attain: they become architectural forces and, indeed, engender musical form.

In this connection a characteristic trait in the structural picture of this sonata and of almost all Chopin's works should not be overlooked, a trait to which the attention it deserved has never been given. Almost invariably Chopin builds his works *from themes alone,* without "bridges" or "episodes." Incredible as this seems with regard to a work of large dimensions such as this sonata, it is nevertheless a fact proved by a brief survey.

The sonata opens with a "Slow Introduction" of four bars (1 to 4), whereupon another four-bar group of introductory accompaniment follows (5 to 8), preparing the actual theme. Now the principal theme enters, forming a period of sixteen bars (9 to 25) and is repeated (25 to 41). Then the second theme follows without any connecting episode, merely prepared through a slackening in tempo and dynamics. This second theme, again sixteen bars long (41 to 57), is in turn repeated, the repetition being expanded—actually expanded and not prolonged through episodes—to twenty-four bars (57 to 81). Again without any bridging insertion, the third thematic group (81 to 104), also complete in itself, follows. With this the exposition is at an end. The development section and the recapitulation are no less concise and clear-cut in their design. As for the development, though it is of course based on combinations and variations of all four previous thematic shapes (introduction, first, second, and third themes), yet it is never interrupted by episodic expediency, and it pursues its course with such musicianly impetus that its whole first part (105 to 136) appears to the listener almost as one group. The following second part, from bar 137 on, may be classed either still as development or as recapitulation, whichever term one wishes to apply; at any rate, it remains a varied reiteration of the first Allegro section. Then, after a short intimation of the third thematic group (stretto), which thus appears to be the only "interpolation" in the whole movement, a true recapitulation, that is, a resumption of the second and third thematic sections, follows, now in the key of the tonic (169 to 228). Such a recapitulation, achieved not by a stereotyped repetition but by by-passing the beginning of the exposition and gliding directly into its center, is of age-old usage, dating as far back as Haydn's time, when it was termed "simulated recapitulation." Nor is there any genuine coda, but merely the above quoted group of thirteen bars (8 plus 5 bars; see example 419a) with which the movement closes. Similarly concentrated constructions, consisting almost entirely of actual thematic statements, are seen in all the following movements. Owing to the constant melodic refiguration and reornamentation, however, this amazingly direct and symmetrical design arouses no feeling of architectural rigidity. In his basic thematic handling, in the way he centers his constructions on a few variants of one thematic thought and makes these variants the foundations of the work's sections and movements,[4] Chopin, among the composers of his period, comes perhaps closest to the classical ideal— although in his melodic idiom and sensitivity he may be the most romantic of all.

What nevertheless separates Chopin's principle of thematic forming from that of the classics proper is that owing to the conciseness of his constructions just described, in which the thematic "sections" usually consist of not more than a twofold utterance of the theme, these themes in themselves do not undergo a real evolution within the course of a movement. Within a single section Chopin's themes sometimes seem almost static. However, this lack of evolution *within the section* is, at least to some extent, compensated by a unifying and comprehensive thematic evolution that takes shape during the course of the whole work. Since one theme springs from the other without episode and interruption, we feel in Chopin's music, more strongly than elsewhere, the form-building phenomenon inherent

---

[4] Schumann, in his otherwise enthusiastic critical survey of Chopin's B-flat minor sonata, deplores the lack of thematic unity between the four movements. While this comment proves again that Schumann expected and demanded such unity between movements, it also illustrates the almost mysterious nature of thematic phenomena, which are so different and individual with each composer that even a mind as intensely "thematic" as Schumann's overlooked them in this instance.

in the gradual transformation of one thematic thought. When in the B-flat-minor sonata the thought of the Introduction hurries, over its threefold thematic transformation (as a first, second, and third theme), to the action and counteraction in the development and becomes at last the emphatic concluding group of the movement; when subsequently this concluding group is, in a new transformation, taken over as the Scherzo theme and finally becomes the Funeral March—then a dramatic story of convincing logic and power has been told; it is, in fact, almost completed. For the architectural and emotional weight of this Funeral March scarcely admits of further thematic intensification. Consequently, the following transformation, the Finale, is rather a sublimation of the thematic thought into almost substanceless whispers. Here we have a romantic version of what we called in the style of Beethoven and the classics "thematic resolution."

All this is, of course, quite contrary to the conceptions according to which Chopin's music is usually pictured. As Chopin's romantic lyricism is—to some extent justly—regarded as the most characteristic aesthetic quality of his compositions, both the popular and historical view adjudge his art as only loosely based on structural principles and thematic laws. Chopin is labeled as an episodist, in fact as an improviser at heart. Now it is clear that in polyphonic depth Chopin, the poet of the piano, cannot, by the very nature of his medium, compete with the great masters of orchestral and choral writing, though his meticulous compositional lines, even when seemingly only figurate accompaniment, invariably abound with contrapuntal and thematic life. But to see in this lyric and truly heroic romanticist a mere improviser is to miss the core of his creative endeavor. These strict—we might almost call them sturdy—constructions, these resilient yet infrangible thematic mechanisms are indeed the direct opposite of musical improvisation.

As previously indicated, the attempt to blend the often capricious, almost violently personal musical message of the romantic spirit with the firm pattern of classical structural thinking forms in an evolutional sense the most remarkable trait in the achievement of this epoch. The manner and degree in which these attempts succeeded are of particular interest to our subject. And so we may turn to another characteristic figure in this development, to Liszt.

Liszt: *Les Préludes*

In Liszt's music, too, thematic ideas and thematic connections play a greater role than is generally thought. The following description may reveal not only the specific qualities but also some of the limitations of his structural endeavor. As an example we have chosen one of Liszt's most popular orchestral compositions, his symphonic poem *Les Préludes*. Omitting any allusion to the programmatic symbolism indicated by the composer in a poetic epigraph (by Lamartine) and turning directly to the structural shapes, we will try to detect their thematic meaning. In the following, the seven thematic figures of *Les Préludes* are listed:

As may be easily seen, all these themes are derived, more or less literally, from the opening thought. (To facilitate comparison, the two motivic parts in each theme are bracketed *A* and *B*.) Themes I and II, for instance, if we look at them in the preceding example, differ merely in nuance. Of course, if we examine the scoring of the sections in which the themes are introduced, the picture becomes quite different. Theme I, which opens the work, sounds only from the unison of the strings; but the full orchestra is enlisted to introduce theme II (example 431*a*). In this orchestral design it is impressive to note that none of the countervoices to the theme is inserted as mere orchestral padding. They are all thematic. In fact, they themselves express the main theme in different interwoven contours (as indicated by the braces in the following example). Conditions similar to those in theme II prevail in theme III (example 431*b*). Though the theme itself is an almost literal repetition of the initial thought, its orchestral appearance presents a new picture.

Ex. 431

All this might at first glance seem to conform closely with the precepts according to which as described in this study the classics evolved their compositional structures. Nevertheless, upon listening to the work, the over-all effect of the thematic design is somewhat disappointing. We have already heard three sections: first, a slow introduction, then a section of increased tempo and dynamics (Maestoso), finally a slightly calmer, more cantabile section—yet all these parts are centered on themes that by no means represent transformations, not even real variations, but are, adorned with different accompaniments, almost literally identical. Up to this point, as far as the innermost substance is concerned, nothing seems to have happened in this symphonic poem.

Among the further shapes of the work, themes IV and VII are the only ones that, to a limited degree, deserve to be called transformations. In fact, the affinity of theme IV is traceable only if we change a note; namely, the A to a B, as has been done in the following fictitious quotation (compare the actual theme IV in example 430):

Ex. 432

And in this work of considerable dimensions, all the other themes are, in essence, literal reiterations of the opening figure. In addition, the thematic developments *within* the sections appear equally poor. In the whole first half of the work, that is, in the part where the themes and their sections should be established, the courses of the sections are built virtually by letting the particular theme—invariably a short utterance of four bars—sound in constant repetition and transposition. However, a climax of the work's architecture is reached in the second half, when themes IV and VII are heard in different, indeed variegated and impressive, contrapuntal combination. Yet again it must seem disappointing to a discriminating listener that the final summit to which the composer carries him, after this lovely contrapuntal play and interplay, is none other than an absolute repetition of the work's second section (save for added piccolo and percussion). To use such primitive repetition as the architectural solution of a great composition, without transforming it to any higher expression of the original idea, contradicts all the more profound concepts of musical form.

The above mentioned brevity of Liszt's themes may itself be cited as a weakness. If in Chopin's sonata the architecture seemed centered on short motivic thoughts, we must not forget that from these motifs (*using them as "contours"*) Chopin developed broad, impressive themes. Liszt's "themes," however, are but ever repeated short figures that by their nature do not admit of any wider "contoured" treatment.

Nevertheless, the thoroughness and extended scope of Liszt's thematic elaboration is unquestionable, in spite of his failure to materialize its deepest meaning. This may be shown in a last example from *Les Préludes*. Although in principle any part of the work would have served as an illustration, a page scored for full orchestra is chosen to make the idea transparent in all its richness:

The main melodic course of these bars is found in the violins (theme VII), to which the double bass adds a counterpoint that is actually simply a variant of the theme above. Another contrapuntal imitation is heard in the woodwinds. This main melodic design is supported by a series of chords, one to a bar (sounded by the horns, trumpets, violas, and cellos), which might easily be mistaken for mere padding. Yet even these chords are clear thematic utterances. The group is preceded by an extended section in which theme IV was the leading melody, and thus the chords in question, in their repeated progression from A-flat to G (together with C to D-flat as the inversion), echo the most emphatic particle of that theme. And since theme IV highlighted the whole preceding section, its sudden complete disappearance would have broken the structural continuity.

There is still another instrument heard in the example quoted: the harp. And even its inconspicuous pluckings—which might seem merely to lend additional sparkle to the orchestra—even they express the work's main motif (E-flat, G, A-flat). Such meticulous treatment shows how deeply Liszt's mind was rooted in thematic conceptions. This must be stressed, as the popular view often associates Liszt, the composer, with the shallow virtuoso piano arrangements of his youth.

Nevertheless, though thematic through and through, Liszt's music is, in the truest sense, an aberration from the highest concept of thematic forming of his epoch. A master at carrying thematic consistency into the smallest ramifications of his brilliant orchestral design, he was nevertheless unable to develop, to transform a thematic beginning into genuine thematic variety, and his compositions often have a touch of the "textbook for thematic forming." Though applying complete thematic consistency, Liszt schematizes and externalizes the innermost idea of the great phenomenon.

One strange but perhaps not too surprising consequence is that Liszt's music is frequently regarded as altogether lacking in thematic consistency, and for that matter, in melodic invention. Although such a view is false, there is a sound instinct behind it. This view merely substitutes an imaginary cause for the final effect made by his music. The cause, that is, the alleged lack of thematic unity, is nonexistent. Liszt's compositions are, on the contrary, strongly united; they are uninterrupted series of all too obvious thematic connections. That his initial themes are at times primitive, even insipid, in itself by no means certifies a lack of inventive power. Often the strength of a composition depends on the implications and consequences which an initial thought is led to produce rather than upon the particular quality of the thought itself.

"What could be more vulgar than the opening of the Finale in Beethoven's Seventh Symphony? Yet what a wonderful musical structure Beethoven built from this melody."

The reader who perhaps rebels at the wording of this statement may be interested to hear that these are not the author's words but those of Peter Ilyich Tchaikovsky. And the significant point with regard to this utterance is that the world has come to regard the man who made it as the melodist par excellence. He is the composer of whom most people think that not structure, but melody, melody alone, must to him have been the determining factor in music.

In this connection we are fortunate that Tchaikovsky has left us the inestimable gift of his recorded opinion on musical composition and its problems. As Tchaikovsky's music is the next object of our thematic inquiry, some parts of these historic remarks may be cited in the following.

In a letter to Nadejda von Meck of July 17th, 1878 (that is, at the time when his Fourth Symphony was completed) Tchaikovsky states:

Although I cannot complain of poor inventive powers or imagination, I have always suffered from lack of skill in the management of form. Only persistent labor has at last permitted me to achieve a form that in some degree corresponds to the content. In the past I was careless, I did not realize the extreme importance of this critical examination of the preliminary sketch. For this reason, *the succeeding episodes were loosely held together and seams were always visible*. That was a serious defect, and it was years before I began to correct it, yet my compositions will never be good examples of form because I can only *correct* what is wrong with my musical nature— I cannot change it intrinsically. But I see with joy that I am progressing slowly, and I ardently desire to take myself as far along this road to perfection as I can go.[5]

---

[5] All quotations from Tchaikovsky's letters are in the translation given in the book about Tchaikovsky, *Beloved Friend*, by Catherine Drinker Bowen and Barbara von Meck, Random House, New York. The italics (apart from those of the word "correct") are not Tchaikovsky's but are inserted by this author.

These are revelations of the first order. They are, be it repeated, of particular weight, since they come from this protagonist of melodic and emotional expression. Those who are so blithely confident that musical creating lies in establishing an esthetic short circuit from the emotional source to the finished work, in disregard of any connecting wire of technique, should seriously consider this statement by a great composer. Discovering with what his mind was really occupied while pouring out his works, they might come to a more realistic view of the process of musical creation.

Moreover, that Tchaikovsky by "lack of skill in the management of form" was indeed referring to inner, thematic form and not to its outer schemes is proved by another letter written the day before the one just quoted. (The two letters were actually two parts of one great confession about his ideas on compositional creation.) In it he expressly refers to the outer form, saying:

You ask if I stick to established forms. Yes and No. In certain compositions, such as a symphony, the form is taken for granted and I keep to it—but only as to the large outline and proper sequence of movements. The details can be manipulated as freely as one chooses, according to the natural development of the musical idea.

Thus it is clear that the schemes, the established patterns of form, did not present an important problem to Tchaikovsky; in fact, they were not even of any particular interest to him, just as they have never been to any composer of creative imagination. But how to bring about inner coherence in his music and how to improve his capacity in this respect became his "ardent desire." No doubt, Tchaikovsky had an innate musicianly desire for thematic structure. With what eager interest and admiration he must have studied the wonders of Mozart's and Beethoven's transformations.

Tchaikovsky: *Symphonie pathétique*

If we look at Tchaikovsky's later works, such as the fourth and fifth symphonies and especially his last and most mature work, the sixth, the *Symphonie pathétique*, we realize his clear consciousness of the necessity of an absolute thematic bond between the movements of a symphonic whole.

The melodic line of the principal theme of the *Pathétique* is quoted as example 434a. Comparing this to the famous theme in five-quarter rhythm of the second movement, the Allegro con grazia (b), it is clear that the idea of the twofold rise (B, C-sharp, D, C-sharp, and D, E, F, E) from the first theme, is entirely integrated in the second. In the first theme the two phrases are each repeated with a little embellishing variant (marked b). And even this embellishment reappears, if not in notes then in fluency and character, in the triplets of the second theme.

The third theme, however, at least in its beginning (c) only touches (in its contour from B to C, and D, E, F-sharp, E) on the original shape. But from the theme of the ensuing Finale (d), omitting repetitions and interpolations, which are not given in our quotation, the direct line of the original is again heard in full clarity.

Ex. 434

As the second themes of all other movements likewise mirror the first movement's second theme, this seems once more an architectural concept entirely in accordance with the Beethovenian pattern.

In order, however, to decipher the full and final meaning of Tchaikovsky's conception of structural formation, we must try to follow the thematic course of a part of his work in detail. Some special aspects may become apparent.

The symphony opens with a short introductory Adagio commencing thus:

Ex. 435

A melodic line rises in the bassoon, the thematic meaning of which is obvious: these phrases are clearly a (slightly improvisatory) anticipation of the following Allegro theme. However, a counter-voice to this line is heard deep in the double-bass and, as will be seen, it represents a second motivic figure from which, in addition to the first, the themes of the work are built.

The first appearance of the Allegro theme differs somewhat from the previously quoted main version, which enters later. This first version reads:

Ex. 436

Though the kernel of the main version is audible here too, the present shape has a different construction. Its first and second halves, in their contrasting figurations, convey quite separate pictures. The thematic meaning of this will soon become clear. In the present version the concluding passage echoes, at least in indication, the descending scale in the lower voice of the Slow Introduction. And the thematic intention of this becomes obvious in the following repetition of the theme, as its second half now reads:

Ex. 437

After the first version of the Allegro theme has thus been twice sounded, the previously quoted main version (example 434*a*) enters. As this more expanded and more elaborate version represents the actual principal theme, it may be quoted again, now in its full course:

Ex. 438

Here the theme is heard in its full melodic intensity. The rise from bar 30 to bar 38 is of great power, though the passage formed by bars 37 and 38, notwithstanding its dynamic pulsation, has a touch of sequential routine. In the following part (39 to 43) one has even more strongly the feeling that the inventive power has run out. Why has the composer added these shallow descending scales, certainly not a worthy continuation to the beautiful first part of the theme? A primitive answer would be: Because the thematic period required a conclusion. This is, of course, true, yet a melodic mind such as Tchaikovsky's could easily have found numerous other more impressive ways of finishing the theme. The reason that the composer nevertheless decided upon these scales is that he needed them as a thematic bridge. The following group reads:

This shape is a contrapuntal statement consisting of two equally important figures. The first figure (sounding in the violins) is derived from elements of the theme's first version, while the second figure (first sounding in cello and bass, later in the woodwinds) is formed by these very descending scales from the "problematic" part of the main theme described above. This scale motif, as we remember, was introduced in the symphony's opening, reiterated in both versions of the first Allegro theme, and is now reintroduced as an important figure in the present group. Thus we understand why the composer centered the second part of the main theme on these scales. Though the scales in themselves do not represent a very original utterance, he needed them for the sake of structural unity, to justify the following, otherwise rather loosely connected themes.

The group quoted in the last example is structurally interesting for further reasons. From its figures a rather extended section is developed. Although this section is centered on the passages of sixteenth notes on which the second half of the main theme was also centered, any reference to the main theme itself is missing in this new section. Thus, to avoid a thematic break which would disturb the listener, who, consciously or subconsciously, expects a natural evolution of the Allegro theme proper, the composer finally returns to the latter. He does so in a most emphatic manner, with blaring trumpets and trombones plunging into the midst of the figurate passages:

Ex. 440

This is a most effective way of restoring thematic unity, as it were, by force. However, it remains a tour de force. Is this, then, one of the "seams" to which Tchaikovsky refers in his letter? For the part without the main theme is not merely a small melodic excursion; it is a real section in the full sense of the word. Moreover, it is dangerously close to the symphony's beginning, where, according to all laws of structural logic, the evolution of the main utterance constitutes the only organic course.

Thus we see here a solution exactly opposite to that in the aforementioned "problematic" conclusion of the main theme. There the composer's anxiety for structural unity was the stronger force; therefore he finished the theme with scales, although in expressiveness and beauty they yield a rather poor result. Now his desire for variety and emotional display remained victorious, but through this a picture develops that causes the work to disintegrate somewhat.

Similar conditions frequently become apparent in the course of the symphony. One group is the most organic expression thinkable of the work's structural idea; the next escapes, in fact jumps, into extraneous regions.

The second theme, now entering, combines both expressive and structural power. It is a shape as laden with melodic impulse as it is structurally convincing. Not only is the main theme's basic pattern slightly, yet clearly, reciprocated and led to a (transposed) climax in the second theme,

but also the characteristic phrase from the first theme (marked *a*) now appears in inversion as an equally characteristic figuration of the second. Moreover, the second part of the theme, too, is centered on the "scales," which here appear as an intensely melodic utterance (marked *b*).

Immediately after the theme, however, another group follows, commencing thus:

The basic pattern I and I*a* is visible here too. Yet this group, actually an annex to the second theme, is now developed to a large section, and the beautiful and important second theme itself is almost forgotten, except for some small parts which now appear in the form of casual counterpoint. Only much later does the second theme reappear in intensified instrumentation, whereupon the whole section is led, very effectively, to a dreamlike conclusion marked *ppppp*.

Finally, however, this almost overlong exposition must come to an end and the composer must find his way back to the main thought, or, speaking in technical terms, to the development and recapitulation. To introduce the first theme immediately after the lyric pianissimo conclusion of the second theme's section appears impossible, and it seems that the composer has again too freely given vent to his melodic inclination; now he is in need of a bridge. On the other hand, he has not much time; the return to the first theme is urgent; thus he inserts a sudden fortissimo outburst of a few bars in which two indications of the first theme's beginning are included. Yet the whole group, in all its dramatic gesture, has a distinct quality of a forced, rather hollow sequence; in short, we are once again, here very strikingly, at one of Tchaikovsky's "seams" which runs through the symphonic fabric.

Nevertheless, it was not criticism of Tchaikovsky's magnificent work that engendered the preceding, perhaps all too dissecting analysis. The purpose was merely to draw attention to the violent struggle in which a composer of this era almost necessarily found himself if his melodic imagination was as expansive and his structural sense as strong as were those of Tchaikovsky.

The first of these qualities, his gift for melodic expressiveness, was of course never questioned. But the true significance of this part of his creative capacity can only be understood in its full impact if it is linked with the other side, with his passionate striving toward thematic unity. This trend toward thematic synthesis became in his later, fully mature works an almost fanatical urge. The few examples from the part of his symphony analyzed above represent only a minute fraction of the comprehensive thematic relations, the innumerable thematic implications, which form the structural plan of this one work alone.

But his passion for full thematic unity brought the composer frequently into conflict with his constantly active, restlessly inventive power. Whenever Tchaikovsky commences a larger composition, his ideas and shapes branch in various directions, and only his consummate thematic skill brings them back—retransforms them, as it were—into architectural unity. The third movement of this sixth symphony, for instance, in the charm of its scurrying 12/8 rhythm, is, no doubt, a musical enunciation the decisive picture of which arose in the composer's mind quite independently from the first and second movements. Yet its themes do become, even if only gradually, reflections of the themes of these preceding movements.

Thus the essence of Tchaikovsky's structural achievement is not to evolve one thought into a large variegated course, as did the classics, but to forge different, often contrasting ideas into thematic unity. Even in this way, however, judged by the final effect, Tchaikovsky achieves structural oneness—indeed, he performs what amounts almost to miracles of thematic unification. Unhesitatingly he grasps the most diversified thoughts wherever he can catch them in their ethereal flight, includes them in his work, and lo! they become parts of one logical whole. Somehow even his "seams" fit charmingly into the design, as through them we feel the ardent, often almost successful endeavor to bridge the unbridgeable.

Of course, the dilemma is not Tchaikovsky's alone. It is the dilemma of an age whose musical language is rooted in the idea of unity but whose artistic desire strives for differentiation. In the realm of the opera, by the very nature of this form of art, these contrasting forces become interestingly apparent.

Opera was the only compositional category that was not developed to a pattern of thematic unity in classical times. Although in Mozart's and Beethoven's music the thematic principle was carried to its greatest intensity, it did not fully penetrate the operatic domain—not in a sense that would have forged the various parts of an opera into a structural unit. The prevailing idea of the libretto, in which the musical sections were interrupted by long recitativical and even spoken parts, in itself excluded real unity. But even when the spoken parts were eliminated and the recitatives reduced, the inner construction remained still more or less a succession of musically independent scenes or "numbers." True, in the operas of Mozart, Beethoven, Weber, and other composers of this period, signs of occasional thematic interconnections between different arias, finales, and so forth become apparent. A desire for unity is shown by sometimes resuming important initial sections or effects at the end of the opera, and a growing sense of architectural proportions is certainly alive in Mozart's last operatic creations, increasing in Beethoven's *Fidelio* to an almost symphonic concept. All in all, however, viewed from a specifically musico-structural angle, opera remained an accumulation of single pieces.

It is well known that Wagner changed this picture fundamentally. However, this change was obviously destined to take place, in one way or another, as the logical consequence of the evolution. The thematic idea was now much too firmly entrenched in the minds of all composers of higher structural conception to allow them to ignore it in any musical sphere. We can observe its working very clearly in Verdi's later operas, where, it should be stressed, it was materialized in a manner entirely independent of Wagnerian influence.

Verdi: *Don Carlo*

To give an illustration of this most interesting type of operatic unity, some basic thematic features from the fourth act of Verdi's

Don Carlo may be described. The act opens with the following line:

Ex. 443

Examining the composition, we discover that *the whole picture of this fourth act is in essence developed as a continuous paraphrase of this opening period.* If in the above example we consider that the pianissimo phrase is merely an echoing repetition, the content of the first eight bars presents itself as a melodic rise to two accented peaks, one on the G (bar 5), the other on the D (bar 8). A contour formed by these two peaks, which are separated by a falling fourth, or, if we lift the second peak an octave higher, by a rising fifth, would read somewhat like this:

Ex. 444

This contour, as will be seen, forms the pattern according to which almost all the forthcoming groups are shaped. However, it forms only the pattern, the skeleton, around which an abundance of different shapes grow. These shapes are, in turn, invariably derived from parts of the above-quoted opening group, as from bars 1 to 4, the series of grace notes, or from the melodious figure of bars 5 and 6, or from the expressive descent to the tonic (bars 12 and 13).

The following group is in the usual piano score somewhat obscured, and we must turn to the orchestral version to make it clear. This group is a literal repetition of the monophonous opening period, but it is now, through an added web of motivic figuration, transformed into a rich polyphonic utterance. Since Verdi's imaginative power becomes in this shaping beautifully transparent, we do not hesitate to quote this group in full (bars 14 to 28), even with the prolongation (29 to 32) with which the orchestral introduction to this scene comes to a close:

To call this a figurate enrichment of the opening group is of course an understatement. In reality Verdi ingeniously combined two separate musical utterances, setting one above the other. If we decipher the thematic content of the superimposed (figurate) group, we realize that it, too, is built according to the aforementioned pattern centered on the two peaks, with the fifth between. Here the peaks are F (bar 14) and C (bar 19). Moreover, the annexed prolongation in its rise from C (bar 29) to G (bar 32) also revolves around the same idea. And even the detail of the figuration (see braces in bar 14 and following) constantly expresses the prime motif in charming miniature, a feature echoed in the accompanying chords which spell the phrases F, D, C-sharp (bars 15 and 16), and F, D, C (17 and 18). Both in the detail and in the wider contour we see the thematic pattern at work.

Now the orchestral introduction is at its end, and the singer (personifying Filippo, the king) enters. But the fascinating idea of developing a scene from one constantly enriched basis continues. For the opening group that was first (in bars 1 to 13) heard alone, then was, with added figurations, repeated and enlarged (14 to 32), is now sounded for the third time [6] (bars 33 to 48), once more enriched by a newly added part: the human voice. (The reader should pursue this course in the score, as it is impossible to print all these extended sections.)

The fact that must make a tremendous impression on every musical mind is that not just some "contrapuntal lines" are here combined but three full utterances, almost three musical pieces in themselves, which have become one in a gradual, organic evolution. Thus the listener is caught as if under a magic spell, since each new part adds more importance to the whole, though the entire course seems more and more familiar the further it progresses. Besides, the newly

---

[6] The only alteration is that the grace-note group, which in the opening of the scene was on A, appears now on D.

added part, the voice, though it is a fully independent musical utterance, again repeats, in its emotional uplift from B-flat–A to E–D, the basic pattern:

Io la ri - ve - do an-cor

From here on, after a brief recitativical, though no less thematic, interlude, we proceed to the climax. Again the design is repeated, but it is now transformed into the concentrated form of an *aria*. The opening of this arioso section is quoted as example 447*a*. Again we find the grace-note group opening the section; we find the figure from bar 14 (example 445), though now changed into a melodious arioso accompaniment, sounded by the horns; and we also hear the solo voice, the actual "aria," in its surge toward the accented B-flat, initiating the basic motif. This solo part, this well known *pièce de résistance* of every bass singer, now progresses to a climax (example 447*b*).

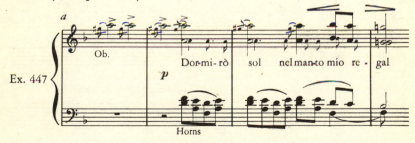

Ex. 447 *a*

Ob.

p Dor-mi- rò   sol   nel man-to mio re- gal

Horns

b

dor - mi - rò   sol   sot - to la vôl - ta   ne - ra (etc.)

dim.

With its peaks on D and A (forming here a falling fourth instead of a rising fifth because of the range of the voice) the basic pattern again clearly forms the structural essence of this shape. Until its end the scene now dwells on this design.

All this is much more than merely the expression of operatic emotion in an effective musical idiom. For by enlivening his lines with thematic continuity, Verdi was able *to dispose of the old division between recitativical and closed musical sections.* Since he develops the whole scene into one organic musical picture, the (thematic) recitative becomes a part of the aria, while the aria itself is but an intensified expression of the recitative.

On this basis the structural idea of the following scenes and their thematic interconnections can be quickly sketched. The second scene, programmatically an encounter of two supreme forces, the King and the Grand Inquisitor, opens with the following group:

Ex. 448

As a first obvious analogy to the opening of the preceding scene, the three C's, now sounding as fortissimo strokes of the full orchestra, catch the eye. But then follows the "theme." This mystically melodious shape, introduced to characterize a new personality, is consequently a musical utterance completely different from the foregoing ones. Yet in its two peaks on A-flat–G and E-flat–D (see asterisks), which are thus separated by a fifth, the literal pattern from the preceding scene becomes audible. In other words, Verdi uses the technique of thematic transformation—clear thematic transformation in the classical sense—to connect one scene of his opera with the other. Moreover, the contrapuntal chords of the trombones that accompany the bass melody in bars 3 to 5 echo the grace notes from the opening scene, thus increasing the idea of thematic parallelism.

From this opening group an entire extended section is developed which, forming an intrada to the actual second scene, is structurally but an elaboration on the group quoted in the last example. But now the Grand Inquisitor begins his aria, centered on a new melodic utterance,

Ex. 449

Nel-l'i-span-o   suol (etc.)

yet again and again we hear the two accents, "the peaks" (on F and C) separated by the fifth.

The analogy penetrates even the detail. Compare the orchestral accompaniments of the arias from the first and second scene:

The King (first scene)

Ex. 450

The Grand Inquisitor (second scene)

The idea of letting the enunciations of the two great opposing personages evolve as two contrasting variants of one identical musical impulse is of course, no less from a *theatrical* than from a structural angle, an effect of particular subtlety and strength. Connections which the text cannot and should not speak out are brought to the listener's consciousness.

This is a specifically operatic application of the technique of thematic transformation. Indeed, thematic transformation appears as a most effective and most logical means *both to differentiate and to unite* the various figures and events of an operatic plot. The same phrase which, announcing the King, was heard as the grace-note group by the strings and horns, or at the beginning of the aria by the wailing oboe, now sounds with the entrance of the Grand Inquisitor in bold strokes from the full orchestra. The tender, elastic eighth-note accompaniment to the King's aria has become in the Grand Inquisitor's aria an austere melodic line of almost pompous quarter-notes (example 450). And the change apparent in the themes themselves is especially impressive, as the same basic pattern which when uttered by the King expresses woeful passion, when referring to the Cardinal conveys a mystic threat (example 448) or implacable yet restrained fervor (example 449).

Again the scene changes completely when the Queen enters. Her part begins with an emphatic group in which some musical high points of the following aria are anticipated. Then the actual aria commences, introduced by accented strokes on C-sharp (*a* in the following example), again recalling the grace-note group of the act's opening, now changed to an utterance of nervous despair. In the course of the aria the original design appears as though dissolved into its particles. We hear the basic motif in constant agitated reiteration, until in the concluding period (*b* in the following example) the melodic idea embarks on its decisive formulation:

These are no longer particles but a beautiful and most dramatic expression of the full thematic pattern, centered on the two peaks G-sharp and D (note Verdi's accent), separated by a falling fourth. As the first peak, the G-sharp, is here the melodic high point, the descent to the second "peak," the low D, is from a vocal angle a particularly effective feature.

A thematic picture similar to that in these first scenes is maintained throughout the act. Naturally, the literal pattern formed by the two peaks separated by a fifth cannot be continued indefinitely, but the same inner idea of driving to accented high points with following stepwise descents remains the thematic basis—a basis reinforced through innumerable smaller analogies and motivic interconnections. The reader, by following Verdi's score, can easily verify the truth of this in concrete detail. In fact, incredible as it may seem, he will detect that this idea of thematic affinity is not confined to one act but is enlarged to the wider scope of two or three basic thematic thoughts extended over the whole opera. Of course, within the homogeneity that unifies the entire work, each act, or even sometimes a large section, has its specific gradation of motivic combinations, yet an over-all thematic idea unites the whole.

A glance at the beginning of the opera may prove that this is more than a mere allegation. A marchlike intrada opens the work, reading:

Ex. 452

These fanfares hardly lead one to expect the tragically passionate shapes encountered in the fourth act, and an attempt to stress similarities might be refuted from the outset. Yet when, a few bars later, the curtain rises, the opening fanfares are repeated, now forming an orchestral accompaniment to a choral section, the melodic line of which interprets the fanfares in this way:

Ex. 453

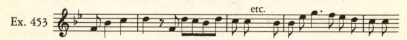

Now the idea can no longer be mistaken. For again we hear the twofold rise, first to D then to G, thus even in pitch identical to the pattern of the opening theme in the fourth act. The peaks are merely exchanged, as in the fourth act G comes first and D follows.

Though we could examine only a small part of this great operatic picture, the existence of deeply rooted affinities binding the work together can surely no longer be doubted. Hidden beneath various appearances though these affinities are, they are nevertheless so intense and appear so regularly that they must have been consciously planned by the composer. Indeed, it is the classical technique of transformation on which Verdi's idea of creating an architectural whole is centered—though here the whole is not symphonic but operatic.

Nevertheless, compared with the classical type, Verdi's transformations appear somewhat generalized. Although strict in their thematic essence, they usually elaborate on the mere patterns of the shapes in question, seldom on their full melodic courses. It is a fascinating spectacle. Mozart and Beethoven, the pioneers and true masters of thematic transformation, did not fully transfer this method of structural thinking, which was theirs inherently, into the operatic realm. When Verdi and Wagner effectuated this transference, the principle itself was already on the way to its dissolution. However, the manner in which Verdi applied it was obviously the form most appropriate to his operatic conceptions, in fact, the perfect symbol of the colorful diversity of his librettos. Every person, every scene has its own character and problem, as each has its own theme. Yet one basic dramatic idea, or, musically speaking, common structural pattern, unites the whole.

Thus the question arises: How was this same principle of thematic unity materialized in Wagner's operas?

Wagner: *Tristan und Isolde*

The striking feature of which everyone thinks first when Wagner's operatic technique is discussed is the *leitmotif*. It is well known that this refers to a technique whereby persons or ideas from the operatic plot are associated with certain shapes that emerge in the musical course whenever their programmatic correspondents appear on the stage or are alluded to, even indirectly, by the text. Of course the device as such—to correlate musical phrases with programmatic ideas—is of old usage, though Wagner developed it to a systematic technique, especially in his later operas.

However, it is perhaps significant that the term "leitmotif" was not invented by Wagner himself but by his friend Wolzogen. For

Wagner was well aware that, though the leitmotif idea created a more intimate and more specific connection between music and text than had ever been thought possible, it alone was not sufficient to produce a structural whole in opera. By filling the score with obvious motivic references, the higher structural postulate that the compositional course has to be formed in thematic consistency and thematic logic was by no means entirely fulfilled.

In this sense we see in Wagner's operas an almost double thematic picture not unlike that encountered in Berlioz's *Symphonie fantastique:* a surface picture formed by the frequent reiteration of the obvious thematic figures, the leitmotifs, and beneath it a second, less obvious picture brought about by the normal imitations, variations, and transformations of the basic material. And though the popular interest in Wagner's structural conceptions is mainly centered on the external leitmotif technique, his achievement of forging an opera into one architectural whole by inner thematic consistency is in an evolutional sense at least as important. Of course, in practice the two principles cannot always be clearly distinguished. For, naturally, the composer is not anxious to make the listener constantly aware whether a shape is a leitmotif or a regular thematic figure. On the contrary, by letting, on the one hand, leitmotifs whenever possible emerge as parts of the organic thematic design and, on the other, by endowing ordinary thematic phrases with leitmotivic effects, Wagner develops a convincing entity from two phenomena that are separate in principle: thematic structure and thematic symbolism.

We may try to demonstrate the double effect of this structural endeavor by a description of some important thematic elements in Wagner's *Tristan und Isolde.* The opera opens with three famous bars, centered around an accented harmony known among musicians as the "Tristan chord":

Ex. 454

How many treatises have been written about this one chord, trying to "explain" its harmonic mystery! However, in accepted theoretical, that is, harmonic terms, this chord cannot be explained. Of course one can parse the chord, classifying it as a manifold suspension, the resolutions of which are resolved again. But does this bring us closer to an understanding of the meaning of this harmony as a compositional utterance?

However, the chord—or rather the reason that the composer chose it—is easily understood from a thematic angle. For, compressed into one chord, the musical story of the whole opera is latent in this initial harmony.

As is easily seen from the following example, the opening period of the Prelude to *Tristan*, reading,

Ex. 455

is a series of three almost identical groups, in each of which the important chord forms the accented center. The chord itself is a summation of two fourths, one placed above the other. In each chord one fourth is augmented, the other perfect.

The chords of the three groups, the three "Tristan chords," show a particular relationship. The lower part of the first chord, F–B, appears as the upper part of the second chord (now with an altered accidental reading F-sharp–B). Analogously, the lower part of the second chord, A-flat–D, becomes the upper part of the third chord, now notated as G-sharp–D.

In this way the whole opening period seems as though it were released, in a widening cycle, from the first chord. Adding to the atmosphere of mystic symbolism that emanates from this shaping is another feature: the melodic course of each of the three groups is formed by two lines (marked by braces) of which one mirrors the other in contrary motion. For instance, in the first group the two lines read F, E, D-sharp, D, and G-sharp, A, A-sharp, B.

If it was the composer's intention, through a shaping *based on two corresponding elements*—*two* fourths that form the harmonic utterance and *two* melodic lines that are a shape and its inversion—to express the programmatic symbolism of *Tristan und Isolde,* he certainly accomplished it in a construction of almost hypnotic power. And if these symbols were to be called leitmotifs, then we must admit that the leitmotif technique appears here carried to the very depths of the work's structure and content.

From the beginning we may turn to the end of the opera. Does the opera's musical and dramatic resolution, the so-called "Love-Death," bear any structural connection to its beginning? If we know how to read, we will detect that the "Love-Death" grows as a melodic radiation from these same opening chords. Comparing the series of three chords as they appear at the opening of the opera (example 456a) with the melodic rise of the "Love-Death" (b),

Ex. 456

we see (by means of the braces) that the picture of the "Love-Death" is an absolute image of the scheme expressed by the three chords. The reader is urged to check the validity of this statement, which is not an approximation but literally true. Only one accidental is omitted (in the phrase marked c); otherwise the succession and pitch are preserved to the last detail (although in an enharmonically changed notation). As the chords themselves grow, by their own magic mechanism, one out of another, the whole design is already determined by the opening chord.

The thematic symbol of these ceaselessly interlacing fourths—
theme and symbol are indeed one in this work—reaches in the
"Love-Death" its climax, but we find it throughout the whole work
as the structural basis of the opera's most emphatic parts. In the
fifth scene of the opening act, when Tristan appears before Isolde
for the first time, the winds blare irresistible, endlessly sustained
fortissimos, which no musical ear, having once heard them, will
ever forget:

and this group is but another expression of that theme which later
appears as the "Love-Death" and, therefore, of the fourths forming
the opera's mysterious opening chord.

The union of the lovers, the central scene of the second act, is
full of such thematic and symbolic pairs of fourths. The agitated
theme in the second act's Prelude, picturing Isolde's impatience for
the arrival of Tristan, displays the fourths forged into one melodic
line. Compare:

Save for the accidentals, this theme reiterates the opening chord
even in pitch, the second (upper) fourth mirroring the version in
which the fourth appears in the preceding example (Tristan's entrance).

Tristan and Isolde's reunion, then, presaged by characteristic
successions of rising fourths (example 459a), culminates in an outburst (example 459b) which, viewed as one line, forms a perfect and
augmented fourth:

This symbolic shaping is continued in the following breathless outcries:

This is symbolism in utter intensity. For by linking (see braces) the detached exclamations of the lovers at the moment of their first union, the hidden theme of the "Love-Death" sounds through.

No doubt, again symbolically, Brangäne's warning voice is heard as a contrary motion of the same theme:

And when the opera reaches its very end, the mystic chord sounds once more, together with a melodic line mirroring the pattern of the work's opening, now at last resolving the tensions into final harmony. Compare the beginning (*a*) with the ending (*b*) of the work in these sketched excerpts:

Ex. 462

Thus we see as the core of Wagner's leitmotif symbolism a method of thematic forming which not only is of inexorable strictness but, in addition, has the capacity of creating musical form. Indeed, it was neither the leitmotif as such, nor the "infinite melody," nor even the lack of "numbers" that made opera become an architectural unit. (The lack of closed "numbers" is merely a surface feature, since Wagner's seemingly continuous scores are often interrupted by musical entities complete in themselves, such as the "Prize Song," the "Fire Spell," funeral or wedding marches, and so forth.) But when the mind of a genius evolves a thematic plan like the one described above, through which the whole work, theme by theme and scene by scene, grows out of a few opening chords, so that the initial cry of longing is finally transfigured into an all-embracing manifestation such as the "Love-Death," then a historic course is completed: *opera has become a unified musical form.*

In this achievement of building opera by thematic evolution, it is especially memorable that Wagner did not simply transplant the thematic technique of his classic-romantic predecessors but transformed and adapted it to his own theatrical purposes. If to the taste of today Wagner's operas may sometimes appear as debatable, this may have many reasons, not the least of which may be his texts. The erotic philosophism in the Tristan libretto, for instance, notwithstanding the timeless idea underlying this great poem, scarcely seems appropriate to an operatic work of general appeal. Several sections, such as King Marke's meditations on discovering Isolde in Tristan's arms, or even the greater part of the third act, are, from the point of view of theatrical dynamism, unwieldy interpolations. Be this as it may, the contention that it constituted a negation of the innermost operatic idea to have taken over conceptions of thematic development, which allegedly are inherently "symphonic," into the realm of operatic structure is pure nonsense. The sections which in this terminology would have to be considered as specifically symphonic, such as the "Love-Death," are also the strongest from an operatic angle. And whenever the thematic and symbolic evolution of the work coincide most intensely, there, too, the operatic strength and effect of the whole are at their peak.

Strauss: *Till Eulenspiegel*

Among the composers after Wagner, we may, as a last example before drawing some general conclusions, turn to Richard Strauss. The same idea of using thematic transformation as a means of connecting the various persons and events in an operatic plot that we saw at work in the operas of Verdi and Wagner reappears, again in a different form, in the works of Strauss. Strauss, the protagonist of program music, applies this idea of developing a programmatic plot by thematic transformation, not only in his operas, but even in his orchestral compositions. The following six shapes are the main thematic figures from Strauss's symphonic rondo *Till Eulenspiegel:*

Ex. 463

These six themes symbolize important experiences from the life of Till, the immortal jester of old folklore. While in some of these themes Till himself seems to speak, as they sound as if the composer may have imitated or even used real folk tunes, in other themes the composer seems to speak in his own right, reacting to the jests or describing them. Different, therefore, not only in shape but even in idiom, as are themes I and II (the "composer's utterances"), from IV and VI (Till's tunes), we discover that at the base of all themes lies a common contour which could be notated as follows,

Ex. 464

In theme VI only some accidentals have to be changed to recognize the full identity. These six shapes comprise the entire thematic material from which the great and manifold musical picture of *Till Eulenspiegel* is developed.

Now it is perhaps too strong a statement to call the figure in our last example a contour. It is—at least with regard to some of the themes—merely a structural scheme unifying the different parts of the work; certainly we are here far removed from the classical identity of full melodic contours sounding from the different themes of a work. Yet it is fascinating to observe how even the meager identity of scheme suffices to bind the various parts of the composition into an irresistibly convincing whole.

The last examples led us close to our own time. The question may now be raised: What picture, *from a thematic aspect,* does our current period present?

To answer this question, the meaning that the term "thematic" has assumed in our analysis must first be clearly recalled. For certainly this meaning is different from that which is in common usage today. In present usage "thematic structure" means merely that a work is built from themes, these themes being held together by more or less frequent and obvious resumptions and perhaps connected by equally obvious motivic features. Our analysis, on the óther hand, establishes the thematic phenomenon as a continuous transformation of one initial thought which builds the work by appearing in ever new disguises or, to use Whitehead's expression (from the epigraph to our study), as the enduring "reiteration of a pattern's succession of contrasts."

Returning to our question, the answer must be that, *understood in this specific sense,* the thematic phenomenon has almost disappeared from the music of our time. Of course, a kind of "thematic structure" is still applied and spoken of today, but the dissolution of its deepest principle, signs of which were apparent in the post-classical era, though there still balanced by a strong and effective impulse to retain thematic consistency, has become almost complete in a great part of the musical production of our time.

In some ways this development is understandable. The most conspicuous factor from a technical point of view in the new, so-called "modern" musical movement, which set in toward the turn of the century, was a decisive new orientation of the *harmonic* concept. This process of new orientation may not yet have come to a close, its definitive direction not having as yet become clear. However, as so often happened in music history, whenever a striking innovation of one kind became the center of artistic endeavor, this was usually accompanied by a loss of understanding in other respects. For instance, as previously described, in the time between Bach and the classics the idea of contrapuntal intensity receded when new aspects of compositional proportions and new ways of orchestral handling were championed. In a similar manner, in our time, the idea of thematic unification, especially in its highest form as a work's architectural basis, paled—in fact, almost vanished—as it was pushed aside by the fascination of the new harmonic concept, by the scintillation of the new orchestral colors and effects, which became the center of compositional interest.

This shift in attitude concerning the role of the thematic idea was supported by another fact of a more intangible nature. Parallel to a short-lived trend that banned "emotion" from musical creation ("matter-of-fact" art), perhaps even as a reaction to it, a tendency seems to have become prevalent to view composing as a process of purely instinctive "inspiration," from which rational elements are almost excluded. Accordingly, if a young composer of today were to show too much interest in questions of aesthetics, music history, or the deeper problems of structure, he might run the risk of having the strength and genuineness of his creative vocation doubted. Consequently, young composers often renounce historical and "theoretical" interest altogether. *Yet this conception of a composer as a purely instinctive agent is entirely contradicted by historical fact.*

The great composers, almost without exception, were serious, thinking, searching minds, expressing their inspiration *by means of* conscious construction. Invariably eager to expand their spiritual horizon, alert to the philosophical and even the scientific questions to which their circumstances gave them access, they occupied themselves ceaselessly with both the general and the concrete technical problems of their art.

Schumann himself, the very protagonist of romanticism, speaks of "the consciousness of the poetic mind." What a world of meaning is comprised in this phrase.

And one has only to read Mozart's letters to his father to realize what a deeply analytical musical mind was his. Constantly striving to get at the core of the compositional idea, he ponders over every single passage. Whenever the father suggests a change which seems to him advisable from a general viewpoint, the son invariably proceeds to the compositional principle involved, applying it to the specific technical detail in question. Also, how revealing is Mozart's remark (reported by Niemetschek): "People err who think that my art has come easily to me. Nobody has devoted so much time and thought to composition as I. *There is not one composer of rank whose music I have not studied industriously many times.*"

To quote another illuminating example: we learn that Tchaikovsky speaks in a letter to his friend about an idea that obviously haunted him; namely, to devote some time to the study and the writing of a textbook on the history of music. Similarly, Chopin once told George Sand of his intention to write a book in which his method and technique of composition were to be explained. Although these great composers never carried out these plans, the intention alone bears sufficient testimony to the direction in which their minds worked.

But in the creative domain of our time an attitude of neglect toward theoretical, technical problems can frequently be observed. As for the thematic idea in particular, the knowledge of its central role in the compositional process has vanished. Not that thematic thought as such has disappeared. References to thematic features are, now as before, common musical parlance. Nevertheless, one has the feeling that the contemporary composer considers thematic connections mainly as interesting accessories with which he embellishes his work. He is satisfied that they bear witness to his skill, though at the same time he takes pleasure in the thought that they come about subconsciously, unknown even to himself. Comparing this with the thematic spirit of the preceding period, when a musical work was from the outset *conceived* as an interweaving of numerous transformations, clearly defined in their place and function within the work's whole, we must admit that the thematic principle in its higher meaning has practically ceased to exist. With the loss of its conscious, systematic use as a form-building force, the power which this great phenomenon exerted in the process of musical composition has almost vanished.

However, music cannot exist for any length of time without the stimulation of the force which from time immemorial has engendered its structural forms. Not until a new agent, comparable in vitality to the thematic idea, has been invented, can this life-giving principle be abandoned. And it seems that our time is gradually awakening to the necessity of a return to thematic thinking. Thematic permeation—permeation in an inner, creative sense—seems to grow ever stronger in recent works of our foremost composers, often perhaps without their being fully aware of the intensity of this trend. The tendency to resume ancient patterns, even though often only in name, such as concerti grossi, ricercari, passacaglias, and the like, is highly significant. And even the most radical trend in the modern movement, the so-called "twelve-tone" music, reveals a vehement desire to lead music back to a thematic concept. Such attempts—quite apart from the question whether they are made in the right or wrong direction—certainly appear indicative of the time's irresistible urge to recapture the lost key, to base musical expression once more on structural, indeed, on thematic formation.

12

SOME FINAL CONSIDERATIONS
AS TO THE NATURE AND RANGE
OF THE THEMATIC PROCESS

Our analysis is driving to its conclusion. Before adding some final remarks, the author wishes to relate a personal incident from his early life that came to mind while writing this book.

As a young student of composition, he once caused an uproar in the class by asking a question which, as the reader may remember, was raised earlier in this study: Why is it that we cannot produce a convincing musical composition by taking a group or a section from one work and linking it to that of another—even assuming an affinity of key, rhythm, and tempo? I feel as strongly as anyone that this cannot be done, but how is it to be explained in musical, structural terms?

After the surprise caused by my unconventional question had subsided, the professor began to advance some explanations. He spoke of the divergent character and mood necessarily emanated by groups from different works. Realizing, perhaps, the vagueness of this reply, he shifted to more specific points. He stressed the necessity of key relation, tempo, and the like, though I had already anticipated these items, and then proceeded to motivic affinity as an essential factor in musical composition.

However, I was persistent. The question had grown in my mind during an analysis of the thematic content of Mozart's G-minor Symphony. "What is the motivic affinity," I wanted to know, "between the first and second themes in Mozart's work of which we have just been told that its two themes form entirely contrasting statements. And yet, why can neither of them be replaced by a theme from another Mozart symphony? Why is it not even considered feasible to exchange the whole Finale of this symphony with that of another symphony of Mozart's?"

I received no answer that day. However, the professor, a man both of profound musicality and of deep sincerity, invited me, weeks later, to a private discussion and said: "I have thought a great deal about your questions. But I do not know an answer. And I admit that it does not seem to me sufficient simply to say that there are always things in art and music that cannot be explained theoretically. Naturally, in every art there are mysterious forces that resist analytic dissection. But your questions seem to me so specific that, if theory professes at all to be a guide in the technique of the compositional process, there must be an answer. Yet again I confess I do not know what it is."

This little classroom incident returned to my mind when, years later, I tried to pierce the deeper meaning of form in music. I realized that my early questions had not sprung merely from the speculation of a youthfully eccentric mind. To ask *why in music one group can be followed only by certain other groups and not by random groups which happen to fit in key, rhythm, and the like* should constitute a serious question to every musician. In fact, far from being primitive or naïve, it is the fundamental question on which the problem of compositional mechanism is centered. It must first be solved if we wish at all to arrive at a satisfactory explanation of musical structure and form.

From the host of examples presented, our readers will themselves draw the answer to the question: It is the thematic force which makes it impossible to replace a group, section, or movement of a logically built composition by a part from another work. Our readers also know that current theory, although stressing the necessity of such consistency in principle, does not provide any concrete answer to the problem through an actual demonstration of facts.

This omission was of far-reaching consequences for our whole esthetic and analytical approach to music, and it has made itself felt even in musical practice both in composition and in performance. To understand the curious situation in which current theory here finds itself, we must first examine the, so to speak, "official concept" of thematic consistency.

However, it turns out that this is very difficult. Current explanations concerning this matter are vague. It is virtually impossible to discover what, according to the official view, thematic consistency actually means and what parts and sections of a composition it is said to unite. The standard encyclopædias, lexicons, and textbooks certainly do not give more than evasive, even contradictory generalizations. In fact, thematic consistency is not even treated in these diverse works of reference as an individual subject; it does not seem to constitute a problem of investigation at all. Thus, to arrive at any tangible result one must glean what one can from remarks interpolated in discussions of other topics.

On consistency within one movement, we gather from *Grove's Dictionary*—the authoritative source for so many musical matters—that "the use of a conspicuous figure taken from the introduction as a central idea for the following Allegro" was much practiced by classical composers. However, *Grove's Dictionary* also stresses that "the second subject necessarily presents a different aspect altogether and is in marked contrast to the first." As for consistency between the movements, it asserts that, at least in Beethoven, there is an "ideal continuity and oneness which is musically felt even when there is no direct external sign of the connections. In a few cases, however, there are signs of more than this." Yet examples that follow to prove the point refer merely to some minute, insignificant particles by which, in a very few, specific cases, movements are supposedly connected. And the whole description makes it clear that even these almost trifling instances are considered exceptions.

Riemann's *Musiklexikon,* the German counterpart of *Grove's Dictionary,* from a different point of departure, arrives at similarly indefinite results. Riemann declares: "Thematic forming means the development of longer pieces from a limited number of characteristic motifs, especially by endowing also the parts between the themes with motifs from the main themes." A further statement of Riemann's, however, almost directly contradicting the one just quoted, reads: "The presupposition for the use of several themes in one piece (for instance, a sonata) is a characteristic difference of the main motifs, in spite of conformity in rhythm and tempo."

The *Encyclopædia Britannica,*[1] finally, also holds that a musical work must be built in artistic unity, but at the same time asks: "Why

[1] All quotations from the *Encyclopaedia Britannica* are taken from the 11th edition, as subsequent editions avoid any detailed analytical reference.

do classical sonatas maintain this scheme of self-centered movements with no community of theme?" It seems to find the solution in that "the treatment by each movement of its own thematic material is so complete that there is little or no scope for one movement to make use of the theme of another."

What clear, common meaning can we possibly deduce from these sweeping declarations? In essence only a negative one; namely, the firm contention that, as a rule, the different movements of a work (obviously above all referring to the sonata type) do *not* show any thematic connection. But even with regard to the various themes of one movement, the necessity of a "characteristic difference of their main motifs" is stressed, while at the same time it is alleged that the parts between the themes should be "endowed with motifs from the main themes."

How is it possible that such conceptions could have become general, since they are not only in glaring contradiction to all the facts of the great compositional practice but are even contradictory in themselves? On the one hand we are assured that the themes of the different movements or even of one movement are not connected, and on the other that thematic forming means the development of a larger piece from a few motifs.

In trying to interpret this contradiction, the very wording of the definitions above may serve as a starting point. The current theoretical view, when speaking of *thematic* affinities, actually alludes only to *motivic* affinities, that is, affinities through particles. This fact is of the utmost consequence. A retrospective consideration of the phenomena demonstrated in our analysis will make us realize of what fundamental importance is the distinction between mere motivic and real thematic connections, although, to avoid collision with a long-practiced terminology, our study itself did not always emphasize this distinction meticulously.

However, this matter must be clarified: we must recognize motivic and thematic consistency as two different, though complementary, structural forces. Thematic consistency is the great phenomenon that forms the structural core of the foremost works in musical literature. In hundreds of examples we have seen *a full theme,* or a large part of it, reappear as the contour of another theme; or we have seen a theme formed by combining two preceding themes or decisive parts of them. Always it was the similarity of the actual thematic lines, of their real melodic courses, which produced that affinity through which the work became so impressively one whole. But affinities of this nature are not pointed out in current theory, which, as a rule, conceives "thematic affinity" as being brought about merely by motivic particles.

Now it must be stressed that affinity through motifs is also an important factor in music. In many of our examples we have seen thematic affinity complemented by motivic connections, that is, by the reappearance of previous particles. In fact, as is the case with most terms, a clear distinction cannot always be maintained in practice. There is no rule stating exactly how long or short a shape must be in order to be considered respectively as a motif or a theme. Nevertheless, affinities brought about, on the one hand, by short motivic phrases, or, on the other, by extended thematic contours exert quite different compositional effects.

But the focal point of the whole question is this: thematic affinities which, as was shown in this study, form the architectural core of so many great works are invariably brought about through transformation. A second theme, or the theme of a new movement, will, in a work of convincing structure, never be a mere repetition or even variation of a former theme, but will be a new utterance, a transformation, the identity of which is "hidden" beneath a new surface. Motivic affinities, on the other hand, are very often obvious, perceptible features—often, though not always, for there are frequent instances when even motifs appear in another theme not literally but transformed.

Here we are at the root of the contradiction in which theory is caught with regard to thematic consistency. The current theoretical view, when investigating the possible affinity of themes, sections, or movements, bases its entire examination on obvious, and thus, as a rule, motivic, reiterations and reminiscences but fails to unravel unity materialized by *real* transformation either motivic or thematic. Linked to this failure, however, there is a strong, if dim, realization that compositions must be built from a common ground. Yet unable to substantiate this concretely, the whole formulation of thematic consistency necessarily dissolves into confusion and contradiction.

With regard to the concept and meaning of the term "transformation," it is necessary to add a few remarks. In a strict sense transformation refers to shapes that are formed from preceding ones. To develop a whole work from such transformations was, as we know, the central structural idea in the music of the last centuries. However, especially in the latter part of the evolution, in the romantic and postromantic period, this technique often took on forms for which transformation no longer seems an adequate expression. Let us take, for instance, two of the most significant themes from Strauss's *Till Eulenspiegel,* quoted in the preceding chapter:

Ex. 465

Would it not be misleading to consider either of these two shapes as actually "transformed" from the other? What melodic similarity can here be pointed out, what common characteristic motifs discerned? Theory would certainly deny any affinity between these themes, which are contrasting not only in character and mood but even in idiom. Surprisingly enough, however, the notes of both themes are exactly the same, except that in the first theme a G-sharp and B are inserted as passing discords which do not appear in the second. And since this identity of substance is found in all six themes of *Till Eulenspiegel,* we must conclude that this is not a chance coincidence, but that a structural force is here at work, uniting the whole composition. However, this cannot be properly termed "transformation," as it is not the true forging of one theme into another but is, instead, a particular process of thematic creation, *in which variegated ideas and expressions converge into one architectural entity.*

In the light of this we see that transformation is not the last word in thematic structure. The differentiation may go further. And the final question underlying our analysis is not whether shapes are "similar" but whether the composer in forming them endowed them with qualities that assure some bond between them.

Of course, in our initial presentation we were often forced to stress the similarities to make our subject clear. However, the core of our problem lies not in the fact of these similarities but in the thematic process which brought them to life. That several shapes in a composition reveal resemblances may be a curious, intriguing feature, but it cannot be worthy of interest and emphasis in a higher sense. But the realization that the edifice of a great composition, such as a Beethoven symphony, a Chopin sonata, a Verdi or Wagner opera, must have grown *from a concept* of the different variants of one musical thought and the emotional possibilities involved—this is the realization of a central phenomenon of musical composition in all its strength and mystery.

With regard to the focal themes that form a work's architecture, the working of this phenomenon was demonstrated in the course of our analysis by means of numerous examples. But in the second part of this study—the part which, from a specifically technical angle, formed the center of our investigation—this demonstration was extended to the work's whole structural mechanism. There the groups between the themes as well as the secondary voices were included; and it was further described how the sustained application of the phenomenon not only unifies the different parts of the composition but also develops the whole course to a dramatic enunciation. Although for practical reasons such detailed analysis could be maintained only for a limited number of compositions, this should have sufficed to convince one that the idea of thematic consistency does not merely bring about affinity between themes but constitutes a continuous process, connecting, indeed, creating the whole of the work.

With this we are virtually at the end of our inquiry. The implications to be drawn must be left to the reader, since it seems possible that the composer, the performer, the aesthetician, and the historian will each see the subject from his own point of view. One thing that was stressed from the beginning may here be repeated: the purpose of this study was to describe an existing but little explored sphere of compositional phenomena, certainly not to develop a "theory," to set up a system of rules of composition.

Of course, in this connection the question may be asked whether the principle here described was applied without exception by all great composers in all of their works. Though the whole content and spirit of our analysis tends to an affirmative answer,[2] it must be said that while thematic consistency does seem to constitute a generally

---

[2] It should be understood that the works quoted in this study constitute but a fraction of the material analyzed.

valid principle in great musical literature, nevertheless the degrees of intensity with which it was applied differed greatly among composers and in different works of the same composer. We occasionally encounter works, even among the most "thematically" minded composers, in parts of which the existence of a clear thematic unification would seem questionable. However, in this respect the following should also be understood. Since the thematic process is centered on the intricate phenomenon of transformation, it is inherent in its nature that shapes which were intensively transformed and retransformed may sometimes be no longer recognizable as originating from a common ground. In such instances it may be difficult *to prove* the unity of the work, even though its existence be felt beyond a doubt. Even Beethoven, the composer whose music emanates thematic spirit in its most comprehensive, most concentrated, and most effective form, even he, once in a while, presents us with a structural design the unifying thematic plan of which may be deciphered only with effort. Indeed, some of his most impressive thematic constructions lie on the border line between being matchless master strokes of transformation or utterances wherein the thematic bond has almost dissolved in that very transforming process by which they were created.

There are, for instance, the themes of the first and last movements in the Seventh Symphony. The Finale begins with some introductory bars (*a* in the following example), whereupon the Finale theme itself (*b*) enters:

Certainly this theme seems to have no possible kinship with that of the first movement, the Vivace, quoted in the following example. Only if we overlook the double bar line before the Finale theme and include the introductory bars, does the thematic identity between the themes of the first and last movements become transparent:

Ex. 467

This unexpected identity is confirmed by the second movement, the Allegretto, in an equally extraordinary manner (now transferred to minor). Compare in the following example the theme of the first movement (*a*) with that of the Allegretto (*b*).

For the sake of completeness the third movement, the Scherzo, is also quoted. While the initial note repetitions of the Vivace theme are converted in the Scherzo into a triad, the following main part of the Scherzo theme (embedded in the falling seventh) clearly echoes the theme of the Vivace. Compare the two themes: Vivace theme (*c*) with Scherzo theme (*d*).

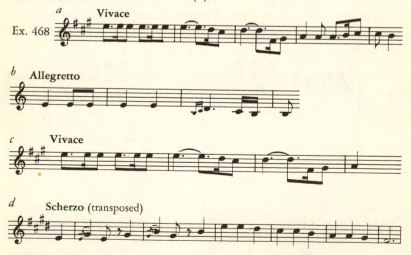

Ex. 468

In the almost infinite structural diversity represented in Beethoven's works, we may even encounter examples where it actually seems impossible to demonstrate thematic affinity convincingly. Do these exceptions then contradict the universal principle which he otherwise followed so meticulously?

Beethoven himself perhaps answers this question.

As is generally known, the first bar in the third movement (Adagio Sostenuto) of Beethoven's Piano Sonata, opus 106, the so-called "Hammerklavier," was added by the composer when the work was already at the publisher's. The *Encyclopædia Britannica* recalls Beethoven's note to his publisher saying that he wished this bar to be added in order to establish a similarity between the openings of the two movements. The encyclopædia considers this remark as proof that the intention to produce a similarity between these movements must have constituted an exception; otherwise Beethoven would not have pointed it out in this instance. The logic of this argumentation is so flimsy that it hardly warrants debate. However, there is a more interesting point involved. For the "similarity" between the openings of the two movements (produced by the added bars) is *by no means one which would ordinarily be considered a thematic resemblance.* The two openings read:

These two beginnings must, in the current view, appear as entirely different shapes. The bond which unites them is the very epitome of thematic transformation, for only a *contour* of the Adagio theme (A, C-sharp, C-sharp, A) sounds (in transposition) as B-flat, D, D, B-flat) from the Allegro.

This is a "similarity" which—with its melodic line changed by inserted notes, its different rhythm and harmonic function—would, *were the idea not expressly confirmed by Beethoven himself,* certainly never be accepted by current analysis as a thematic affinity.

Another example, though of a different kind, speaks no less strongly.

In a museum in Vienna, a number of notebooks are preserved containing Beethoven's handwritten sketches of many of his compositions. In the second half of the last century a Viennese music teacher named Nottebohm published some of these sketches, thus making their contents generally accessible. Of the Third Symphony, the so-called "Eroica," a particular abundance of sketches is preserved, and Nottebohm tells us that the Trio to the Scherzo of the symphony appears in no less than four successive versions. However, he publishes only the first and the fourth.

If we consider the Trio theme as it appears in the symphony itself (example 470*a*) and the version in which this theme appears in the fourth, the last sketch (*b*), it is hardly possible to point out any actual affinity between these shapes and the well known theme of the first movement *c*:

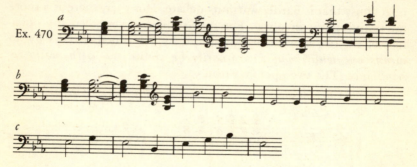

Ex. 470

An attempt on this basis to prove that Beethoven formed the themes of the various movements from one common thought would be refuted as artificial. Nevertheless, the sketchbook lucidly demonstrates the true process by which the Trio theme came into existence. Looking at the version in which the theme appears in the *first* sketch,

Ex. 471

we can hardly believe our eyes. For this first original version of the Trio theme mirrors the main theme of the symphony so distinctly in the rhythm and spirit of its whole shaping that the nature of the themes as two conceptions of one identical thought cannot be doubted.

The fact that the idea of thematic identity is the basis of compositional formation in the great works of musical literature does not, at the conclusion of this analysis, need confirmation. Yet the specific emphasis added by the last examples may not be without importance. For here Beethoven himself appears as a witness and testifies. And his is a testimony that is difficult to set aside.

Nevertheless, we should avoid again focusing our thought on "similarities," even though they be pointed out by Beethoven. For above and beyond even Beethoven himself stands the principle of musical creation of which he is both personification and symbol. What Beethoven and all great composers give us is more than the substance of their works, magnificent as it may be: it is the dynamism and mystery of that creative process through which music becomes an expression of life itself.

Having worked our way through the various stages of this investigation, we may have become increasingly aware of the fascinating fact that music is created from sound *as life is created from matter.* In the organic sphere one cell engenders the other in its own image, yet each of the innumerable cells is different from all the others. By a magic interplay between these identical yet different cells, the higher forms of life come into existence.

In an astoundingly analogous way one musical motif, one theme releases another as an expression of its own innermost idea, yet the latter is a being entirely different from the first. The theme lives through the motifs from which it is formed, the work through its themes; yet the theme and the highest unit, the work, are each entities in their own right, announcing their own message. And the act of creation is centered in this very process by which a musical idea emerges as a consequence of another, as a thing which is a part of the given world, yet which has never existed before.

This process takes shape, consciously or instinctively, in the composer, the performer, and the listener, and only because "creation" works by its own nature in all of them does music become the great wonder that it is. Moreover, it works in each of them, and in every individual, in a different way. The work of musical art, though at first seemingly an objective fact, thus becomes, through the complexity and abundance of its interconnections, a violently dynamic, ever changing manifestation. If these identical yet contrasting ideas speak to us from the different voices and harmonies of a composition, from the manifold groups, sections, and movements, then their meaning and that of the work as a whole will vary with the numerous possibilities of interrelations by which the listener may comprehend them according to his own ever latent creative impulse. His musicianly and structural, his emotional and critical impulses, perhaps his historical conceptions, will live, respond, and struggle throughout the work.

It has been our endeavor to bring the working of this process more lucidly into relief. And it is hoped that this book may serve as an incentive to further thought, for the range and nature of the thematic phenomenon in its stylistic and historical expansion are as infinite as music itself.

INDEX OF NAMES AND COMPOSITIONS